SAP® S/4HANA Product Cost Planning

Configuration and Master Data

Tom King

Thank you for purchasing this book from Espresso Tutorials!

Like a cup of espresso coffee, Espresso Tutorials SAP books are concise and effective. We know that your time is valuable and we deliver information in a succinct and straightforward manner. It only takes our readers a short amount of time to consume SAP concepts. Our books are well recognized in the industry for leveraging tutorial-style instruction and videos to show you step by step how to successfully work with SAP.

Check out our YouTube channel to watch our videos at https://www.youtube.com/user/EspressoTutorials.

If you are interested in SAP Finance and Controlling, join us at http://www.fico-forum.com/forum2/ to get your SAP questions answered and contribute to discussions.

Related titles from Espresso Tutorials:

- ▶ Stefan Eifler: **Quick Guide to CO-PA (Profitability Analysis)**
  http://5018.espresso-tutorials.com

- ▶ Paul Ovigele: **Reconciling SAP CO-PA to the General Ledger**
  http://5040.espresso-tutorials.com

- ▶ Ashish Sampat: **First Steps in SAP Controlling (CO)**
  http://5069.espresso-tutorials.com

- ▶ Marjorie Wright: **Practical Guide to SAP Internal Orders (CO-OM)**
  http://5139.espresso-tutorials.com

- ▶ Ashish Sampat: **Expert tips to Unleash the Full Potential of SAP Controlling** *http://5140.espresso-tutorials.com*

- ▶ John Pringle: **Practical Guide to SAP Profit Center Accounting**
  http://5144.espresso-tutorials.com

- ▶ John Pringle: **Practical Guide to SAP Cost Center Accounting**
  http://5192.espresso-tutorials.com

- ▶ Stefan Eifler, Christoph Theis: **Value Flows into SAP ERP FI, CO, and CO-PA** *http://5199.espresso-tutorials.com*

- ▶ Tom King: **Practical Guide to SAP CO Templates**
  http://5262.espresso-tutorials.com

Tom King
SAP® S/4HANA Product Cost Planning—Configuration and Master Data

ISBN:	978-3-96012-908-0
Editor:	Karen Schoch
Cover Design:	Philip Esch
Cover Photo:	iStockphoto.com	sykono No. 171301497
Interior Book Design:	Johann-Christian Hanke

All rights reserved.

1st Edition 2019, Gleichen

© 2019 by Espresso Tutorials GmbH

URL: *www.espresso-tutorials.com*

Feedback
We greatly appreciate any feedback you may have concerning this book. Please send your feedback via email to: *info@espresso-tutorials.com*.

Table of Contents

Introduction

I have often been frustrated searching through books and the internet to try to find solutions to specific requests that I have encountered in product costing. There are a few very fine books covering the entire subject of Product Cost Controlling, including the SAP Press book "Product Cost Controlling with SAP" by John Jordan (Rheinwerk Publishing) and "Practical Guide to SAP® CO-PC (Product Cost Controlling)" by Tanya Duncan (Espresso Tutorials). These books by their nature can devote only a small amount of space to the Product Cost Planning module of Product Cost Controlling. They provide good coverage of the configuration processes and an overview of what Product Cost Planning does, but they contain few examples and only minimal discussion of the effects of selecting one configuration over another. When searching the internet for blogs or other posts concerning product costing with SAP, the information provided can be either very basic or tends to be an answer to a specific question. The help documentation provided by SAP is another source that can be used for research, and it contains a lot of details. However, there are few, if any, practical examples, and some of the details are left up to the reader to try to decipher and test.

I have written a set of two books on this topic, aiming to satisfy my need to view the subject of product costing as a whole and to fill in the missing details using practical examples which highlight the impact of configuration choices. There are so many facets to Product Cost Planning (CO-PC-PCP) that the topic had to be split into two books. Book 1 covers the major configuration tasks and how this is used both in unit costing and in cost estimates with quantity structure. The emphasis of this book is to give an understanding of how material and manufacturing overhead costs are assigned to materials. Cost estimates with quantity structure have many further options and features for fully defining the product costs; these topics make up Book 2 of this set. The basic structure for costing functions in S/4HANA is the costing variant, and this is the backbone of CO-PC-PCP. Costing variants are also used in other modules such as Cost Object Controlling (CO-PC-OBJ), but details included in these books only cover configuration that pertains to Product Cost Planning; however, the basic concepts are applicable to the other modules as well.

The examples used in these books are based on a fictitious company: Universal Writing Utensil Corporation, and have no true basis in fact. I wish to express my apologies in advance to any of you who are working in the ballpoint pen manufacturing industry! My aim was to define a consistent base for comparing cost estimates at each stage in the process, and the manufacturing processes appear to be disparate enough to demonstrate many of the aspects of product costing.

S/4HANA is the latest generation of the ERP software suite offered by SAP. There are many similarities with the older ERP releases, and S/4HANA is essentially a souped-up version of those earlier releases, with a new database structure designed for an enhanced user experience. The basic functionality remains the same, and most of the transactions have been translated to use the new database structure. In addition to the standard SAPGUI transactions, there are many Fiori apps that duplicate or extend the functionality of several of the older transactions. Where both Fiori and SAPGUI transactions coexist, screenshots in this book use the Fiori equivalent. Configuration examples use the traditional SAPGUI screen shots, as the majority of configuration has no Fiori equivalent. The system used for the examples runs S/4HANA on-premise version 1809. Although this book is written from the S/4HANA point of view, the concepts introduced are applicable to the earlier ERP versions as well. Also note that throughout this book, when the image of a Fiori app button is used, the image for the corresponding SAPGUI transaction is shown in parentheses. For example: 🔘 (🔳) indicates the button for switching currencies. 🔘 is the Fiori button and 🔳 is the SAPGUI version of the same button.

We have added a few icons to highlight important information. These include:

Tips

Tips highlight information that provides more details about the subject being described and/or additional background information.

Examples

Examples help illustrate a topic better by relating it to real world scenarios.

Attention

Attention notices highlight information that you should be aware of when you go through the examples in this book on your own.

Finally, a note concerning the copyright: all screenshots printed in this book are the copyright of SAP SE. All rights are reserved by SAP SE. Copyright pertains to all SAP images in this publication. For the sake of simplicity, we do not mention this specifically underneath every screenshot.

1 Introduction to product cost planning

Product Cost Planning (CO-PC-PCP) is the controlling module that is used for assigning costs to materials. How these costs are assigned is based on a significant amount of configuration that is used to control not only the accumulation of costs, but also the purpose of the product cost itself. Many of the basic constructs used for controlling cost estimates for materials are also used in other CO modules including CO-PC-OBJ (Cost Object Controlling).

1.1   Purpose of product cost planning

The concept of a standard cost has been developed over time to represent the monetary resources required to manufacture or procure a specific item or material. This standard is used for valuing stock in inventory, for measuring profitability of a product, and for serving as a benchmark for determining purchasing and manufacturing variances. Since this is really an estimate, the standard cost of a material can be different than the actual cost it took to make or buy it, and variances must be accounted for.

A cost or price can be directly assigned to a material without the need to resort to cost estimates generated within the SAP ERP system. Transactions such as MR21 (Price Change) and MR22 (Debit/Credit Material) allow you to directly change the price of a material without reference to any other document within the system. These prices are then used to value inventory and help determine profitability. In addition, inventory valuation can also be represented by the moving average method in which the costs are calculated by taking purchasing or production costs for a specific order and blending them with the value of material that was already in inventory. Using these methods can bring up questions about the means for how these costs were generated, and whether these costs fully reflect the true value of the material.

Standard costs versus moving average costs

 A *standard cost* is a specific price assigned to a material. The value of the inventory is based on that standard, and every valuated goods movement uses that value. If the actual price for purchasing or making that material is different to the standard, then the difference between the standard value and the actual value is posted in a variance account. Materials are assigned price control "S". *Moving average costs* are used to account for fluctuations in the procurement price of a material. If a goods receipt occurs when there is no inventory, the value is determined directly from the actual price of the procurement process. Valuated goods movements take on the value assigned at this point. The next time the material is procured, the actual value of the quantity procured is added to the current inventory value. This total value is divided by the quantity in inventory to produce the moving average price. For example, if there are 100 units of material A in inventory with a value of $1.00 per unit, and an additional 50 units of A are purchased at a value of $2.00 per unit, the resulting inventory value will be $200.00 (100 multiplied by $1.00, plus 50 multiplied by $2.00). The moving average price becomes $200.00 divided by 150; i.e. $1.33 per unit. Valuated goods movements use the $1.33 value from then on. In this case, the material is assigned price control "V".

CO-PC-PCP is a module within Product Cost Controlling (CO-PC) that allows prices to be set for materials based on planned costs associated with manufacturing, purchasing, and managerial overhead functions. Costs planned in Controlling are assigned to the materials using consistent methodology to provide an accurate reflection of the true value of a given material. This methodology enables you to set both cost of goods manufactured (COGM) and cost of goods sold (COGS) prices for each material. It also provides a way to break down these costs into specific components such as raw material, labor, energy consumption, or administrative processes, in order to analyze the costs of different materials. This information can be used to help determine the best means of procurement. Should the material be manufactured in-house, subcontracted to an outside processor, or purchased?

The costs calculated in CO-PC-PCP are the basis for comparing the planned or standard cost for a material against the actual cost incurred when manufacturing or purchasing that item. Cost Object Controlling (CO-PC-OBJ) uses the CO-PC-PCP standards to calculate variances that can be attributed to specific causes associated with the manufacturing processes. In addition, costs of different methods of production can be compared to determine the most cost-effective approach for manufacturing. Costs of outside manufacturing or straight purchases of the materials can also be compared to in-house manufacturing to help determine the best make-or-buy decision for the company. Only the details provided using CO-PC-PCP enable such a decision to be made with confidence.

1.2   Product life cycle

The popularity and usefulness of products is not constant. The first huge cellular phones of decades ago morphed into flip phones and then into smart phones. Even smart phones must be frequently changed out every year or two as new features hit the market and the older phones cannot keep pace with the newer requirements. After a while, the older phones can no longer be used and have to be replaced. This illustrates the impact of the product life cycle. In general, the life cycle can be broken down into seven stages:

▶ Research—the company begins looking for something new

▶ Development—turning the research idea into a marketable product

▶ Introduction—the product enters the marketplace

▶ Growth—sales grow based on market acceptance

▶ Maturity—product sales reach a plateau

▶ Decline—the "next big thing" is introduced and sales decline

▶ Obsolescence—demand for the product has virtually ceased

The stages are not necessarily constant. For example, a product can go through several stages of growth and decline during its life cycle. Figure 1.1 gives a pictorial view of a typical product life cycle. CO-PC-PCP has been designed to provide useful costs at each stage.

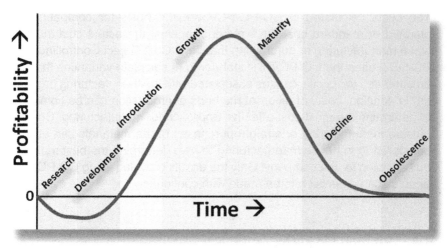

Figure 1.1: Simple product life cycle

Of course, the simple product life cycle shown in Figure 1.1, does not pertain to every product. Some of the alternatives are shown in Figure 1.2, but there can be an infinite number of permutations. The CO-PC-PCP module supports all types of life cycles.

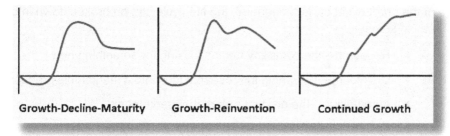

Figure 1.2: Alternative product life cycles

1.2.1 Research stage

During the research stage, the need for a new product is determined. This could constitute anything from a completely new innovative item in the marketplace to an improvement to an already existing product. The process for procuring this product has not yet been finalized, but it is important to generate expected costs to help establish the viability of this product in the marketplace. At this stage, there is no sellable material and no manufacturing process established. Costs can only be estimated based on expected component costs and estimates of what the manufacturing or procurement costs will be. Cost estimates associated with this stage of the life cycle are covered in Chapters 2 and 3.

1.2.2   Development stage

During the development stage, work is performed to fine tune how the product will be made. A material ID is typically assigned to the product at this point. Manufacturing routings have not been finalized and only trial production runs are made. The product is not ready to sell, but the cost picture is becoming clearer. At this point, it is important to know the costs as closely as possible is in order to set the customer pricing when the product is finally introduced into the marketplace. Determination of costs for this stage is covered in Chapter 3.

1.2.3   Introduction stage

The new product is being sold to customers in low volumes. The initial manufacturing routings and bills of material (BOMs) have been determined, but manufacturing lot sizes are small. The initial standard costs are determined using the newly created BOMs and routings, and it is possible to more accurately gauge profitability. At this stage, small lot sizes keep manufacturing costs high. Chapter 6 covers the determination of costs for this stage. The cost of the raw materials used to make up the BOM is covered in Chapter 5.

1.2.4   Growth stage

The product has been successfully introduced to the market and demand for the product is ramping up. Sales and administrative costs remain high. Due to demand growth, manufacturing bottlenecks can occur. It is necessary to start looking at alternative means of making or procuring the product. Standard costs are determined as in the introduction stage. Alternative cost estimates can be created to determine the viability of alternative procurement strategies.

1.2.5 Maturity stage

The product has reached a point where demand is predictable. Sales and administrative costs should have leveled off and begun to decline at this point because the product is established in the market. The focus in manufacturing and procurement is on continuous improvement. Is there a less expensive method for manufacturing the product? Can alternative components be used in the manufacturing process? The product costing tools of CO-PC-PCP can be used to help determine this.

1.2.6 Decline stage

Product demand is down, which impacts the manufacturing batch sizes and run frequency. A standard cost is still required and is based on the manufacturing structures, just as before. Sales and administrative costs also start to diminish. From a product costing point of view, products in the decline stage are processed similarly to those in the introduction, growth, and maturity stages.

1.2.7 Obsolescence stage

The product is no longer being manufactured. There can still be inventory kept for the product, but as there is no requirement to make the product, there is no need to maintain a BOM and manufacturing routing, and no desire to do any more manufacturing. Value is assigned for inventory purposes only. There can still be sales and administrative costs to consider, but these are minimal. CO-PC-PCP provides a means for assigning the value to materials at this stage of the product life cycle.

1.3 Introduction to the cost component split

Analyzing product costs can be difficult. All costs assigned to a material cost estimate are associated with either primary or secondary cost elements. There can be a multitude of costs represented by the various cost elements. Trying to perform an analysis at that level of detail would be complex and time-consuming.

A powerful feature of SAP product costing is the ability to view costs by what is known as a *cost component split*. Cost elements are used in the assignment of costs in controlling, and this includes the costs associated with a cost estimate. The cost component split allows for individual cost elements to be assigned to a cost category or component for analysis purposes.

Cost elements

 A *cost element* identifies a type of cost posted in the CO module. Primary cost elements are associated with general ledger accounts, and the CO posting is tied directly to the financial posting in the FI module. Secondary cost elements are used for moving costs between cost objects in the CO module and are independent of primary general ledger postings. With the introduction of S/4HANA and the Universal Journal, secondary cost elements have themselves become accounts. However, the purpose of the secondary cost elements in S/4HANA has not changed from the earlier ERP versions.

A good example of this is illustrated using labor cost assignment. Multiple accounts/cost elements are used to represent different details of the cost assigned for wages. Straight time pay is associated with one account, insurance costs to another account, vacation pay to yet a different account, and so on. Trying to analyze cost estimates broken down into the individual details by cost element would be overwhelming. Instead, all the costs associated with wage rates can be assigned to a single cost component, enabling the analysis of overall labor costs at a glance.

1.3.1 Cost components

A *cost component* is a specific grouping of costs represented by cost elements and origin groups. These groupings are used to classify costs and determine how these costs are used in a material cost estimate. Certain costs, such as sales and administrative costs, are used in Cost of Goods Sold (COGS) but excluded from Cost of Goods Manufactured (COGM), which is used for measuring manufacturing performance. Cost components are designed to make this distinction possible.

Origin groups

 An *origin group* is used to represent a subdivision of a cost element. Its main purpose is to enable the assignment of a single cost element to multiple cost components. This is especially useful for segregating specific material-related costs in the cost estimate. Origin groups can be part of the base cost definition when allocating costs using an overhead costing sheet. When defined as part of the allocation base, the overhead is only applied to that base for those materials assigned to the specific origin group. Origin groups can also be assigned to purchasing conditions to allow those condition costs to be included in a raw material cost estimate (see Chapter 5).

A maximum of 40 different cost components can be assigned to a specific cost component structure. A cost component can have the combined fixed and variable portions assigned to it, or it can be divided into two separate groupings of fixed costs and variable costs. If the decision was made to differentiate fixed and variable costs, then a maximum of 20 cost components is possible per cost component structure.

Fixed versus variable costs

 A *fixed cost* is one for which the expected amount to be spent is the same regardless of production level or revenue. The planned amount is the expected spend amount. A *variable cost* is a cost that can change based on some level of activity, such as production. Variable costs in SAP are usually planned in conjunction with a quantity of activity represented by an activity type. Fixed costs may be activity-dependent or activity-independent. Variable costs are always activity dependent. Many companies want to distinguish between fixed and variable costs to provide a better understanding of the total cost of production.

Costs are assigned to material cost estimates in multiple ways. They are associated with materials that make up the components of a manufactured product, as part of activity type allocation, as part of overhead costing sheet allocation, or are even directly assigned as part of a unit cost estimate.

An *activity type* is the instrument used for allocating costs from a cost center to another cost object in the CO module. Cost objects in this case include material cost estimates. An activity type is assigned a secondary cost estimate, a unit of measure, and a value for the unit of measure. When a quantity of activity is allocated, the value assigned to that quantity is "moved" from the sender cost center to the receiving cost object. In product costing, activity types are used to allocate production costs to the cost estimate. The cost component split associated with the activity price is then used in the material cost estimate.

Activity types and the cost component split

 Activity types can either be assigned a cost in cost center planning, or they can have costs calculated for them. In order to fully utilize the cost component split, make sure the structure is defined as a primary cost component split and the activity prices are calculated using transaction KSPI. Otherwise, only the cost element of the activity type determines the cost component used in the cost estimate. Calculation of activity prices creates a much richer view of costs in the cost estimates.

1.3.2 Cost component views

Cost component views provide different ways of looking at costs assigned to a material. Configuration for what to include in the cost component views is handled in the main cost component configuration task. From the IMG menu, select CONTROLLING • PRODUCT COST CONTROLLING • PRODUCT COST PLANNING • BASIC SETTINGS FOR MATERIAL COSTING • DEFINE COST COMPONENT STRUCTURE or run transaction OKTZ. Select COST COMPONENT VIEWS, as shown in Figure 1.3. Double click on the COST COMPONENT VIEWS folder to display a list of the available views. The folder is highlighted when active.

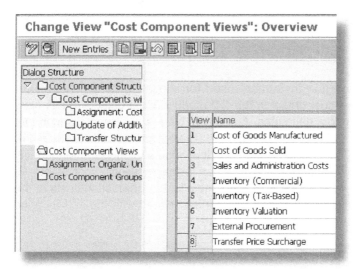

Figure 1.3: Cost component view configuration

Each view is assigned characteristics to determine which cost components are to be included in the calculation of the value for that view. Double click on a specific view to display the characteristic assignments. Figure 1.4 shows the options selected for cost component view (COST COMP. VIEW) 1—cost of goods manufactured (COST OF GOODS MFD).

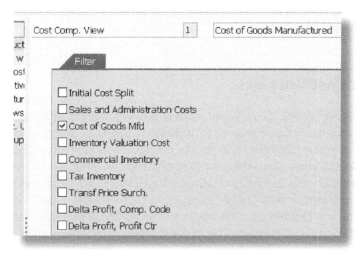

Figure 1.4: Single cost component view details

Multiple selections can be made. The selections correspond to the setup options of the cost component, shown later in Figure 1.12. If the selected option is active for the cost component definition, then that cost component is included in the cost component view defined here. For this example, all cost components with the COST OF GOODS MANUFACTURED option selected in section ❹ of Figure 1.12 are included in the specific view of the cost estimate. Figure 1.5 shows a cost estimate with five cost component views defined.

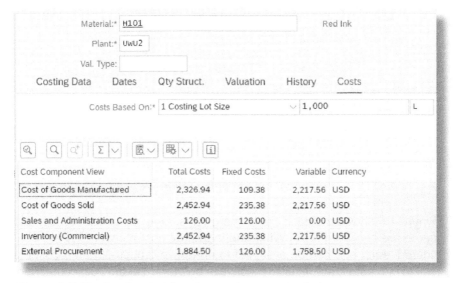

Figure 1.5: Cost estimate showing cost component views

The cost estimate can only display five of the defined views. In this instance, views 1, 2, 3, 4, and 7 have been selected for display. The differences in the costs depend on the selections made in Figure 1.4 for each of the views and the configuration of each of the cost components, as defined in Section 1.3.5. See Chapter 4 for information on how to set up the available views in the cost estimate.

1.3.3 Cost component groups

Different cost components can be combined into groups for a more macro view of the costs. For example, if there are three cost components which identify manufacturing costs, they can all be assigned to the same group to display all manufacturing costs together.

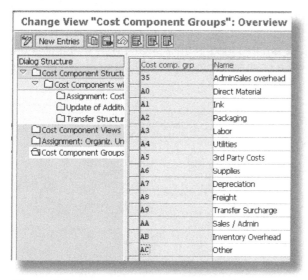

Figure 1.6: Cost component group configuration

Figure 1.6 shows the definition of the groups. Only the group number and name are assigned here. When the individual cost components are configured, each one can be assigned to up to two groups. When a cost estimate is created, the resulting costs can be viewed at the cost component level or subtotaled by cost component group. The costs of all cost components with a common group assignment are added together and shown at the group level in the cost component report. Cost component groups are independent of cost component structures and may be reused in multiple structures.

1.3.4 Cost component structure

The first step for defining the cost components is to create a cost component structure. Click on New Entries , as shown in Figure 1.7.

The cost component structure ID is two characters long. There is also an activation selection, a primary cost component split selection, and a structure name. The ACTIVE checkbox is always disabled when making modifications to the cost components or any of the other structure-related data to ensure that any cost component split changes are carefully controlled. After making the necessary changes, reselect the ACTIVE checkbox before saving the configuration.

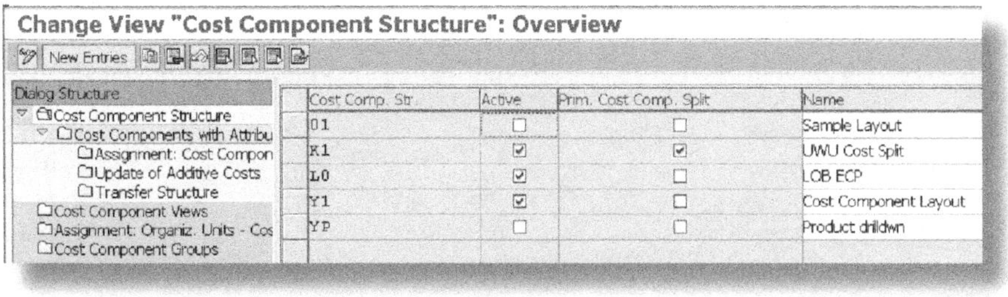

Change View "Cost Component Structure": Overview				
New Entries				
Dialog Structure	Cost Comp. Str.	Active	Prim. Cost Comp. Split	Name
▽ 🗂 Cost Component Structure	01	☐	☐	Sample Layout
▽ ☐ Cost Components with Attribu	X1	☑	☑	UWU Cost Split
☐ Assignment: Cost Compon	L0	☑	☐	LOB ECP
☐ Update of Additive Costs	Y1	☑	☐	Cost Component Layout
☐ Transfer Structure	YP	☐	☐	Product drildwn
☐ Cost Component Views				
☐ Assignment: Organiz. Units - Cos				
☐ Cost Component Groups				

Figure 1.7: Cost component structure definition

Selecting the PRIM. COST COMP. SPLIT checkbox determines whether a primary cost component split is used instead of just a COGM cost component split. A COGM cost component split would use the cost elements assigned directly to activity types when determining the cost components included in a product cost estimate. If the primary cost component split is selected, then costs planned for activity types in cost center planning are also divided into components. This only occurs if activity prices are calculated using transaction KSPI. Selecting the primary cost component split is useful to provide a more thorough analysis of material costs.

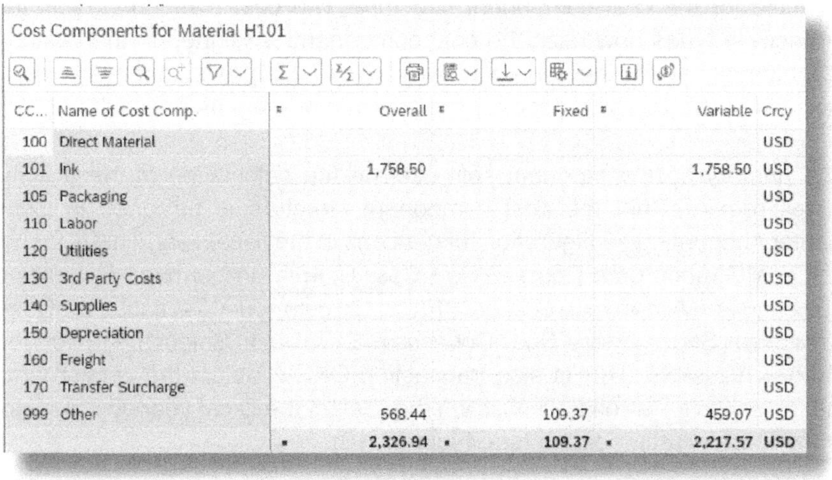

CC...	Name of Cost Comp.	Overall	Fixed	Variable	Crcy
100	Direct Material				USD
101	Ink	1,758.50		1,758.50	USD
105	Packaging				USD
110	Labor				USD
120	Utilities				USD
130	3rd Party Costs				USD
140	Supplies				USD
150	Depreciation				USD
160	Freight				USD
170	Transfer Surcharge				USD
999	Other	568.44	109.37	459.07	USD
		2,326.94	109.37	2,217.57	USD

Cost Components for Material H101

Figure 1.8: Cost estimate cost component split with primary not set

Figure 1.8 shows the cost component view of a cost estimate where the PRIM. COST COMP. SPLIT checkbox has been deselected for the cost component structure. The cost elements associated with the activity types are assigned to cost component 999 (OTHER).

CC...	Name of Cost Comp.	Overall	Fixed	Variable	Crcy
100	Direct Material				USD
101	Ink	1,758.50		1,758.50	USD
105	Packaging				USD
110	Labor	286.26		286.26	USD
120	Utilities	94.04		94.04	USD
130	3rd Party Costs				USD
140	Supplies	78.76		78.76	USD
150	Depreciation	109.38	109.38		USD
160	Freight				USD
170	Transfer Surcharge				USD
999	Other				USD
		2,326.94	109.38	2,217.56	USD

Figure 1.9: Cost estimate cost component split with primary set

Figure 1.9 shows the cost component split view for the cost estimate of the same material where the PRIM. COST COMP. SPLIT checkbox has been selected for the cost component structure. The cost component split for the activity types now uses the cost components assigned to the cost elements planned for the various activity types. This provides a much more granular view of what constitutes the makeup of the material cost.

The primary cost component split used in the calculation of the activity prices requires that the cost component structure is assigned in Cost Center Accounting configuration for versions in the fiscal year. This is found in the IMG menu path CONTROLLING • COST CENTER ACCOUNTING • PLANNING • ALLOCATIONS • ACTIVITY ALLOCATION • PRICE CALCULATION • SETTINGS FOR COST COMPONENT SPLIT • DEFINE COST COMPONENT STRUCTURE. Select the option for MAINTAIN VERSIONS. This is also transaction OKEV. Select the version and the folder SETTINGS FOR EACH FISCAL YEAR. Select the fiscal year and then go to the PRICE CALCULATION tab (see Figure 1.10).

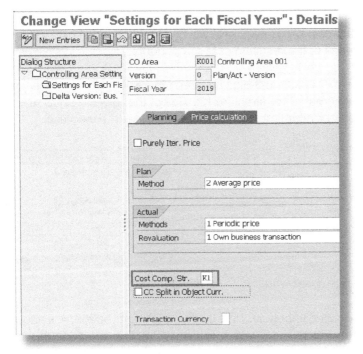

Figure 1.10: Cost center accounting price calculation configuration

Make sure that the cost component structure is assigned to this version and year (COST COMP. STR.). This should be done for each fiscal year that is defined.

1.3.5   Configuring cost components

After the cost component structure is defined, the cost components can be created for that structure. The cost component structure is used for both cost planning and for actual costing with the material ledger. Adding cost components to a structure after turning on material ledger actual costing causes issues with the calculation of the actual cost component split for cost objects that are open at the time of the change. Please refer to SAP Note 434873[1] for more details and links to other notes relating to this

---

[1]   SAP Note 434873—"Actual cost component split—cost component structure change"

issue. Prior to doing any configuration of the cost components, plan out the details of how the cost component split will be used and how costs will be combined into each of the resulting cost components.

A cost component ID is a 1- to 3-digit number. Figure 1.11 shows the list of cost components created for structure K1. Select the folder Cost Components with Attributes after first selecting Cost Component Structure.

Dialog Structure	Cost Comp. Str.	Cost Compo	Name of Cost Comp.
▽ ☐ Cost Component Structure	K1	100	Direct Material
▽ 🗐 Cost Components with Attribu	K1	101	Ink
☐ Assignment: Cost Compon	K1	105	Packaging
☐ Update of Additive Costs			
☐ Transfer Structure	K1	110	Labor
☐ Cost Component Views	K1	120	Utilities
☐ Assignment: Organiz. Units - Cos	K1	130	3rd Party Costs
☐ Cost Component Groups			
	K1	140	Supplies

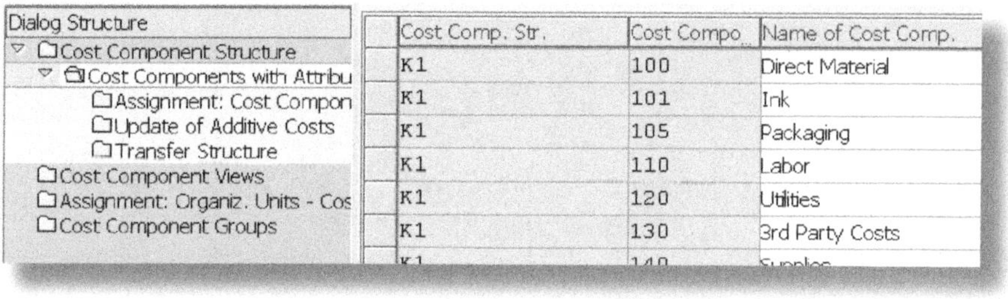

Figure 1.11: Define cost components for the structure

To create a new cost component, click on the [New Entries] button. A window is displayed (see Figure 1.12) which is used to define the attributes of the cost component. If an existing cost component definition needs to be changed, select the cost component in the list in Figure 1.11 and then click on the 🗐 button.

The configuration here controls which cost component views will use the costs assigned to this cost component and which of two cost component groups can be used for further summarization in reports. Up to 40 different cost components can be defined. However, if there is a need to differentiate between fixed and variable costs for the cost component, then there is a maximum of 20 cost components that can be used.

Referring to Figure 1.12:

❶ Cost Share defines whether the cost component is relevant for variable costs only, or for fixed and variable costs. If Fixed and Variable Costs is selected, the cost component uses both a fixed and a variable portion, essentially taking up two cost component slots.

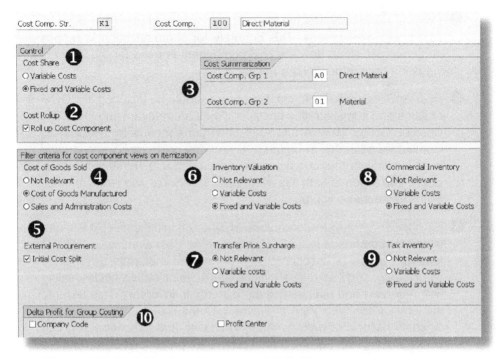

Figure 1.12: Individual cost component definition

❷ COST ROLLUP defines whether the values assigned to the cost component are included from lower levels of a multi-level costing structure. If a material is transferred from another location or a material from the same location is used in a BOM, its cost component costs are included in the total cost component split for the cost estimate. Two sets of cost component costs are maintained for the cost estimate. These are the top level, which includes only costs that were added to the material at the material itemization cost level, and lower levels, which include all the costs by cost component from all the lower costing levels. This configuration defines whether this cost component is included in the lower levels and if the cost is included in the specific cost view for the top level. As an example, COST OF GOODS MANUFACTURED costs could be included in the cost rollup, whereas SALES AND ADMINISTRATIVE COSTS would not.

❸ COST SUMMARIZATION assigns the cost component to up to two different cost component groups. This is purely for summarization in reports and does not affect how the cost component is used for the different valuation requirements (see Section 1.3.3).

❹ COST OF GOODS SOLD controls if the costs should be included in COGM or sales and administration costs, or if they are relevant for either. The COST OF GOODS MANUFACTURED selection corresponds to the COST OF GOODS MFD selection in Figure 1.4, and this cost component is used in all views with that characteristic selected. SALES AND ADMINISTRATION COSTS corresponds with the view selection SALES AND ADMINISTRATION COSTS in the same figure.

❺ EXTERNAL PROCUREMENT determines whether an initial cost split is maintained for purchased materials. Select INITIAL COST SPLIT to enable this feature. The costs associated with purchased materials can include other costs, such as delivery costs and administrative costs dealing with receiving and maintaining the material in inventory. This ties into the INITIAL COST SPLIT view in Figure 1.4, and if that view is selected, all costs associated with material purchases and subcontracting can be viewed together, giving a total picture for purchased costs within a higher level cost estimate.

❻ INVENTORY VALUATION defines the standard price of the material used in material movements and inventory valuation. The selections are either NOT RELEVANT, VARIABLE COSTS, or FIXED AND VARIABLE COSTS. The costs associated with any cost component where costs are relevant for this are added together to determine the standard price in the cost estimate. If costs are relevant, then these costs are displayed in the INVENTORY VALUATION COST view, as assigned in Figure 1.4.

❼ TRANSFER PRICE SURCHARGE is assigned to the cost component for which transfer pricing surcharges are maintained. A transfer price surcharge defines the intercompany profit when transferring a material from a plant in one company code to a plant in another company code. The corresponding view associated with this is TRANSF PRICE SURCH. in Figure 1.4.

❽ COMMERCIAL INVENTORY defines costs that are included in commercial inventory cost estimates. These costs can be updated in the ACCOUNTING 2 tab of the material master, which can be viewed in Figure 1.21. This ties to the COMMERCIAL INVENTORY view in Figure 1.4.

⑨ TAX INVENTORY defines costs that are included in tax inventory cost estimates. These costs can also be updated in the ACCOUNTING 2 tab of the material master and ties to the TAX INVENTORY view in Figure 1.4.

⑩ DELTA PROFIT FOR GROUP COSTING entries are required when using group costing. A selection can be made for both COMPANY CODE and PROFIT CENTER by checking each box. If COMPANY CODE is selected, this corresponds to the view DELTA PROFIT, COMP. CODE in Figure 1.4. Profit Center corresponds to DELTA PROFIT, PROFIT CTR.

1.3.6   Cost component cost assignment

The next step in the cost component structure configuration is to assign cost elements and origin groups to each cost component. This is shown in Figure 1.13. If the COST COMPONENT STRUCTURE folder is selected, the cost definitions for all cost components are displayed. If the ASSIGNMENT: COST COMPONENTS folder is selected, then only the cost assignments for an individual cost component are displayed. Click on New Entries to create a new cost assignment, or just update the existing cost estimate ranges. Costs can be assigned as either a range of cost elements or an origin group, or a combination of the two. If only an origin group is defined, that group will apply to all cost elements. If an origin group is assigned to a range of cost elements, then it will only apply if the costs are associated with these specific cost elements.

Cost Comp. Str.	Chart of Accts	From cost el.	Origin group	To cost elem.	Cost Compo	Name of Cost
K1	YCOA		HATL		100	Oject Material
K1	YCOA	51100000		51100000	100	Direct Material
K1	YCOA	54300000		54300000	100	Direct Material
K1	YCOA	54400000		54400000	100	Direct Material

Figure 1.13: Cost component cost assignment

1.3.7   Additive cost configuration

Additive cost estimates are used to include costs in a material cost estimate that cannot be derived from normal methods. When creating an additive cost estimate, itemization costs are assigned a cost element. This can be done manually or derived from the cost element assigned to the specific object type selected. For those itemization items where the cost element is not known, the cost component can be entered, and a cost element determined, based on the assignment in the Update of Additive Costs folder.

First, select the cost component structure from the Cost Component Structure folder. Then, select the Update of Additive Costs folder. Click on New Entries . Enter the cost component structure, the cost component, the chart of accounts, and the cost element. Cost element is required in this case. However, an origin group can also be selected to further define the costs to use. For this to work properly, the cost element and origin group combination must exist in the selected cost component. When an item is then added to the additive cost estimate and only the cost component is entered, the system automatically assigns the cost element from this configuration to the cost estimate. This configuration is shown in Figure 1.14.

Change View "Update of Additive Costs": Overview

Dialog Structure		Cost Comp. Str.	Cost Com	Chart of Accts	Cost Element	Origin group
▽ ☐ Cost Component Struct		K1	160	YCOA	65400000	
▽ ☐ Cost Components w		K1	180	YCOA	94113000	
☐ Assignment: Cost						
☐ Update of Additiv						
☐ Transfer Structur						
☐ Cost Component Views						
☐ Assignment: Organiz. L						
☐ Cost Component Group						

Figure 1.14: Assignment of cost element to additive costs

1.3.8 Transfer structure configuration

If an alternative cost component structure is defined, a transfer structure is created to determine how the costs are transferred from the main cost component structure to the alternative structure.

New Entries: Overview of Added Entries

Dialog Structure	Source Cost Comp Str	Source CCS	Tgt Cost Comp Str	Target CCS
▽ ☐ Cost Component Struct	K1	100	Z9	1
▽ ☐ Cost Components w	K1	101	Z9	1
☐ Assignment: Cost	K1	105	Z9	1
☐ Update of Additiv	K1	90	Z9	2
⊟ Transfer Structur	K1	120	Z9	2
☐ Cost Component Views	K1	130	Z9	2
☐ Assignment: Organiz. L	K1	140	Z9	2
☐ Cost Component Group	K1	150	Z9	2

Figure 1.15: Cost component transfer structure

The lowest level at which a transfer can take place is the cost component level. To create a new transfer structure, first select the cost component structure from the COST COMPONENT STRUCTURE folder, and then double click on the TRANSFER STRUCTURE folder (see Figure 1.15). Click on New Entries to make the assignments. For each cost component in the source structure, enter the source structure ID and cost component, and the destination structure and corresponding cost component. The cost component split is generated for both structures when creating a cost estimate. The alternative structure then needs to be defined in the valuation variant configuration (see Section 1.4.18).

1.3.9 Organizational assignment

A cost component structure is assigned to company code, plant, and costing variant so that it can be used in cost estimates.

Change View "Assignment: Organiz. Units - Cost Component Struct": Over

Dialog Structure	Company Code	Plant	Costi	Valid from	Cost C	Name	Cost Comp Structure (Aux. CCS)
▽ ☐ Cost Component Structu	++++	++++	++++	01/01/2012	Y1	Cost Component Layout	
▽ ☐ Cost Components wi	K101	++++	++++	01/01/2018	K1	UWU Cost Split	
☐ Assignment: Cost	K102	++++	++++	01/01/2018	K1	UWU Cost Split	
☐ Update of Additi	L100	++++	PS06	01/01/2000	L0	LOB ECP	
☐ Transfer Structur							
☐ Cost Component Views							
⊟ Assignment: Organiz. Un							
☐ Cost Component Groups							

Figure 1.16: Cost component structure organization assignment

Figure 1.16 shows the definition. An important feature is the use of wild-cards for the assignment of company code, plant, and costing variant. This greatly reduces the amount of configuration required. The wildcard descriptor is ++++ and can refer to company code, plant, and costing variant. If the wildcard is used for company code for one cost structure, then if a different cost structure is required for other company codes, those company codes must be explicitly defined. When creating a cost estimate, an explicit definition is searched for first, and if that is not found, then the selection defaults to the wildcarded entry. In Figure 1.16, cost component structure Y1 is the default structure for all company codes. However, structure K1 is explicitly defined for company codes K101 and K102. Structure K1 is used for those two company codes. Y1 is used for all other company codes. This includes company code L100 for all costing versions except PB06.

1.4   Introduction to costing variants

SAP uses the term *cost estimate* to denote the aggregation of costs from various sources assigned to an object. The object could be a material, a sales order line item, or a manufacturing order, among other things. The purpose of this book is to show how costs are assigned to materials, although much of what is included also applies to other types of cost estimates.

Among the many reasons for wanting to create a cost estimate, a primary one is to generate a standard cost that can be used for valuation and profitability measurement. Other reasons include creating comparison costs for what-if scenarios, generating commercial or tax-based inventory valuation, and for estimating costs for new products. The requirements for determining the costs differ from company to company as well. SAP handles these different needs and requirements by using a costing variant to specify the purpose and composition of the various types of cost estimates. The costing variant not only controls what costs are included in a cost estimate, it also determines if a cost estimate can be saved and what fields, if any, can be updated in the material master.

The costing variant has many parts that have specific application to the cost estimate. The rest of this section gives an overview of each of the costing variant sections to use as a reference. Specific settings and alternatives are covered by individual topic in later chapters in this book and in its companion book "SAP® S/4HANA Product Cost Planning—Costing with Quantity Structure".

1.4.1 Costing variant configuration

Costing variant configuration for CO-PC-PCP is processed using transaction OKKN, or via IMG menu path CONTROLLING • PRODUCT COST CONTROLLING • PRODUCT COST PLANNING • MATERIAL COST ESTIMATE WITH QUANTITY STRUCTURE • DEFINE COSTING VARIANTS. When first entering the configuration transaction, a list of existing costing variants associated with product costing is displayed, as shown in Figure 1.17. A costing variant must have both a costing type and a valuation variant assigned to it. The combination of the two defines the purpose and the valuation strategy used by the costing variant.

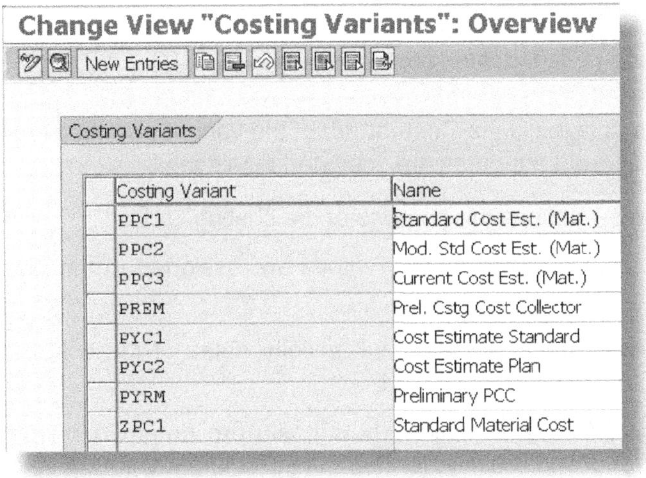

Change View "Costing Variants": Overview

New Entries

Costing Variants

Costing Variant	Name
PPC1	Standard Cost Est. (Mat.)
PPC2	Mod. Std Cost Est. (Mat.)
PPC3	Current Cost Est. (Mat.)
PREM	Prel. Cstg Cost Collector
PYC1	Cost Estimate Standard
PYC2	Cost Estimate Plan
PYRM	Preliminary PCC
ZPC1	Standard Material Cost

Figure 1.17: Costing variant configuration initial window

To modify an existing costing variant, select the variant from the list and click on the button. To create a new costing variant, click on the New Entries button. A costing variant can be copied by selecting the source variant and then clicking on the button. When copying one costing variant from another, the new costing variant must use the same costing type and valuation variant from the source costing variant. If a new costing type or valuation variant is needed for the new costing variant, click on New Entries and

33

then assign the new costing type and valuation variant. The settings from the original costing variant need to be manually copied to the new one.

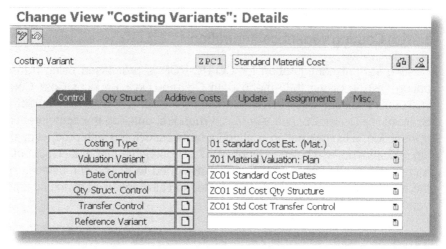

Figure 1.18: Costing variant control tab

The next window displayed is the CONTROL tab of the variant definition (see Figure 1.18). Six different attributes are assigned in this tab:

▶ COSTING TYPE—defines the purpose of the costing variant

▶ VALUATION VARIANT—defines how values are assigned to the cost estimate

▶ DATE CONTROL—defines the default validity dates of the cost estimate

▶ QTY. STRUCT. CONTROL—defines how costs are determined from bills of material and routings for manufactured materials

▶ TRANSFER CONTROL—defines how lower level costs are determined when creating a cost estimate

▶ REFERENCE VARIANT—defines a costing variant that is referenced when calculating costs

Maintenance of these attributes can be performed either from within the CONTROL tab by clicking on the corresponding button for the attribute, or by using the separate configuration transactions provided for the attributes.

To create a new attribute from within the costing variant configuration, click on the corresponding ⬚ button next to the attribute.

1.4.2 Costing type

The costing type defines the purpose for the cost estimate. It determines whether the resulting price is updated for the material and how it is updated. It specifies the date for the cost estimate, the cost component view used when applying overhead costs, and how the partner cost component split is handled for multilevel cost estimates. Costing type configuration is processed using transaction OKKI or via IMG menu path CONTROLLING • PRODUCT COST CONTROLLING • PRODUCT COST PLANNING • MATERIAL COST ESTIMATE WITH QUANTITY STRUCTURE • COSTING VARIANT: COMPONENTS • DEFINE COSTING TYPES. There are three tabs under the costing type definition. The costing types provided by SAP are identified by a 2-digit number. A new costing type must have a 2-character alphanumeric ID to distinguish it from the SAP-supplied costing types.

Price update

The PRICE UPDATE tab defines whether material master fields are updated based on the cost estimate and which fields are updated. Figure 1.19 shows the dropdown selection boxes for the price update determination.

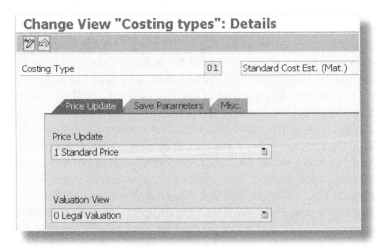

Figure 1.19: Costing type price update

PRICE UPDATE has 5 options:

- ▶ STANDARD PRICE

- ▶ TAX-BASED PRICE

- ▶ COMMERCIAL PRICE

- ▶ PRICES OTHER THAN STANDARD PRICE

- ▶ NO UPDATE

STANDARD PRICE update can only be assigned to one costing type. Costing type 01 comes delivered with this setting. Once this is set for a costing type, it cannot be changed. A cost estimate created using a costing variant with costing type 01 can be released as the standard cost estimate for the material. The standard cost can be seen on two different tabs of the material master. Section ❶ in Figure 1.20 shows the field on the ACCOUNTING 1 tab, and section ❶ in Figure 1.22 shows the field on the COSTING 2 tab. The STANDARD PRICE is used for valuing inventory for materials with price control S, and access to updating this price should be limited.

STANDARD PRICE is not the only price field in the material master that can be updated. Nine other price fields can have values loaded based on the costing type of specific cost estimates. Tax-based inventory prices, commercial inventory prices, and planned prices can be saved. Selecting TAX-BASED PRICE or COMMERCIAL PRICE for PRICE UPDATE in a costing type indicates that the resulting cost estimate is an inventory cost estimate. The costs included in such cost estimates are determined by the setup of the cost components (see Section 1.3). Only the costs from cost components for which COMMERCIAL INVENTORY (see Figure 1.12, section ❽) is enabled can be used for updating the commercial price fields (see Figure 1.21, section ❷). Only the costs from cost components for which TAX INVENTORY (see Figure 1.12, section ❾) is enabled can be used for updating the tax price fields (see Figure 1.21, section ❶). Up to three different prices can be saved for each type of inventory valuation. The specific field is selected when releasing the cost estimate. When using a costing variant with a cost type set up for updating either tax-based or commercial price, the determination of lowest value is used. The inventory cost estimate is compared with the standard cost estimate and the lowest value cost estimate becomes the inventory cost estimate. This type of update is only applicable for manufactured materials and is not allowed for purchased materials.

Figure 1.20: Accounting 1 tab of material master

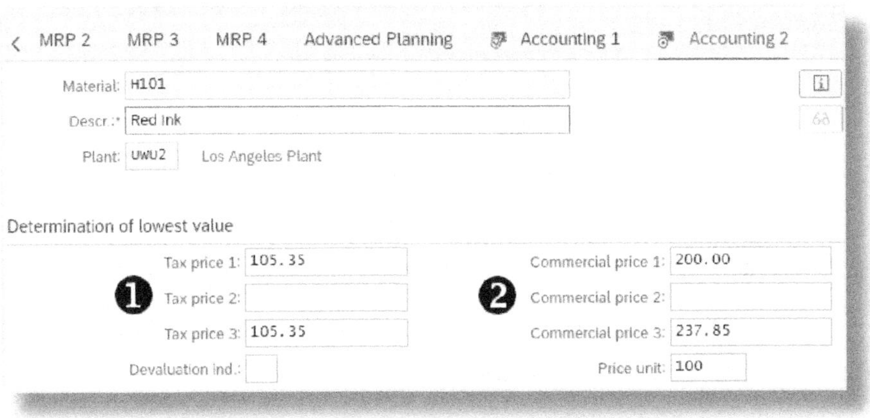

Figure 1.21: Accounting 2 tab of the material master

If PRICES OTHER THAN STANDARD PRICE is selected for the price update for the costing type, then the planned price fields on the COSTING 1 tab of the material master can be updated in addition to the tax-based and commercial valuation fields in the ACCOUNTING 2 tab. All nine fields are available for update.

Updating commercial and tax-based prices

 When prices for either commercial or tax-based inventory fields are updated using PRICES OTHER THAN STANDARD PRICE, the "determination of lowest value" rule is not used. The value of the calculated cost is updated regardless of whether it is lower than the current lowest value price.

The planned price fields on the COSTING 2 tab are shown in Figure 1.22, in section ❷. When these fields are updated, the corresponding planned price date is set to the date of the cost estimate.

‹ Costing 1	Costing 2	Plant stock	Stor. loc. stck	WM Execution	WM Packaging

Material: H101

Descr. Red Ink

Plant: UWU2   Los Angeles Plant

Standard Cost Estimate

Cost Estimate	Future	Current	Previous
Period / Fiscal Year	4 2019	3 2019	0
Planned Price	234.52	227.02	0.00

❶ Standard price: 227.02

Planned prices

Planned price 1:		Planned price date 1:
❷ Planned price 2: 112.85		Planned price date 2: 04/01/2019
Planned price 3: 172.56		Planned price date 3: 04/01/2019

Figure 1.22: Costing 2 tab of the material master

After defining PRICE UPDATE, select an option for the VALUATION VIEW. There are three views used in product costing:

▶ LEGAL VALUATION—value based on company code currency and includes any inter-company profits

▶ GROUP VALUATION—valuation based on group currency excluding inter-company profits

▶ PROFIT CENTER VALUATION—valuation based on profit center view

For standard price update, LEGAL VALUATION should be selected, and this cannot be changed later. For other price update strategies, any of the three types can be used, depending on whether the controlling area definition calls for parallel valuation.

Save parameters

The SAVE PARAMETERS tab (see Figure 1.23) is used to define which date is used when the cost estimate is saved. Settings are made for both cost estimates with quantity structure (covered in Chapters 4, 5, and 6) and for additive cost estimates (covered in the companion book "SAP® S/4HANA Product Cost Planning—Costing with Quantity Structure"). Three selections are possible for each type of cost estimate:

▶ WITHOUT DATE—the cost estimate is saved without the costing date as part of the key

▶ WITH DATE—the cost estimate is saved with the date of the cost estimate

▶ WITH START OF PERIOD—the cost estimate is saved with the date of the start of the period in which the costing date falls

Standard cost estimates must use WITH START OF PERIOD to ensure consistent valuation throughout the period. If additive cost estimates are used, the same strategy for saving should be used as for regular cost estimates.

Change View "Costing types": Details

Costing Type   01   Standard Cost Est. (Mat.)

Price Update | Save Parameters | Misc.

Cost Estimates with Quantity Structure
3 With Start of Period

Additive Cost Estimates
3 With Start of Period

Figure 1.23: Save parameters

Misc.

The MISC. tab (see Figure 1.24) defines both the behavior of overhead cost allocations to the cost estimate and the way in which partner cost component splits are used. COST PORTION FOR OVERHEAD APPLICATION defines which cost component view is used when calculating overhead costs with an overhead costing sheet.

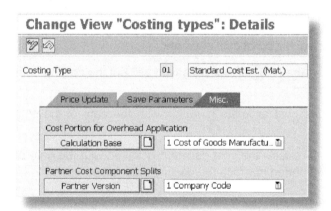

Figure 1.24: Overhead and partner cost component splits

Overhead costs are allocated to a cost estimate using an overhead costing sheet assigned to the valuation variant used for the cost estimate (see Section 1.4.3). The calculation base defines which cost component view is used in the overhead calculation. If COST OF GOODS MANUFACTURED is selected, the overhead only applies to the costs associated with the cost components assigned to that view. For example, costs in a cost component assigned to SALES AND ADMINISTRATIVE COSTS are not included in the overhead calculation because these views are mutually exclusive. If this is left blank, then overhead applies to the entire cost estimate regardless of cost component. To see the definition of the cost component view, click on the [□] button. To see which cost component options are selected for the view, click on the CALCULATION BASE button. Cost component view configuration is explained in Section 1.3.2.

The partner cost component split allows for a detailed look at the contribution costs from various organizational units that make up the supply chain for a material. An organizational unit could be a plant, a profit center, a company code, or a business area. Turning on the partner cost component split gives the ability to understand the cost contributions from the specific organizations when doing group costing. A partner is an organizational unit that provides materials and services used in manufacturing of a product. A direct partner is the specific partner that directly supplies those costs to the current manufacturing level. A partner cost component split contains configuration for general partners and direct partners.

A specific partner version must be selected to enable the partner cost component split for this costing type. Select a partner version from the drop-down list under PARTNER COST COMPONENT SPLITS or create one by clicking on the [□] button (see Figure 1.25). This transfers focus to the partner version configuration transaction OKYB. The IMG menu option for this is CONTROLLING • PRODUCT COST CONTROLLING • PRODUCT COST PLANNING • SELECT-ED FUNCTIONS IN MATERIAL COSTING • DEFINE PARTNER VERSIONS. Select which organizational units are included for the partner cost component split. The PARTNER VERSION button on the MISC. tab of the costing type definition shows the definition of the selected partner version.

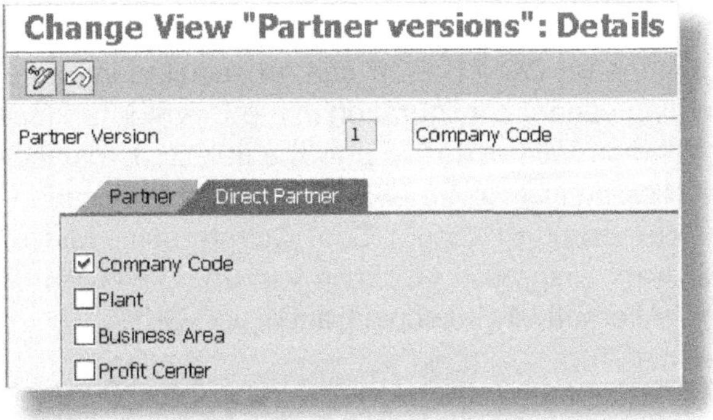

Figure 1.25: Partner version configuration

41

1.4.3 Valuation variant overview

The valuation variant defines how costs are assigned to the cost estimate. The valuation variant configuration has six different tabs which cover the various aspects of determining how costs should be applied:

▶ MATERIAL VAL. defines the method for costing purchased materials

▶ ACTIVITY TYPES/PROCESSES defines the method for including the costs of internal activities and business processes in the cost estimate

▶ SUBCONTRACTING defines the methods used to calculate the cost of outside processing of goods supplied by the company

▶ EXT. PROCESSING defines the costing strategy for external manufacturing in which only the manufacturing operation within a route is handled by an outside company

▶ OVERHEAD is used to configure the overhead costing sheets used to apply costs to both manufactured and purchased materials

▶ MISC. is used to create costing relevancy factors that can be assigned to components or operations used in manufacturing

An additional feature of the valuation variant is that it can be defined at the plant level. Each plant can have its own specific valuation variants with different parameter settings to account for the costing requirements at the various sites. For example, if plant UWU3 has specific overhead calculation requirements that differ from those of other plants, then a plant specific valuation variant can be set up with a different overhead costing sheet defined on the OVERHEAD tab. Any cost estimate for a material within that plant would then use that overhead costing sheet instead of the one used for the other plants.

Valuation variant configuration for CO-PC-PCP can be selected in one of three ways. From the costing variant configuration in the CONTROL tab (see Figure 1.18), click on VALUATION VARIANT to jump to the selected valuation variant configuration, or click on ▣ to be able to create a new variant. The IMG menu path is CONTROLLING • PRODUCT COST CONTROLLING • MATERIAL COST ESTIMATE WITH QUANTITY STRUCTURE • COSTING VARIANT: COMPONENTS • DEFINE VALUATION VARIANTS. Alternatively, execute transaction OKK4.

1.4.4   Valuation variant—material valuation

Figure 1.26 shows the strategy sequence for determining the cost of pur-chased raw materials. Up to five different strategies can be selected. If a cost is not found using the first strategy, then the system goes to the next strategy, and so on, until a cost is found or the last strategy is reached. This is shown in section ❶ of Figure 1.26. For each strategy selected, there is a checkbox to indicate whether additive cost estimates are to be included in the cost estimate with this strategy.

Section ❷ is only displayed if one of the strategies defined in section ❶ is PRICE FROM PURCHASING INFO RECORD. If this strategy is selected, another set of strategies is defined to determine how the cost is pulled from the purchasing information record master data or from purchase orders for the material. A DELIVERY COSTS link is also provided in the configuration in order to assign origin groups to specific purchasing conditions. This is used to define which cost components are to be used to represent the purchasing costs for the material. This configuration is covered in more detail in Chapter 5.

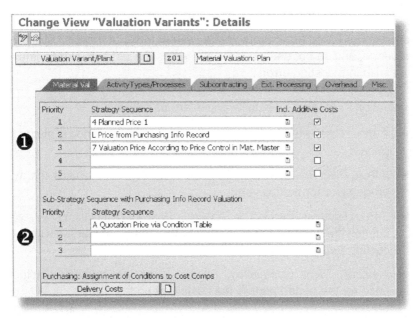

Figure 1.26: Raw material pricing definition

1.4.5   Valuation variant—activity price values

Click on the ACTIVITY TYPE/PROCESSES tab to configure the valuation behavior of activity types and business processes when included in the cost estimate. Figure 1.27 shows that a strategy sequence is also used for activity type and business process cost calculations.

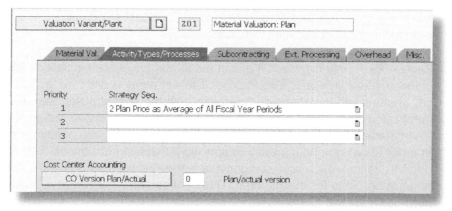

Figure 1.27: Activity price determination

If a price is not found for a strategy, the system looks at the next strategy in sequence, and so on, until no more strategies are defined. Not finding a price results in a costing error.

The valuation strategies for activity prices are as follows:

▶ 1 PLAN PRICE FOR THE PERIOD—uses the costing period's planned price

▶ 2 PLAN PRICE AS AVERAGE OF ALL FISCAL YEAR PERIODS—takes the average price for the full year

▶ 3 PLAN PRICE AS AVERAGE OF REMAINING PERIODS OF FISCAL YEAR—calculates the average price for all periods in the year starting with the costing period

▶ 4 ACTUAL PRICE OF PREVIOUS PERIOD—uses the calculated actual price for the period prior to the costing period

▶ 5 MOST UP-TO-DATE ACTUAL PRICE IN THE PAST—looks at the costing period and takes the latest calculated actual price prior to the costing period

▶ 6 MOST UP-TO-DATE PLAN PRICE—looks at the costing period and takes the latest planned price prior to the costing period

▶ 7 ACTUAL PRICE FOR THE PERIOD—uses the actual price for the period of the cost estimate

The COST CENTER ACCOUNTING section defines which controlling cost version is used when retrieving activity prices. This version is not the same as the costing version used when creating cost estimates. Click on the CO VERSION PLAN/ACTUAL button to see the list of defined CO versions. CO version 0 should be used for standard cost estimates.

1.4.6 Valuation variant—subcontracting

The strategy sequence for determining the subcontracting price is similar to the sequence for material valuation of purchased materials. However, the two strategies using condition types to divide the costs into material and delivery costs are not available for subcontracting. This means that it is not possible to split subcontracting costs in the same way that raw material costs can be split. In addition, specifying planned prices for subcontracting in the material master, as is done for raw material costing, is not allowed for subcontracting. This is because the material cost is developed from a combination of the subcontracting price plus the components in the BOM. The subcontracting cost must be derived from either a purchasing information record or from purchase order information. Figure 1.28 shows the configuration of the strategy sequence.

Figure 1.28: Subcontracting price determination

Up to three strategies are defined for selecting the costs included in the subcontracting price. If more than one strategy is defined, and when the first one does not produce a valid cost, the next strategy is used. This continues until the last defined strategy is reached. If no strategy can find a cost, an error is displayed, and the cost estimate fails.

The QUOTATION IN PURCHASING selection defines whether to use the planned or actual quota arrangement when determining the vendor to use in the vendor selection process. Quota arrangements are used to divide procurement among multiple vendors, or even multiple types of procurement such as outside purchasing and in-house production. When searching for a vendor, if a quota arrangement is defined for the material, the quota arrangement is used before looking for a low-cost vendor.

1.4.7   Valuation variant—external processing

External processing differs from subcontracting in that instead of shipping off components to a vendor to return a new product, work in process is sent as part of a manufacturing order, to execute a specific order operation, and is then returned to complete processing in the sending plant. External processing is defined as an operation within a routing.

Click on the EXT. PROCESSING tab (see Figure 1.29). This shows that a strategy sequence also exists for the determination of the external processing cost that is similar to the one for subcontracting. External processing uses the same strategies for finding costs as for subcontracting. There is an additional strategy (PRICE FROM OPERATION) which allows for a value to be assigned to the routing operation to define the processing cost. A price can be specifically loaded in the operation and can be used for determining the processing cost. This is analogous to the material master prices which can be used for raw material costing.

Valuation Variant/Plant	⬜	Z01	Material Valuation: Plan

Material Val.	Activity Types/Processes	Subcontracting	Ext. Processing	Overhead	Misc.

Priority	Strategy Sequence	
1	1 Price from Operation	🔽
2	3 Net Quotation Price	🔽
3		🔽

Figure 1.29: External processing price determination

1.4.8 Valuation variant—overhead calculations

To apply overhead to a material cost estimate, specific overhead costing sheets must be assigned to the valuation variant. Figure 1.30 shows that overhead is allocated differently for purchased materials than it is for manufactured materials. Separate costing sheets can be defined for each. OVERHEAD ON FINISHED AND SEMIFINISHED MATERIALS includes not only materials manufactured in a plant, but also materials that are transferred from plant to plant. The OVERHEAD ON MATERIAL COMPONENTS section is used for overhead costing sheets for purchased materials.

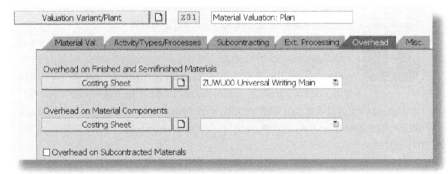

Figure 1.30: Overhead allocation assignment

Clicking on the OVERHEAD ON SUBCONTRACTED MATERIALS checkbox enables overhead from the material component overhead costing sheet to be applied to subcontracted materials.

1.4.9 Valuation variant—price factors

Price factors are used to define a percentage relevancy of the cost of a routing operation or a material component in costing. There are two pre-defined costing relevancy IDs: "X" for 100% relevancy and " " (blank space) for 0% relevancy. Each routing or recipe operation and each BOM component include a field where costing relevancy is defined. This normally defaults to "X" (100% relevancy), but this can be overridden. Inventory cost estimates are the only types that can use costing relevancies other than 0% or 100%. Price factors can be defined to specify different percentages. However, standard cost estimates, modified standard cost estimates, current cost estimates, and order cost estimates can only use 0% or 100% relevancy to costing. If a BOM item or routing operation uses a different price factor, it is always treated as 100% for these types of cost estimates. Alternative price factors are only valid for inventory cost estimates as defined in the costing type definition (see Section 1.4.2).

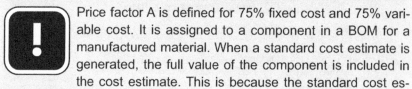

Price factors in costing

Price factor A is defined for 75% fixed cost and 75% variable cost. It is assigned to a component in a BOM for a manufactured material. When a standard cost estimate is generated, the full value of the component is included in the cost estimate. This is because the standard cost estimate costing type is not defined for inventory costs, and any non-blank factor assigned to the component is then treated as 100% relevant by the system.

Figure 1.31 shows how to configure the price factors from the valuation variant configuration. Click on the MISC. tab, then on PRICE FACTORS to modify the percentages of an existing price factor. The 0% factor and the 100% factor cannot be modified. Click on ⬚ to assign a new factor to a costing variant.

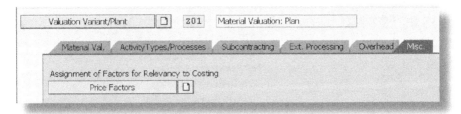

Figure 1.31: Price factor configuration

Figure 1.32 shows the configuration. This configuration can be processed using either transaction OKK7 or IMG menu path CONTROLLING • PRODUCT COST CONTROLLING • PRODUCT COST PLANNING • PRICE UPDATE • PARAMETERS FOR INVENTORY COST ESTIMATE • DEFINE PRICE FACTORS. The valuation variant can be wildcarded using the string +++. If the wildcard is used, the relevancy factor will be valid for all valuation variants. The system first looks in the configuration for a specific valuation variant. If that matches the costing variant assignment, then that factor is used. If there is no match, the system then looks for the wildcard variant definition, if any. To create a new factor for a valuation variant, select the costing relevancy ID and then define the percentages used for relevancy for both fixed and variable costs. A price factor can be defined with different percentages for fixed and variable costs. The value entered is a multiplier, and 75% should be expressed as 0.75.

Price Factors			
Valuation Variant	Costing Relevancy	Fxd Prc. Factor	Var. Price Factor
004	A	0.750	0.750
	Q	0	

Figure 1.32: Price factor definition

In order to assign a costing factor to a valuation variant, that factor must be pre-defined. This is done using transaction OKK9 or by using IMG menu path CONTROLLING • PRODUCT COST CONTROLLING • PRODUCT COST PLANNING • PRICE UPDATE • PARAMETERS FOR INVENTORY COST ESTIMATE • DEFINE RELEVANCY TO COSTING. Figure 1.33 shows that a 1-character factor and text are all that is required when defining the relevancy factor.

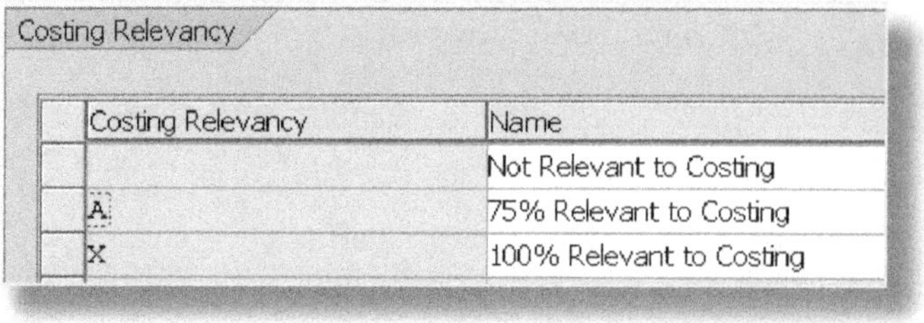

Costing Relevancy	Name
	Not Relevant to Costing
A	75% Relevant to Costing
X	100% Relevant to Costing

Figure 1.33: Costing relevancy definition

1.4.10 Valuation variant—plant specific

Valuation variants can be set up to be specific to a plant. To create a new plant-based definition of the valuation variant, click on the [□] button next to the VALUATION VARIANT/PLANT button. Click on [New Entries] and the definition of the general variant is displayed with the plant ID field blank. Enter a valid plant ID and make the necessary changes. All tabs of the valuation variant can be customized for the specific plant. Click on the VALUATION VARIANT/ PLANT button and select the plant to make changes to an existing plant-specific valuation variant. Figure 1.34 shows the definition on the OVER-HEAD tab for VALUATION VARIANT Z01. Note that this differs from the definition shown in Figure 1.30. Plant UWU3 uses overhead costing sheet ZUWU03, whereas other plants use the default overhead costing sheet ZUWU00 for overhead calculations.

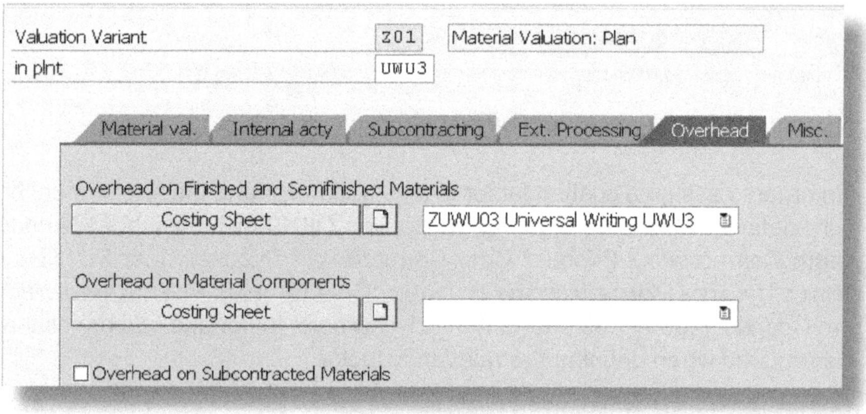

Valuation Variant	Z01	Material Valuation: Plan
in plnt	UWU3	

Material val. | Internal acty | Subcontracting | Ext. Processing | Overhead | Misc.

Overhead on Finished and Semifinished Materials
Costing Sheet | □ | ZUWU03 Universal Writing UWU3

Overhead on Material Components
Costing Sheet | □ |

☐ Overhead on Subcontracted Materials

Figure 1.34: Plant specific valuation variant

1.4.11 Date control

Returning to the costing variant CONTROL tab definition (see Figure 1.18), the DATE CONTROL section defines the defaults for the validity dates for the cost estimate, the valuation date for the assigned costs, and the validity date for the quantity structures used in generating the cost estimate. Date control configuration is processed using transaction OKK6, the IMG menu path CONTROLLING • PRODUCT COST CONTROLLING • PRODUCT COST PLANNING • MATERIAL COST ESTIMATE WITH QUANTITY STRUCTURE • COSTING VARIANT: COMPONENTS • DEFINE DATE CONTROL, or by clicking on the DATE CONTROL button or button. Figure 1.35 shows the configuration parameters.

Figure 1.35: Date control configuration

COSTING DATE FROM defines the date assigned to the cost estimate. COSTING DATE TO defines the last date that the cost estimate is valid. QUANTITY STRUCTURE DATE refers to the date during which a quantity structure such as a BOM or routing is valid. Quantity structures have validity dates assigned to them, and only if the quantity structure is valid for the date selected for the cost estimate, will a quantity structure be considered when generating a cost estimate. VALUATION DATE refers to a date from when valuing costs are pulled into the cost estimate. If there is a requirement to create a 2019 cost estimate using 2018 costs, then the valuation date must be set to a 2018 date.

When creating a cost estimate, the date control uses the defaults configured for each of these dates. The MANUAL ENTRY checkbox determines if the dates can be overridden when creating a cost estimate. If the manual override is deselected, then only the default date can be used. The override is useful when making a cost estimate for a future time, or when attempting to analyze the effect of valuation changes or quantity structure changes. The following values are available for use as defaults:

▶ COSTING DATE FROM—the same date that was selected for the COSTING DATE FROM field. For example, set the default for VALUATION DATE to be COSTING DATE FROM to ensure that the valuation date is the same as the costing date.

▶ COSTING DATE TO—the same date that was selected for the COSTING DATE TO field

▶ QUANTITY STRUCTURE DATE—the same date that was selected for the QUANTITY STRUCTURE DATE field

▶ REQUIREMENTS DATE—the date of the MRP requirement

▶ VALUATION DATE—the same date that was selected for the VALUATION DATE field

▶ START OF MONTH—the beginning day of the calendar month in which the cost estimate was created

▶ END OF MONTH—the ending day of the calendar month in which the cost estimate was created

▶ START OF NEXT FISCAL YEAR—the initial date of the fiscal year following the current fiscal year

▶ END OF NEXT FISCAL YEAR—the end date of the fiscal year following the current fiscal year

▶ START OF CURRENT POSTING PERIOD—the initial date of the current fiscal period

▶ END OF CURRENT POSTING PERIOD—the last date of the current fiscal period

▶ START OF NEXT MONTH—the beginning date of the calendar month following the current month

▶ END OF NEXT MONTH—the end date of the calendar month following the current month

- ▶ END OF CURRENT FISCAL YEAR—the final date of the current fiscal year

- ▶ MAXIMUM VALUE—December 31, 9999

- ▶ NO DEFAULT VALUE—no date is selected, and the date must be manually filled in

- ▶ CURRENT DATE—the date the cost estimate is generated

- ▶ END OF POSTING PERIOD IN WHICH "COSTING DATE FROM" FALLS—the end of the period for the date assigned to COSTING DATE FROM

- ▶ END OF FISCAL YEAR IN WHICH "COSTING DATE FROM" FALLS—the end of the fiscal year for the date assigned to COSTING DATE FROM

Select the default date that best matches the criteria for the costing variant. For example, if a cost estimate should remain valid after the current fiscal year, then choose MAXIMUM VALUE. If the cost estimate should expire at the end of the fiscal year, then choose END OF FISCAL YEAR IN WHICH "COSTING DATE FROM" FALLS.

1.4.12 Quantity structure control

In the QTY STRUCT. CONTROL section of the costing variant CONTROL tab (see Figure 1.18), a quality control definition is selected, determining which BOMs and manufacturing routings or task lists are used for generating costs for manufactured materials. Configuration can be processed in several ways: using transaction OKK5, or IMG menu path CONTROLLING • PRODUCT COST CONTROLLING • PRODUCT COST PLANNING • MATERIAL COST ESTIMATE WITH QUANTITY STRUCTURE • COSTING VARIANT: COMPONENTS • DEFINE QUANTITY STRUCTURE CONTROL, or by clicking on QUANTITY STRUCTURE CONTROL or on ⬜. Figure 1.36 shows the initial window when entering the configuration transaction. There are two tabs: BOM is used for the bill of material definition, and ROUTING is used to define which task lists representing routings or recipes are to be used to generate manufacturing costs in the cost estimate. Like the valuation variant, quantity structure control can be customized for a specific plant because specific plants can have different requirements in manufacturing.

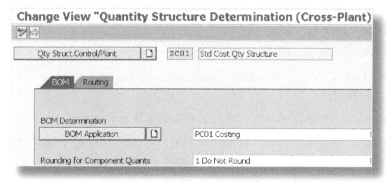

Figure 1.36: Quantity structure determination—BOMs

BOM configuration

The BOM DETERMINATION configuration defines what types of BOMs are used for costing purposes. A material can have several different types of BOMs created for it which have different uses. For instance, there are BOMs that are specific to manufacturing and others that can be specific to costing. Click on BOM APPLICATION to view or edit the selected BOM application configuration. Click on ☐ to create a new BOM application definition. ROUNDING FOR COMPONENT QUANTS defines how certain component quantities are treated in the cost estimate. See Section 6.2 for more details.

Routing configuration

The ROUTING tab of quantity structure determination (see Figure 1.37) is used to define which routing alternative should be used in the cost estimate. Choose an automatic routing selection strategy in the ROUTING DETERM. section. An automatic routing selection strategy is made up of a list of task list types and task list statuses arranged by search priority. Task list types include N for routings, 2 for recipes, and R for rate routings, among others. In general, a task list contains a list of operations to be performed. In manufacturing, this defines the steps that are used to manufacture a product. Different task list types are used by different types of manufacturing. For example, routings (N) are used in production orders, and recipes (2) are used in process orders. When a route or recipe is created, it is given a status which indicates whether it can be used for planning, production, or costing purposes. The selection strategy entered here determines whether a specific task list type and status combination can be used for costing and the order in which task list types and statuses are searched to find the proper task list used for the cost estimate.

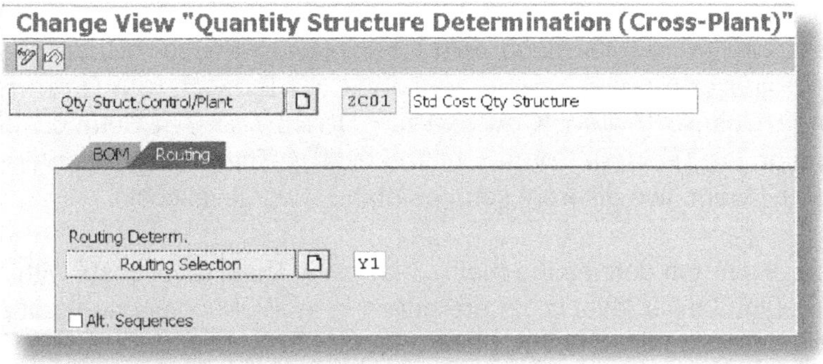

Change View "Quantity Structure Determination (Cross-Plant)"

Qty Struct.Control/Plant | ZC01 | Std Cost Qty Structure

BOM Routing

Routing Determ.
Routing Selection | Y1

☐ Alt. Sequences

Figure 1.37: Routing selection configuration

Click on the ROUTING SELECTION button to make changes to the selected strategy. Click on the  button to create a new strategy. See Section 6.3 for further details.

The ALT. SEQUENCES checkbox determines whether the cost estimate looks for an alternative operation sequence if one is defined for the material being costed. Alternative sequences can be selected in a routing or recipe based on certain characteristics, such as lot size. For costing purposes, if this is set and the route is defined for alternative sequences, then different costing lot size selections are able to use different cost sources based on the operations used.

1.4.13 Transfer control

A product's bill of materials can include both purchased items (raw materials) and semi-finished materials. When generating a cost estimate for the product, the prices of those raw and semi-finished materials must be known to be included in the cost. If a cost estimate does not yet exist for a BOM item, then the system creates a cost estimate so that the costs can be included. If cost estimates already exist for the components, then the system has to decide whether to create new cost estimates. Transfer control settings tell the system how to handle this situation. It defines whether a lower level cost estimate is recreated to be included in the current cost estimate, and how that lower level cost estimate is generated. If no new lower level cost estimate is to be created, then costs are copied from the existing cost estimate, depending on the settings in the configuration. Select a setting from the Transfer Control selection in the Control tab of the costing variant (see Figure 1.18). Configuration is processed using transaction OKKM, or IMG menu path Controlling • Product Cost Controlling • Product Cost Planning • Material Cost Estimate with Quantity Structure • Costing Variant: Components • Define Transfer Control, or by clicking on the Transfer Control button or ⬜. This configuration distinguishes between two different sources of the lower level costs.

The Single-Plant tab defines the method for using lower level costs within the same plant. Lower level costs are pulled in as BOM components of a manufactured material within the plant. Figure 1.38 shows the configuration parameters for transfer within the same plant.

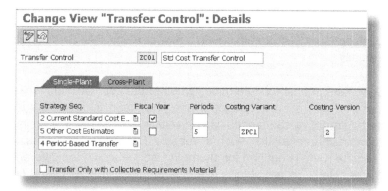

Figure 1.38: Transfer Control within the same plant

The strategy sequence defines up to three different types of cost estimates which can be selected for transfer. If an existing cost estimate of the type defined in the first strategy sequence step is not found, then the system searches the next strategy until either No Transfer is found or there is no further strategy available. If no cost estimate is found, then a new cost estimate for the lower level material is created when costing the higher-level material. There are six possible strategies:

▶ No Transfer—no transfer of costs from a lower level cost estimate. A new cost estimate is created.

▶ Future Standard Cost Estimate—the system searches for a marked future standard cost estimate.

- ▶ CURRENT STANDARD COST ESTIMATE—the system searches for a released standard cost estimate.

- ▶ PREVIOUS STANDARD COST ESTIMATE—the system searches for the previous standard cost estimate.

- ▶ PERIOD-BASED TRANSFER—the system searches for cost estimates that have the same costing variant, costing version, and period. Only those costs are transferred from an existing cost estimate.

- ▶ OTHER COST ESTIMATES—allows for transfer of cost estimate using different costing variants or different costing versions.

The FISCAL YEAR checkboxes indicate whether only cost estimates of the current fiscal year should be transferred. If these are selected, only cost estimates of lower level items that were created in the current fiscal year can be transferred. These should be selected for costing variants used for standard cost updates so that future fiscal year product costs are consistent.

The PERIODS fields provide a method of restricting which cost estimates are transferred based on number of periods in the past (for all strategies but PERIOD-BASED TRANSFER) or in the future (for the FUTURE STANDARD COST ESTIMATE strategy only) that the cost estimate was created. Depending on the FISCAL YEAR setting, this can also include cost estimates created in previous fiscal years. If the cost estimate fits within the period constraint, then it is transferred to the higher level. If the PERIODS field is left blank, this is interpreted as 0, which would normally indicate the current period. This is true if FISCAL YEAR is not set. If FISCAL YEAR is set and PERIODS is blank, then the system assumes that the latest cost estimate from within the fiscal year can be transferred. Use PERIOD-BASED TRANSFER to force the cost estimate to be from both the current fiscal year and current period.

The COSTING VARIANT and COSTING VERSION selections are only available for OTHER COST ESTIMATE. This is the only strategy that allows for the transfer of costs using different costing variants and costing versions. This should not be used for standard cost estimates.

The TRANSFER ONLY WITH COLLECTIVE REQUIREMENTS MATERIAL checkbox should be selected if existing costing data is transferred based on the collective requirements setting in the material master. Cost estimates are transferred if the collective requirements indicator is set. If the individual requirements indicator is not set, then a new cost estimate is created for that material. Do not set this indicator if the cost estimates of both types of materials should be transferred.

The CROSS-PLANT tab contains the definition for using lower level cost estimates when the lower level represents a material transfer from its plant to another plant. The use of lower level cost estimates within the same plant versus transfers from another plant can be different depending on need.

Figure 1.39: Cross-plant transfer control

Figure 1.39 shows the setup for transferring cost estimates between plants. The configuration for this tab is the same as the configuration for the SINGLE-PLANT tab.

1.4.14 Reference variant

The reference variant is a tool which copies an existing cost estimate and then re-costs only certain parts of the cost estimate. This is useful in a several ways. First, since an existing cost estimate is used as the basis of the new cost estimate, there is no need for the system to search for the quantity structure (BOMs and routings) to determine how to cost the material. Only existing items in the cost estimate are re-costed based on the reference variant definition. The other item costs are copied directly from the original cost estimate. This speeds up the execution of the cost calculation. Reference variants allow for cost comparisons based on specific items such as raw material, processing, or overhead costs. Group costing for multiple valuations is another function that benefits from using reference variants. After the original cost for legal valuation is created, costs for the additional valuations can use the reference variant to ensure that the quantity structures for each valuation is the same. Select an existing variant from the REFERENCE VARIANT section of the CONTROL tab of the costing variant. Existing reference variants can be changed, or new ones created, using transaction OKYC, or IMG menu path CONTROLLING • PRODUCT COST CONTROLLING • PRODUCT COST PLANNING • MATERIAL COST ESTIMATE WITH QUANTITY STRUCTURE • COSTING VARIANT: COMPONENTS • DEFINE REFERENCE VARIANT, or by clicking on the REFERENCE VARIANT button or ☐ in the CONTROL tab.

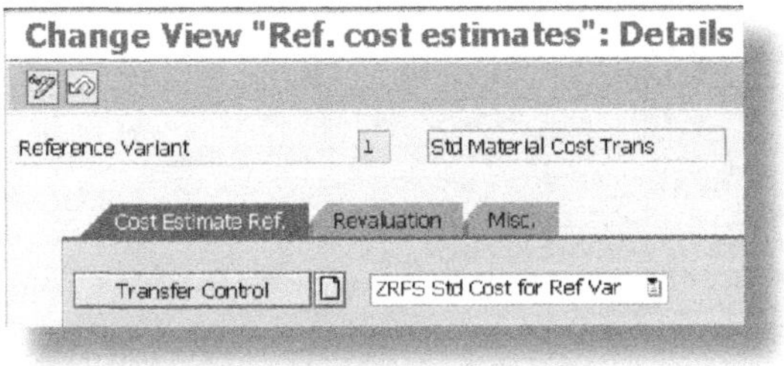

Change View "Ref. cost estimates": Details

Reference Variant   1   Std Material Cost Trans

Cost Estimate Ref.   Revaluation   Misc.

Transfer Control   ☐   ZRFS Std Cost for Ref Var

Figure 1.40: Reference variant transfer control

Configuration for the reference variant begins with the creation of a transfer control setting which is used for copying an existing cost estimate and making it the basis of the cost estimate using this costing variant. Configuration of transfer control was explained in Section 1.4.13, but only the single-plant configuration is relevant in this case. The costs being transferred are always at the same costing level. The COST ESTIMATE REF. tab (see Figure 1.40) is used for configuring the transfer control for this purpose. Select an existing transfer control setting from the dropdown menu. Click on the TRANSFER CONTROL button to view and make changes to the selected transfer control. Click on the ☐ button to create a new transfer control.

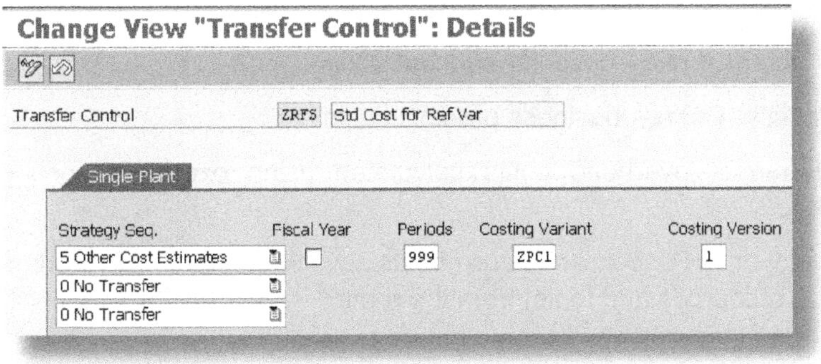

Change View "Transfer Control": Details

Transfer Control   ZRFS   Std Cost for Ref Var

Single Plant

Strategy Seq.	Fiscal Year	Periods	Costing Variant	Costing Version
5 Other Cost Estimates	☐	999	ZPC1	1
0 No Transfer				
0 No Transfer				

Figure 1.41: Transfer control configuration for reference variant

Figure 1.41 shows a configuration for the transfer control, using the latest cost estimate from costing variant ZPC1 as the basis to create the new cost estimate regardless of fiscal year. Note that only the Single-Plant tab is displayed for this definition.

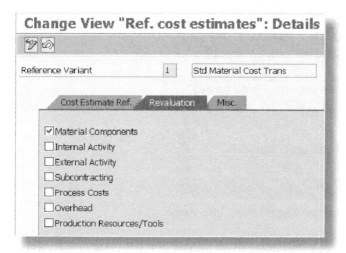

Figure 1.42: Reference variant costs to revalue

The Revaluation tab (see Figure 1.42) defines which costs are to be revalued within the cost estimate. Any option that is selected is revalued; the other options use the value from the copied cost estimate. The different cost sources are defined below:

▶ Material Components—purchased materials in the BOM

▶ Internal Activity—activity type costs

▶ External Activity—costs for external processing

▶ Subcontracting—costs for subcontracting

▶ Process Costs—business process costs

▶ Overhead—overhead costs calculated using overhead costing sheets

▶ Production Resources/Tools—costs associated with PRT (production resources and tools) from the route

Only those costs that are selected in the REVALUATION tab are recalculated when the new cost estimate is created. All other costs are transferred from the reference cost estimate.

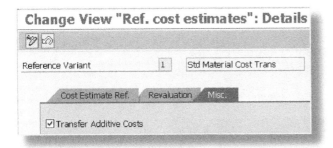

Figure 1.43: Reference variant additive costs

The MISC. tab shown in Figure 1.43 defines whether additive costs associated with the reference cost estimate are included in the new cost estimate.

1.4.15 Costing variant quantity structure parameters

Moving back to the main costing variant window, the QTY STRUCT. tab, as shown in Figure 1.44, is used to define how certain costs are transferred and how the costs are calculated throughout the quantity structure. PASS ON LOT SIZE controls the lot size used to cost lower level materials in a multi-level BOM. There are three possible selections:

► No—the costing lot size of the material master is used for each cost estimate in the multi-level BOM. The resulting lower-level component cost is factored by the BOM quantity in the top-level cost estimate.

► ONLY WITH INDIVIDUAL REQUIREMENTS—The costing lot size of the top-level material is used when costing lower-level materials defined for individual requirements in planning. If this is selected, then TRANSFER ONLY WITH COLLECTIVE REQUIREMENTS MATERIAL should be selected in the transfer control setting (see Section 1.4.13).

► ALWAYS—the costing lot size of the top-level material determines the lot size used for the lower-level materials. The consumption quantities of the BOM components for the top-level costing lot size determine the costing lot size for the components on the next level. The resulting costing lot size of the next level components then determine the lot size of the next lower level of components, and so on, until the lowest level is reached. This can impact which quantity structures are used when costing the lower level items.

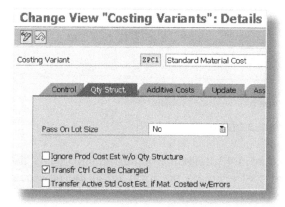

Figure 1.44: Costing variant quantity structure cost transfer

If IGNORE PROD COST EST W/O QTY STRUCTURE is selected, the system is forced to look for existing BOMs and routings in order to determine the quantity structure of the cost estimate. If this is not set and the WITH QTY STRUCTURE setting in the COSTING 1 tab of the material master is not set, then existing cost estimates without quantity structure are searched in order to valuate the components of the material being costed.

TRANSFR CTRL CAN BE CHANGED determines if the transfer control defined for the costing variant can be overridden when creating the cost estimate. If this is not set, the transfer control assigned to the costing variant is always used.

TRANSFER ACTIVE STD COST EST. IF MAT. COSTED W/ERRORS controls how lower-level cost estimates with errors (status KF) in a multi-level BOM affect the top-level cost estimate. If this is set and there is a lower-level cost estimate with errors, the system uses the resulting cost component split of the error cost estimate to pass the costs up to the next level. If no cost component split was generated, the standard cost from the material master is used in its place. The status of the top-level cost estimate is also set to KF (costed with errors). If this is not set, the standard cost from the material master is used as the cost of the component, and a warning is generated at that level. Levels above that are costed without error.

1.4.16 Costing variant additive costs

The ADDITIVE COSTS tab (see Figure 1.45) is used to determine whether additive costs should be included in the cost estimate. An additive cost estimate is a special separate cost estimate for a material, enabling cost items to be entered manually in a similar manner to a unit cost estimate. If additive costs are enabled by the costing variant, the manually added costs are included in the material cost estimate as separate line items at the end of the cost itemization.

The ADDITIVE COST COMPS dropdown menu includes three options for dealing with additive cost estimates:

- ▶ IGNORE ADDITIVE COSTS—additive cost estimates cannot be created, and existing additive cost estimates are not included in the material costs

- ▶ INCLUDE ADDITIVE COSTS—additive costs estimates are included in the material cost estimate, but overhead cannot be applied to these costs

- ▶ INCLUDE ADDITIVE COSTS AND APPLY OVERHEAD—additive costs estimates are included in the material cost and overhead is applied to these costs

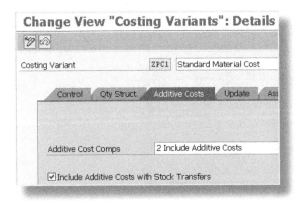

Figure 1.45: Additive cost behavior

The INCLUDE ADDITIVE COSTS WITH STOCK TRANSFERS checkbox determines whether lower-level additive costs from a different plant are to be included as part of transferring the material from one plant to another. If this is not selected, then additive costs from another plant cannot be included in the costs of the materials at the receiving plant.

1.4.17 Costing variant cost estimate update

The UPDATE tab is used to determine what information is saved with respect to cost estimates. Figure 1.46 shows the options available:

▶ SAVING ALLOWED—determines if the cost estimate is saved. If the cost estimate is to be used later, this option must be selected. Otherwise, the cost estimate can only be viewed when it is created.

▶ SAVE ERROR LOG—If SAVING ALLOWED is set and the configuration on the MISC. tab allows the creation of logs, an error log file is created. This provides the default value for error logs when the dialog box for saving is displayed upon exiting a cost estimate.

▶ DEFAULTS CAN BE CHANGED BY USER—determines whether the default settings in the save dialog box can be changed by the user.

▶ ITEMIZATION—the cost component split of the cost estimate is always saved if saving is allowed. Setting the ITEMIZATION parameter means that the itemization is also saved. The value of this can be changed when saving a cost estimate if DEFAULTS CAN BE CHANGED BY USER is set.

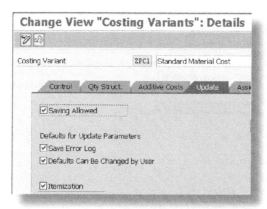

Figure 1.46: Costing variant file updates

1.4.18 Costing variant assignments

The ASSIGNMENTS tab is used to make specific costing structure assignments to the costing variants. This includes which cost component structure to use, the behavior of the various costing versions, whether the cost component split is processed in controlling area currency as well as in company code currency, and whether cross-company costing should be allowed for materials transferred between plants in two different company codes. Figure 1.47 shows the initial window that is displayed when selecting the tab. At this point, only the four different selections which can be updated are shown. Selecting one of the buttons pulls in information about that button at the bottom of the window.

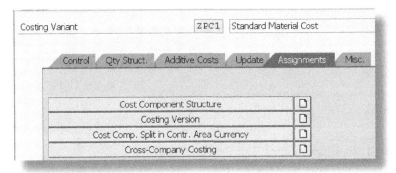

Figure 1.47: Assignments tab

Cost component structure

Click on the COST COMPONENT STRUCTURE button to get a list of cost component structures used by company code. The definition of the cost component structure and assignment by company code is defined in Section 1.3. Clicking on the ☐ button also gives access to the cost component structure configuration. Figure 1.48 shows the default display for assigning the structures. The default is to show the assignment only by company code.

The display can be expanded to show individual plant assignment of the cost component split or the alternative cost component structure, this can be done by selecting the ▦ button and making sure that all fields are included in the display.

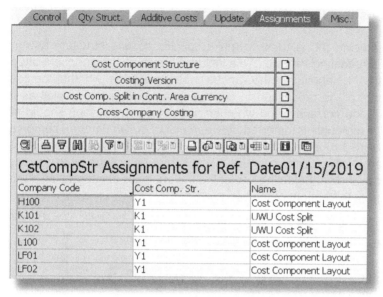

| Control | Qty Struct. | Additive Costs | Update | Assignments | Misc. |

Cost Component Structure	□
Costing Version	□
Cost Comp. Split in Contr. Area Currency	□
Cross-Company Costing	□

CstCompStr Assignments for Ref. Date01/15/2019

Company Code	Cost Comp. Str.	Name
H100	Y1	Cost Component Layout
K101	K1	UWU Cost Split
K102	K1	UWU Cost Split
L100	Y1	Cost Component Layout
LF01	Y1	Cost Component Layout
LF02	Y1	Cost Component Layout

Figure 1.48: Cost component structure assignment

CstCompStr Assignments for Ref. Date01/15/2019

Company Co	Plant	Cost Comp. Str.	Name	Cost Comp. Str.	Name
H100	H10	Y1	Cost Component Layout		
K101	UWU1	K1	UWU Cost Split		
K102	UWU2	K1	UWU Cost Split		
L100	L10	Y1	Cost Component Layout		
LF01	LF01	Y1	Cost Component Layout		
LF02	LF02	Y1	Cost Component Layout		

Figure 1.49: Full cost component structure assignment

Figure 1.49 shows the complete assignment. See Section 1.3 for a description of the cost component structure configuration.

Costing version

The costing version configuration is used to define specific parameters that can be used for each costing version. Within a costing variant, 99 costing versions are allowed. Click on the COSTING VERSION button to see the attributes of the different costing versions, as shown in Figure 1.50.

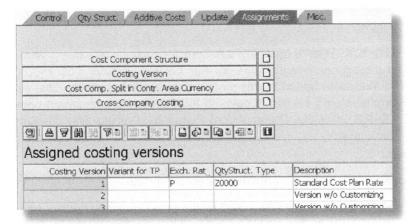

Figure 1.50: Costing version configuration

Actual configuration of the costing version is done using transaction OKYD or by using the IMG menu path CONTROLLING • PRODUCT COST CONTROLLING • PRODUCT COST PLANNING • SELECTED FUNCTIONS IN MATERIAL COSTING • DEFINE COSTING VERSIONS (see Figure 1.51).

New Entries: Overview of Added Entries

Costing Version	Costing Type	Valuation Var	Variant fo	Exch	Qty Str	Description
1	01	Z01		P	Z0000	Standard Cost Plan Rate

Figure 1.51: Costing version configuration—OKYD

Three different parameters can be defined for each version:

▶ VARIANT FOR TRANSFER PRICE—select a transfer pricing variant to determine how transfer prices are calculated when using parallel valuation.

▶ EXCH. RATE TYPE (exchange rate)—select a specific exchange rate to use for inter-country transfers. If not defined, the exchange rate for the valuation variant is used. Different costing variants can use different exchange rates, and the costs of two cost estimates with

67

different versions can be compared to show the effect of exchange rate differences.

▶ QTY STR. TYPE 1 (quantity structure for mixed costing)—assigns a mixing quantity structure for this costing version. Cost mixing strategies assigned to this structure are used in a mixed cost estimate. Mixed costing is covered in detail in the companion book "SAP® S/4HANA Product Cost Planning—Costing with Quantity Structure".

Cost component split in controlling area currency

Cost component splits are determined by default in company code currency. Figure 1.52 shows the company codes for which the cost component split will be created both in company code currency and controlling area currency. If the company code currency is USD and the controlling area currency is EUR, then the cost component split will be created in both currencies using the selected exchange rate calculation.

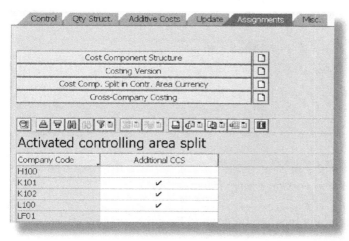

Figure 1.52: Cost component split in controlling area currency

Click on the ▢ button to enter the configuration. This can also be configured using transaction OKYW or via the IMG menu path CONTROLLING • PRODUCT COST CONTROLLING • PRODUCT COST PLANNING • SELECTED FUNCTIONS IN MATERIAL COSTING • ACTIVATE COST COMPONENT SPLIT IN CONTROLLING AREA CURRENCY (see Figure 1.53).

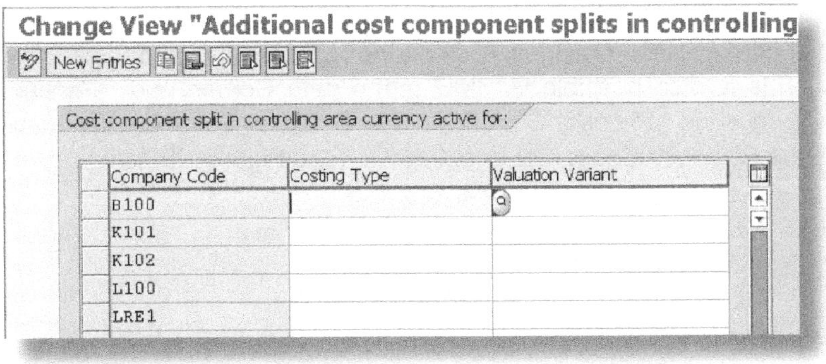

Change View "Additional cost component splits in controlling

Company Code	Costing Type	Valuation Variant
B100		
K101		
K102		
L100		
LRE1		

Cost component split in controlling area currency active for:

Figure 1.53: Split in controlling area currency—OKYW

This can be limited to specific costing types and valuation variants. If these items are blank, then cost component split in controlling area currency is activated for all costing variants.

Cross-company costing

Businesses with more than one company code can have materials transferred between plants residing in different company codes. In these cases, costing between the company codes should be allowed. This is determined by controlling area, as shown in Figure 1.54.

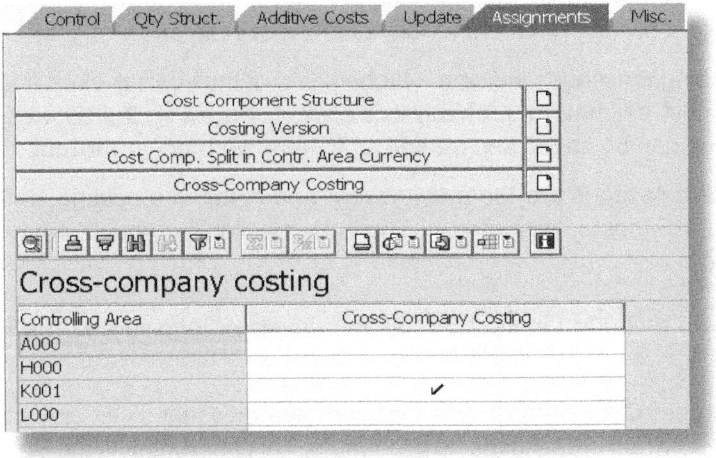

Control	Qty Struct.	Additive Costs	Update	Assignments	Misc.

Cost Component Structure	▢
Costing Version	▢
Cost Comp. Split in Contr. Area Currency	▢
Cross-Company Costing	▢

Cross-company costing

Controlling Area	Cross-Company Costing
A000	
H000	
K001	✔
L000	

Figure 1.54: Cross-company costing

69

This shows that controlling area K001 is set up for cross-company costing. To make configuration changes, click on the [▣] button or run transaction OKYV. This is also possible via IMG menu path CONTROLLING • PRODUCT COST CONTROLLING • PRODUCT COST PLANNING • SELECTED FUNCTIONS IN MATERIAL COSTING • ACTIVATE CROSS-COMPANY COSTING (see Figure 1.55).

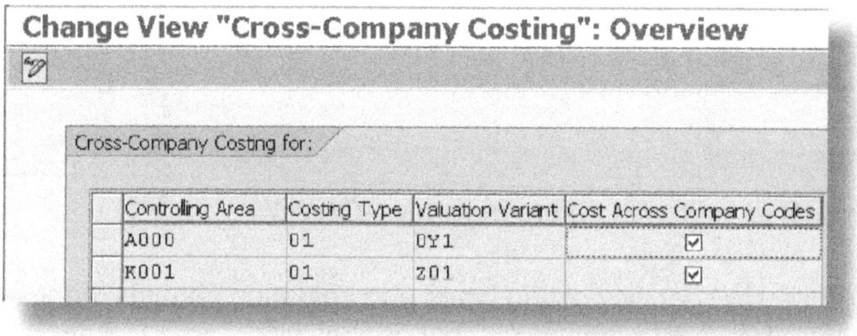

Controlling Area	Costing Type	Valuation Variant	Cost Across Company Codes
A000	01	0Y1	☑
K001	01	Z01	☑

Figure 1.55: Cross-company costing setup—OKYV

1.4.19 Costing variant error processing

The MISC. tab of the costing variant configuration for CO-PC-PCP defines how messages are processed. There are three levels of messages:

▶ Informational messages indicate that some issue occurred in the cost estimate that requires attention, but it does not necessarily cause a problem with the validity of the cost estimate.

▶ Warning messages indicate a higher level of the costing issue and the cost estimate is probably not correct. However, the cost estimate can be saved and treated as if there were not any errors.

▶ Error messages are the most severe and result in a costing status of KF (costed with errors). These cost estimates should not be used.

The dropdown menu in Figure 1.56 has four levels of logging and notification:

▶ MESSAGES ONLINE—logging is disabled, and messages can only be viewed when creating the cost estimate. This also impacts the configuration on the UPDATE tab (Section 1.4.17). Costing runs must have logging enabled.

▶ LOG AND SAVE MESSAGES, MAIL ACTIVE—messages are logged and an e-mail can be sent to the person responsible for fixing the errors.

▶ LOG AND SAVE MESSAGES, MAIL INACTIVE—messages are logged, and no e-mail can be generated.

▶ LOG MESSAGES BUT DO NOT SAVE THEM, MAIL INACTIVE—the messages are collected in a log for viewing online, but the log cannot be saved. If the costing variant is used for costing runs, this setting must not be selected.

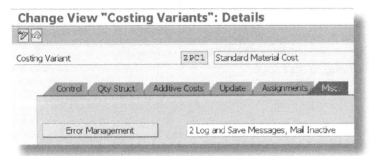

Change View "Costing Variants": Details

Costing Variant   ZPC1   Standard Material Cost

Control   Qty Struct.   Additive Costs   Update   Assignments   Misc.

Error Management   2 Log and Save Messages, Mail Inactive

Figure 1.56: Costing variant error management

Error Management   2 Log and Save Messages, Mail Inactive

User-defined messagesMaterial Cost Estimate

Light	Message Processed	Msg Type	Area	Message	Message Text
			C2	223	A valid bill of material could not be foun
			C2	315	Routing & is flagged for deletion
			CZ	011	Order: Finish dat is before start date, f
			CZ	015	No capacity category maintained in wor
			CE	351	Problems when calculating using metho
			CK	037	Lot size & & taken from costing view
			CK	038	Lot size in material master is & &
			CK	053	Deletion indicator set in material & plant
			CK	054	Deletion indicator set in material & valu
			CK	063	Activity type &2 not assigned to cost o
			CK	064	Assignment of activity type & / cost ce
			CK	065	Activity type & in CO area & cannot be

Figure 1.57: Special error definitions

The ERROR MANAGEMENT button brings up the specific list of messages for which the behavior can be modified (see Figure 1.57). Click on a message number. A list of message behaviors is displayed. The message can be changed so that it is suppressed (*), becomes an informational message (I), becomes a warning message (W), becomes an error message (E), or becomes a termination message (A). A checkmark is placed in the MESSAGE PROCESSED column and MSG TYPE is set to the type of message to which it has been changed (see Figure 1.58).

Figure 1.58: Changed message

2 Cost estimates without reference to materials

Early in the product life cycle, little is known about the costs of a material or even the specific components and operations required to manufacture that material. Costs can be manually specified in unit cost estimates to represent the costs in these early stages of product development. Using special material types, non-productive materials can be defined to represent reusable manufacturing processes and component lists for developing costs.

2.1 Purpose of cost estimates without reference to materials

Using the term "cost estimates without reference to materials" is a bit misleading. What is really intended is the ability to create a cost estimate without having to create a production material to go with it. The research phase of the product life cycle is a time of experimentation, and there is no compelling reason at this point to begin to create materials that will never make it into production. The desire at this stage is the ability to estimate the costs of creating a type of product. If the result is not deemed to be cost effective, then there is no need to move forward with creating a material. SAP provides alternative methods for generating cost estimates without requiring a production material.

2.2 Base planning objects

Prior to the release of S/4HANA, a special method for generating costs was included; it was known as "base planning objects". This feature allowed for the assignment of costs without specifically referencing a material. Base planning objects could reference costs from other base planning objects as well as materials, activity types, and other cost objects. The same processes used for creating cost estimates for base planning objects are also used when creating unit cost estimates. The only difference is that unit cost estimates are assigned to specific materials. Seeing that the base planning object functionality is essentially duplicated with unit cost estimates, base planning objects found themselves on the simplification list when S/4HANA was introduced, and the functionality was made obsolete (refer to SAP Note 2349294[2]). Some of the functionality has been temporarily restored in S/4HANA (see SAP Note 2133644[3]), but I personally believe that this was done to support those customers converting to S/4HANA who were unable to switch over to unit costing prior to the conversion. The intent is that base planning objects will no longer be supported and should no longer be used. Other methodologies exist which virtually duplicate the older functionality.

2.3   Easy Cost Planning for cost estimation

SAP Note 2349294 suggests two alternatives for managing costing simulations. One is to use Easy Cost Planning transaction CKECP to develop ad hoc costs. Easy Cost Planning is a very flexible tool, used to create cost estimates for planning costs for certain CO objects and also for generating ad hoc costs used in "what if" analyses. A full examination of Easy Cost Planning and its uses is beyond the scope of this book. One of the main features of this module is the ability to develop a costing model to generate repeatable cost estimates. The costing model uses templates to generate costing items based on characteristics that are defined with the model. Usually the pre-defined costing model is first selected for the cost estimate. Then, values are assigned to the characteristics. Based on those values and the underlying templates, the cost items are assigned to the cost estimate. Changes and additions can be made to the resulting cost itemization before saving. A fuller explanation of how this works is found in the book "Practical Guide to Using SAP® CO Templates" published by Espresso Tutorials.

2.3.1   Creating a cost estimate with CKECP

Transaction CKECP can also be used without assigning a costing model to the cost estimate. Skip the selection of the costing model and go directly

---

[2]   SAP Note 2349294—"S4TWL—Reference and Simulation Costing"

[3]   SAP Note 2133644—" Error message SFIN_FI 004: Transactions KKE1, KKE2, KKE3 cannot be called"

to the itemization screen to create the ad hoc cost estimate. The cost estimate in the following example is used to determine the cost for a new type of ink that is purple in color.

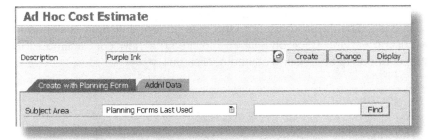

Figure 2.1: Transaction CKECP initial window

Figure 2.1 shows the initial window with the CREATE WITH PLANNING FORM tab opened. Enter the description of the item to be costed. Skip the selection of the planning form and click on the ADDNL DATA tab. The required costing parameters are shown in Figure 2.2.

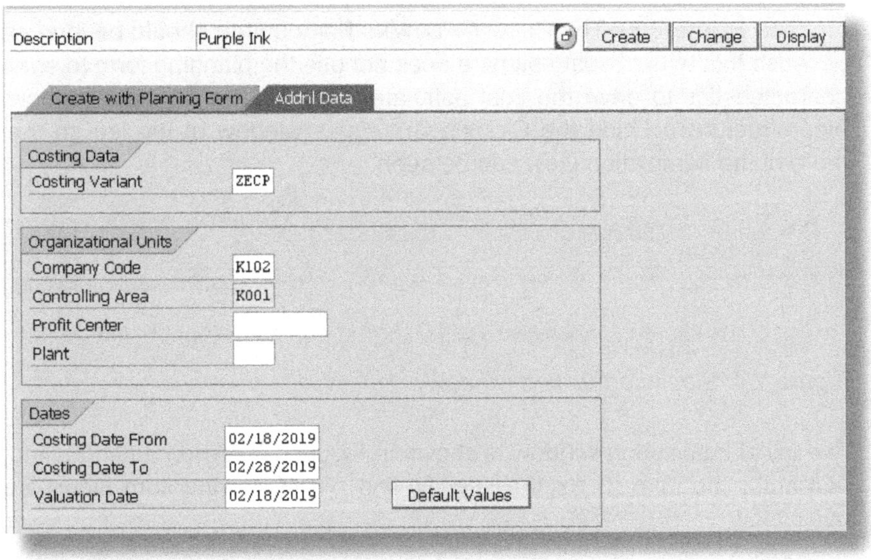

Figure 2.2: Transaction CKECP costing parameters

Because a cost estimate with itemization is being created, a costing variant is required. Only costing variants using costing type 26 (Ad Hoc Cost

Estimate) can be used for creating ad hoc cost estimates with Easy Cost Planning. Either company code or plant must be entered. Company code is necessary to determine the chart of accounts to use. If plant is entered instead of company code, the company code is derived from the plant definition. A profit center can be assigned, if so desired, but it is not necessary in this case. The dates come from the date control definition assigned to the costing variant. Click on [Create] to create a new cost estimate. To make changes to an existing estimate, click on [Change].

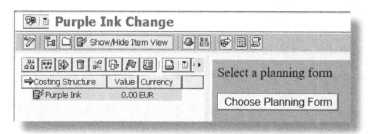

Figure 2.3: Initial cost estimate window

To bring up the itemization window, click on the [Show/Hide Item View] button (see Figure 2.3). The CHOOSE PLANNING FORM button should be ignored because this type of cost estimate does not use the planning form to enter characteristics to drive the cost estimate. Click on the [🖳] button (show/hide structure) to hide the COSTING STRUCTURE window at the left so that more of the itemization view can be seen.

ItmNo	Ite	Resource	Plant/A	Pu	Quantity	Unit	Total Price	Σ	Total Value	Currency	Description	Cost Ele
							0.00		0.00			
									0.00			

Costing Items : Purple Ink

Figure 2.4: Blank itemization window

The initial itemization window is shown in Figure 2.4. When adding a line, first enter the item ID for the specific line. The following item types are available:

▶ *B*—base planning object. Requires base planning object ID, quantity, and cost element if not already assigned to the base planning object itself. Base planning objects are not intended to be used in S/4HANA.

▶ *E*—internal activity. Requires cost center, activity type, quantity of activity, and unit of measure. The cost element comes from the definition of the activity type.

▶ *F*—external activity (external processing of work in process). Requires purchasing information record ID, plant, purchasing organization, quantity, and cost element.

▶ *L*—subcontracting. Requires purchasing information record ID, plant, purchasing organization, quantity, and cost element. The cost element is derived from the account assignment configuration for subcontracting (transaction event key FRL—External Activity).

▶ *M*—material. Requires material number, plant, quantity, and unit of measure. Cost element is derived from the automatic account assignment configuration for transaction event key GBB (inventory posting offset), modifier VBR (consumption).

▶ *N*—external service. Requires service ID, plant, purchasing organization, quantity, and unit of measure. Cost element is derived from the valuation class assigned to the external service activity.

▶ *P*—process (manual). Requires business process ID and quantity. Unit of measure is derived from the business process. The cost element is taken from the business process definition.

▶ *T*—text item. Requires a description. This is not included in the cost.

▶ *V*—variable item. Requires quantity, price, price unit, and cost element. Text describing the cost should also be entered under DESCRIPTION.

There are several buttons which can be used to manipulate the itemization and display details about the itemization:

Cost estimate log—clicking this button displays the message log for the specific costing node represented by the itemization window.

Item information—select an item line and click on this button to get detailed information about the specific object.

Confirm cost estimate—after all changes have been made to the cost estimate, click on this button to save those changes.

Fill column—select the item lines. Then, select the cell to copy by clicking the left mouse button with the [Ctrl] key pressed. Click on the ⬚ button to paste the contents of that cell into the other selected cells of that column.

Revaluate all items—click on this button to revalue all lines in the itemization after making changes.

Revaluate selected items—first, select specific lines from the itemization that have been changed. Then, click on this button to revalue those items, but no other items in the cost estimate.

Explode base planning object—select a base planning object (item category B) from the cost estimate. Click on this button to replace the base planning object line with the individual line items from the base planning object. Although this button still exists as of S/4HANA on-premise release 1809, this functionality should no longer be used.

Change/display costing lot size—click on this button to see the costing lot size of this costing node. The lot size can be changed. This affects only the current costing node, and the costing structure should be revalued after making a change.

Detail display—select a line from the itemization. Clicking this button brings up a window showing the value of all possible columns of the report for this line.

Undo changes—click on this button to undo the recent typing in a field.

Append line—click on this button to add a new line at the end of the itemization.

Insert line—select a line and click on this button to insert an empty line before the selected line.

Delete line—select a line and click on this button to delete that line from the itemization.

Duplicate row—select a line and click on this button to duplicate the selected line.

In addition to the above functions, standard ALV grid buttons for manipulating layouts, filtering, totaling, subtotaling, and exporting data are also available.

Creating the cost estimate for the purple ink

Purple ink will be made at the Los Angeles plant UWU2 in a similar manner to other inks. Dye will be mixed with lubricant, surfactant, and thickener to make the ink. Most of the Universal Writing Utensil inks are made using a single color dye, but the purple dye will be a mixture of red and blue dyes. A new red dye will be tested that should mix well with the existing blue dye. The mixing quantities of the dyes and other chemicals are being tested. Mixing time is still to be determined as well. A standard batch size of the ink is expected to be 1,000 L, and this will be used as the costing lot size.

First, the costing lot size is selected by clicking on the 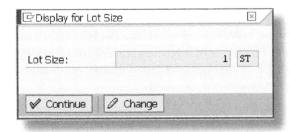 button. The window in Figure 2.5 is displayed.

Figure 2.5: Change costing lot size window

Click on the ⟨✎ Change⟩ button to change the lot size. The default unit of measure is ST (piece), which is an internal unit of measure that has no dimension attribute. This cannot be changed to a different type of unit of measure, such as L (liter), because L is a volume unit of measure. However, since this cost estimate is not associated with a material, the unit of measure can be overlooked and assumed to be L instead of ST. The window in Figure 2.6 is displayed.

Figure 2.6: Changed lot size

79

To accept the change to 1000, click on [💾 Copy Lot Size]. When entering the items for the cost estimate, make sure to keep the lot size quantity in mind because this is the basis for determining the cost. There are five components to the ink. Four of the items are existing materials, and the red dye component is yet to be determined. The four known components are:

▶ R108—blue dye

▶ R105—lubricant

▶ R106—surfactant

▶ R107—thickener

These are all existing materials, and the item type to use in the cost estimate is M.

The MIXING work center at the UWU2 plant uses three activity types assigned to cost center 200101: SETUP, MACHHR, and LABRHR. All activity types need to be accounted for in the cost estimate and they all use item type E.

The red dye component is unknown at this time. Item type V is used for this item.

Before entering the itemization, make sure that the currency is set correctly for the cost estimate. The default currency used for Easy Cost Planning cost estimates is the controlling area currency. Controlling area currency for controlling area K001 is EUR. This needs to be set to company code currency (USD) for the cost estimates for company code K102. Click on the 🔲 button to change from controlling area to company code currency. Next, enter the items into the cost estimate using the rules for the entry of each item type. The resulting cost itemization is shown in Figure 2.7.

Click on 💾 to save the cost estimate. It is saved to the original name assigned to it. In this case the name is "Purple Ink". Use transaction CKECP to display or make changes to the cost. Any of the values assigned to the items can be changed, including the values in the TOTAL PRICE column.

ItmNo	Ite	Resource	Plant/A	Pu.	Quantity	Unit	Total Price	Σ	Total Value	Currency	Description	Cost Ele
1	E	200101	SETUP		1.0	HR	586.25		58.63	USD	Setup Hour	94303000
2	E	200101	MACHHR		5.0	HR	45.00		225.00	USD	Machine Hour	94301000
3	E	200101	LABRHR		10.0	HR	22.75		227.50	USD	Labor Hour	94311000
4	V				250	L	2.81		702.50	USD	Red Dye	51100000
5	M	R108	UWU2		360	L	150.00		540.00	USD	Blue Dye	51100000
6	M	R105	UWU2		100	L	75.00		75.00	USD	Lubricant	51100000
7	M	R106	UWU2		250	L	25.00		62.50	USD	Surfactant	51100000
8	M	R107	UWU2		125	L	35.00		43.75	USD	Thickener	51100000
									1,934.88			

Costing Items : Purple Ink

Figure 2.7: Itemization for purple ink

Easy Cost Planning is useful for creating cost estimates without having to create a material. However, the resulting cost estimates cannot be used as an item in other cost estimates. In this example, the purple ink costs would have to be manually added to a cost estimate for the manufacture of a purple ink pen. This method should only be used for a quick estimation of costs.

2.3.2 Configuring the costing variant for CKECP

The costing variant configuration for ad hoc costing requires only the assignment of a costing type, valuation variant, and an optional date control assignment. The costing type used by transaction CKECP is 26, which is configured using IMG menu path CONTROLLING • PRODUCT COST CONTROLLING • PRODUCT COST PLANNING • AD HOC COST ESTIMATES • DEFINE COSTING VARIANT or transaction IKKZ.

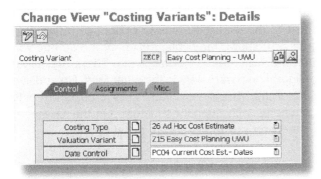

Figure 2.8: Ad hoc costing variant configuration

Figure 2.8 shows the CONTROL tab of the costing variant. There are no configuration options under the ASSIGNMENTS and MISC. tabs. Configuration is much simpler than the costing variant for standard cost estimates covered in Chapter 1. COSTING TYPE must be set to the delivered costing type 26 for ad hoc cost estimates. No other costing type is allowed. The costing type definition shown in Figure 2.9 is also very simple for ad hoc cost estimates and only allows for the selection of VALUATION VIEW. There is no separate configuration for costing types for ad hoc cost estimates. New costing types or changes to existing costing types can only be processed using the ad hoc costing variant configuration.

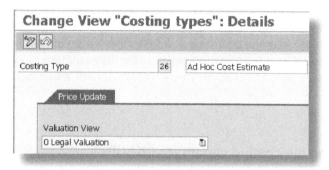

Figure 2.9: Ad hoc costing type

Although any valuation variant can be assigned to an ad hoc costing variant, not all functionality is supported. For example, the price factor configuration on the MISC. tab of the standard valuation variant configuration (see Section 1.4.9) is not useable in ad hoc costing. Certain sources of cost are not as applicable to an ad hoc cost estimate either. The best solution is to create a new valuation variant for the costing variant. This can be done using the 🗋 button, next to the VALUATION VARIANT button, or by running transaction IKKW. Figure 2.10 shows the configuration for the ad hoc valuation variant. Note that the MISC. tab is not available. There are minor modifications in the configuration parameters in the other tabs. No additive cost options are allowed for the MATERIAL VAL. tab. Additive costs are only associated with cost estimates with quantity structure. On the OVERHEAD tab, overhead costing sheets for raw materials are not supported.

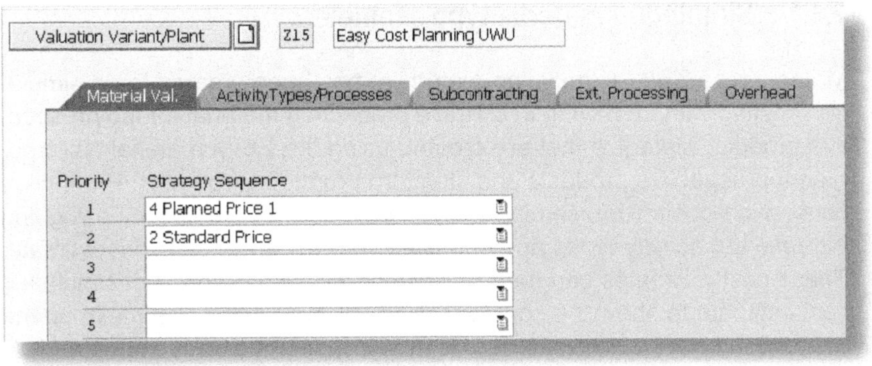

Valuation Variant/Plant	☐	Z15	Easy Cost Planning UWU

Material Val.	ActivityTypes/Processes	Subcontracting	Ext. Processing	Overhead

Priority	Strategy Sequence	
1	4 Planned Price 1	🗎
2	2 Standard Price	🗎
3		🗎
4		🗎
5		🗎

Figure 2.10: Ad hoc valuation variant

2.4 Unit costing

The second alternative to execute cost simulations is to use unit costing. SAP Note 2349294 suggests using the multi-level unit costing with SAP-GUI transaction CKUC (Fiori tile Create Unit Cost Estimate Multi). Another approach is to use the single-level transactions KKPAN (Fiori tile Create Unit Cost Estimate Single) and KKPBN (Fiori tile Change Unit Cost Estimate Single). Multi-level unit costing is covered in detail in Chapter 3.

The drawback of using any of these costing functions is that a material must be created in order for unit costing to work. If company policy indicates that a productive material ID should not be assigned at this stage of the product life cycle, then an alternative plan of action needs to be developed. One suggestion for circumventing this provision is to create one or two separate non-productive material types to hold simulation cost estimates. This method allows for the creation of special reusable building blocks which can represent common manufacturing sequences or common BOM quantities. The costs of these building blocks can be used directly as items in the new simulation cost estimate. Alternatively, if minor changes need to be made to the structure of the building blocks, the cost estimate for that item can be copied directly into the unit cost estimate and the necessary changes made after it is copied. Using this method allows for more flexibility in designing the costs of the prospective product. There is also no reason that these same tools cannot be used to help create the unit cost estimate after the production material is first created.

2.4.1 Simulation material type example

Material type ZSIM (simulation materials) has been created to do simulation costing without having to create a production material for the prospective product. Materials that are created using the ZSIM material type represent prospective products and standard production routings. Production conversion costs representing the routings can be created by assigning the relevant activity types and quantities to a separate unit cost estimate. These cost estimates can then be exploded within the product simulation cost estimate to show the component activity type items that make up the production conversion costs. This is shown in the following example.

The new purple ink product outlined in Section 2.3.1 is being evaluated for mixing at the Los Angeles plant UWU2. The MIXING work center is assigned to cost center 200101 with three activity types planned: SETUP, MACHHR, and LABRHR. Setup for mixing always takes one hour, and there are two people assigned to monitor the mixing process. Total mixing time changes based on the ink being mixed. A standard batch size is 1,000 L. The development team has created a ZSIM material to represent standard mixing called *INK MIXING*.

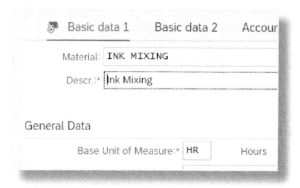

Figure 2.11: Basic data tab of INK MIXING material

The base unit of measure for this material is set to HR (see Figure 2.11). This was chosen because mixing time is measured in hours. Figure 2.12 shows that the costing lot size was selected to be 100 HR for this same material.

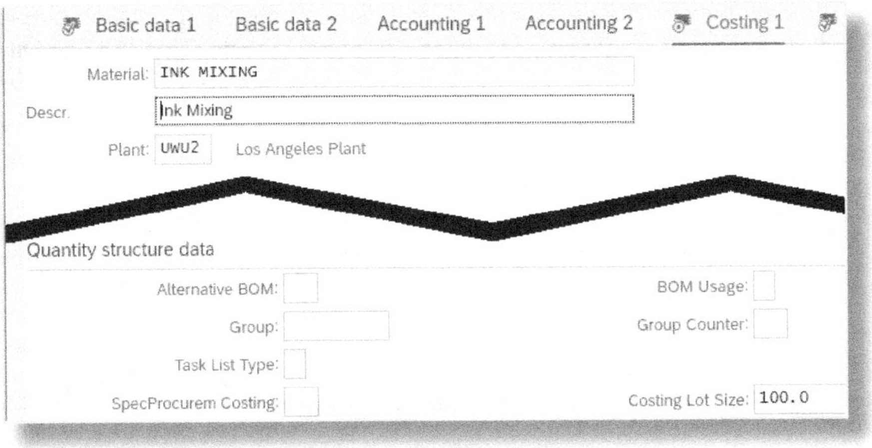

Basic data 1	Basic data 2	Accounting 1	Accounting 2	Costing 1

Material: INK MIXING

Descr. Ink Mixing

Plant: UWU2   Los Angeles Plant

Quantity structure data

Alternative BOM:		BOM Usage:	
Group:		Group Counter:	
Task List Type:			
SpecProcurem Costing:		Costing Lot Size:	100.0

Figure 2.12: Costing 1 tab of INK MIXING material

The resulting unit cost itemization of this material only contains the activity type sources for the mixing process. The cost estimate is created using the Create Unit Cost Estimate Single Fiori app (SAPGUI transaction KKPAN). The details for creating unit cost estimates are covered in Chapter 3. The data entry window for the INK MIXING material is shown in Figure 2.13.

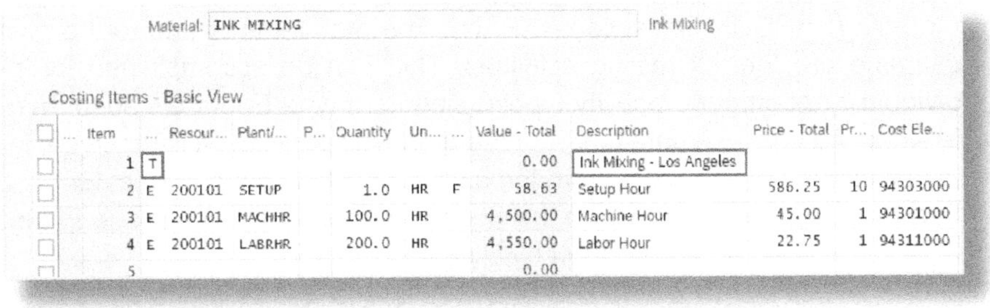

Material: INK MIXING   Ink Mixing

Costing Items - Basic View

	Item		Resour...	Plant/...	P...	Quantity	Un...	...	Value - Total	Description	Price - Total	Pr...	Cost Ele...
	1	T							0.00	Ink Mixing - Los Angeles			
	2	E	200101	SETUP		1.0	HR	F	58.63	Setup Hour	586.25	10	94303000
	3	E	200101	MACHHR		100.0	HR		4,500.00	Machine Hour	45.00	1	94301000
	4	E	200101	LABRHR		200.0	HR		4,550.00	Labor Hour	22.75	1	94311000
	5								0.00				

Figure 2.13: Unit cost estimate entry for INK MIXING

The data has been entered to reflect the 100 HR costing lot size. 1 HR has been entered for setup, 100 HR for the machine hours and 200 HR for the labor hours. Item 1 is a text item (T) indicating that this represents ink mixing at the Los Angeles plant. The resulting cost estimate is saved for later use.

85

The next task for the development team is to create the simulation purple ink material and create an associated unit cost estimate. The ZSIM activity type is again chosen for this. Figure 2.14 shows that the Costing Lot Size for this material has been set to 1,000 to represent the standard mixing size.

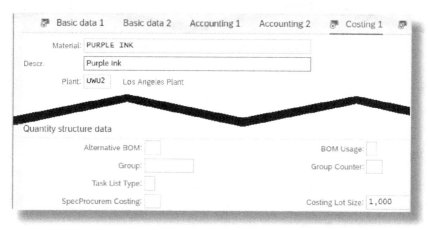

Figure 2.14: Costing 1 tab of PURPLE INK simulation material

The cost estimate is created using the Create Unit Cost Estimate Single Fiori tile (SAPGUI transaction KKPAN). The first items to add to the cost estimate are the ink mixing activities. This can be accomplished by individually entering the activity types using item type E, but because there is already a cost estimate that represents these activities, it is much easier to just copy in the activities from the existing cost estimate. Select Explode Material Cost Estimate... from the Functions dropdown menu (see Figure 2.15). This is accessible in Fiori by clicking on More ∨ .

Figure 2.16 shows the initial window used for the selection of an existing cost estimate. The Cancellation parameter determines how much of a multi-level cost estimate is to be copied. Select All Levels to copy the itemization from every level of the cost estimate. Alternatively, select No. of Levels and enter the number of levels required. If there is a 5-level cost estimate and 3 levels are selected, then the itemization for the top 3 levels is copied into the cost estimate. The materials that account for the two lower levels are copied as M (material) items as part of the third level. In this example, INK MIXING only has one level, so either selection is acceptable.

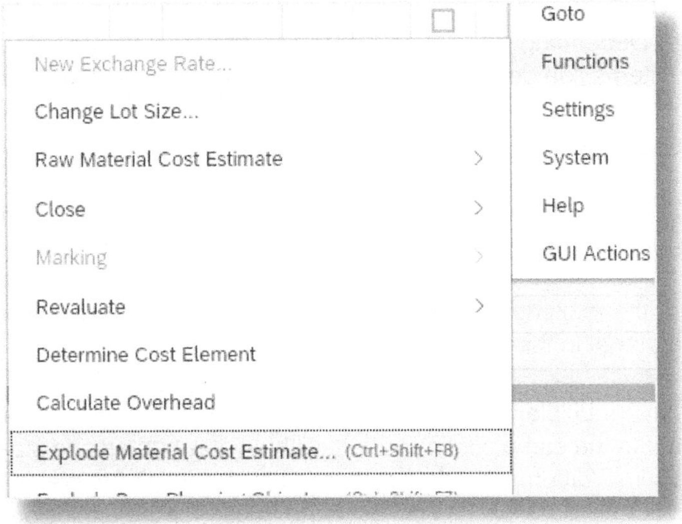

Figure 2.15: Functions menu for unit costing

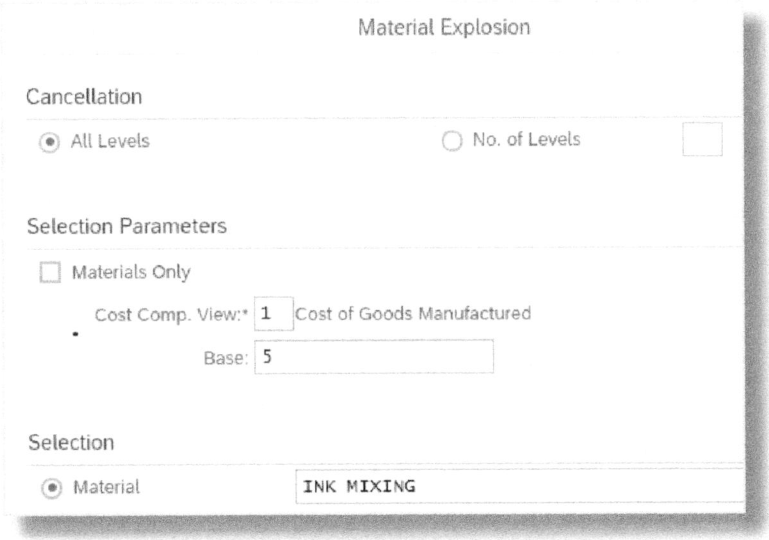

Figure 2.16: Selecting cost estimate material and lot size

The SELECTION PARAMETERS section determines which items are copied and the quantity used to adjust the quantities of the items to be added. If MATERIALS ONLY is selected, only M item types will be copied from the cost estimate. Cost Comp. View selects which cost component view to use to value the items. Depending on the view selected, the costs associated with some of the items can be different. The value entered for Base adjusts the quantities of the items from the original cost estimate's costing lot size. The initial estimate for mixing 1,000 L of purple ink is five hours. Since the original cost estimate for INK MIXING uses a costing lot size of 100, this needs to be adjusted back to 5 for inclusion in the PURPLE INK cost estimate.

Under Selection, the exploded cost estimate's material ID is entered. INK MIXING is the material in this example.

A material can have multiple cost estimates associated with it at any given time. These can use the same costing variant with different dates and statuses, or they can use different costing variants. After selecting the material, the next step is to choose which cost estimate to use for the explosion. Figure 2.17 shows the window for the cost estimate selection.

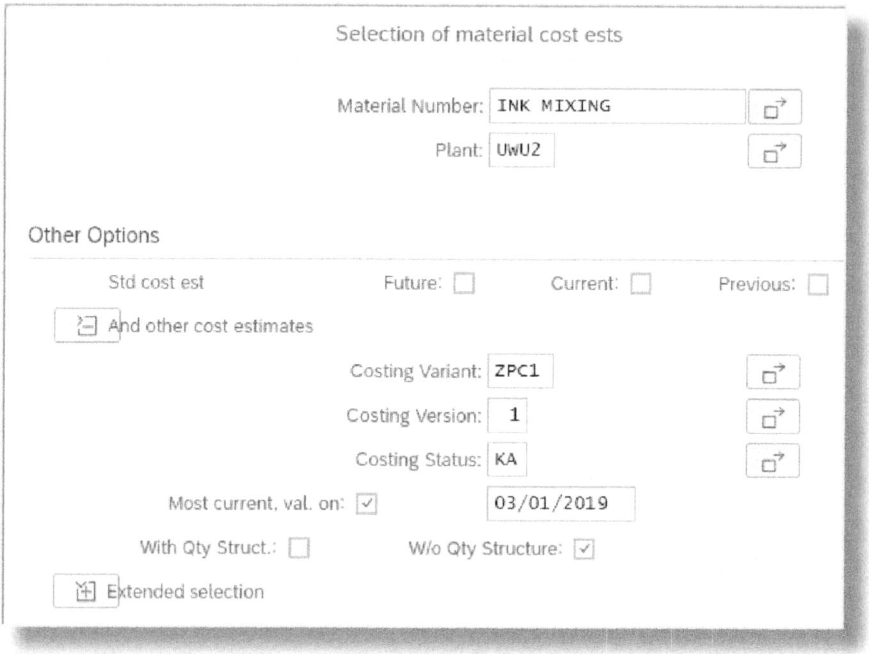

Figure 2.17: Entering search parameters for the cost estimate

There are several options to choose from. The MATERIAL NUMBER is copied from the previous window and the plant defaults to the one used for the PURPLE INK cost estimate. OTHER OPTIONS allows for a more exact selection of a specific cost estimate. If one of the STD COST EST options is selected, the cost estimate associated with the FUTURE, CURRENT, or PREVIOUS costs on the COSTING 2 tab of the material master will be part of the list of cost estimates. Selecting AND OTHER COST ESTIMATES includes all cost estimates that match a specific costing variant, costing version, and costing status. If MOST CURRENT. VAL. ON is selected, only the latest cost estimate that was created on that date or earlier is displayed. If that option is not selected, then all cost estimates from that date onward are included. If the date field is left blank, then all cost estimates that match the costing variant, costing version, and costing status are added to the list. WITH QTY STRUCT. and W/O QTY STRUCTURE are used to specify which type of cost estimate for the material should be searched. Open EXTENDED SELECTION in order to choose configured materials or materials by material class type. Figure 2.17 indicates that only the latest cost estimate with the KA status for costing variant ZPC1 will be in the selection list. This is seen in Figure 2.18.

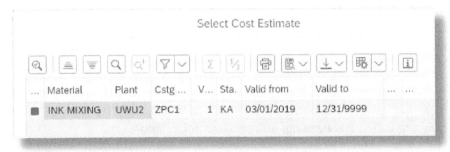

Figure 2.18: Select cost estimate from the list

Double-click on a specific cost estimate from the list. The itemization for that cost estimate is copied to a paste buffer and control is restored to the main itemization input window. The copied cost estimate is now pasted into the PURPLE INK cost estimate. Select PASTE from the More ∨ menu (this is found under the EDIT dropdown menu in the SAPGUI transaction, or by clicking on the 🗎 button).

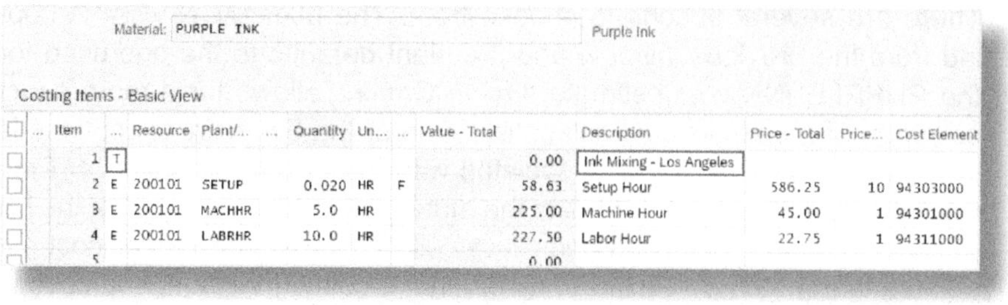

...	Item	...	Resource	Plant/...	...	Quantity	Un...	...	Value - Total	Description	Price - Total	Price...	Cost Element
	1	T							0.00	Ink Mixing - Los Angeles			
	2	E	200101	SETUP		0.020	HR	F	58.63	Setup Hour	586.25	10	94303000
	3	E	200101	MACHHR		5.0	HR		225.00	Machine Hour	45.00	1	94301000
	4	E	200101	LABRHR		10.0	HR		227.50	Labor Hour	22.75	1	94311000
	5								0.00				

Material: PURPLE INK — Purple Ink — Costing Items - Basic View

Figure 2.19: Cost estimate entry window after pasting cost estimate

Figure 2.19 shows the copied items from the INK MIXING material cost estimate. Note that activity type quantities have all been reduced from the quantities required for 100 HR to those needed for 5 HR. However, the SETUP activity should be 1 hour based on the manufacturing requirements. This should be changed in the PURPLE INK cost estimate. Figure 2.20 shows the change. Currently, the 5 HR for MACHHR and 10 HR for LABRHR are correct, but these can be changed at a later date if the development process determines that different times are required.

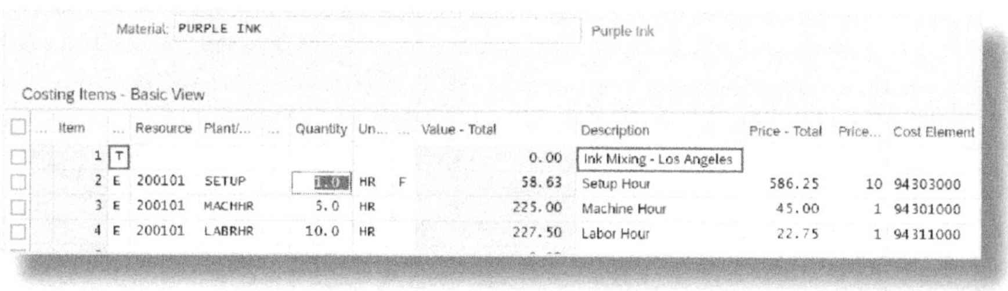

...	Item	...	Resource	Plant/...	...	Quantity	Un...	...	Value - Total	Description	Price - Total	Price...	Cost Element
	1	T							0.00	Ink Mixing - Los Angeles			
	2	E	200101	SETUP		1.0	HR	F	58.63	Setup Hour	586.25	10	94303000
	3	E	200101	MACHHR		5.0	HR		225.00	Machine Hour	45.00	1	94301000
	4	E	200101	LABRHR		10.0	HR		227.50	Labor Hour	22.75	1	94311000

Material: PURPLE INK — Purple Ink — Costing Items - Basic View

Figure 2.20: Cost estimate with updated setup time

Figure 2.21 shows the itemization data entry, including the addition of the five components. The red dye uses item type V because no material is currently set up for that particular dye. When complete, click on Save (⊟ in SAPGUI) to save the preliminary cost estimate.

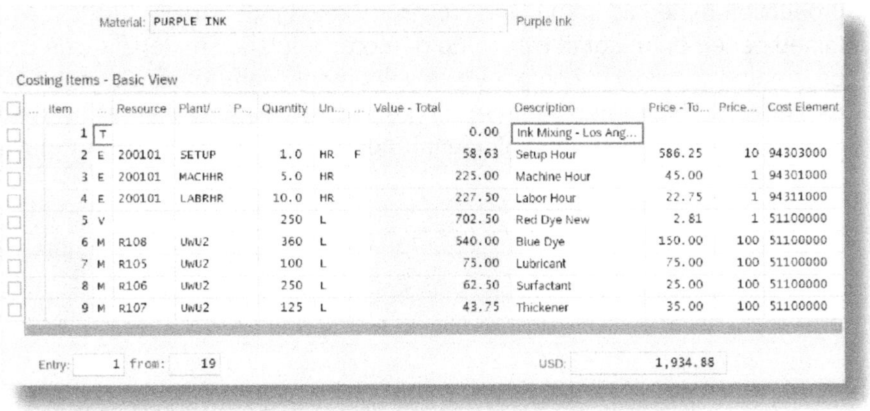

	Item	Resource	Plant/	P...	Quantity	Un...	...	Value - Total	Description	Price - To...	Price...	Cost Element
☐	1	T						0.00	Ink Mixing - Los Ang...			
☐	2	E 200101	SETUP	F	1.0	HR		58.63	Setup Hour	586.25	10	94303000
☐	3	E 200101	MACHHR		5.0	HR		225.00	Machine Hour	45.00	1	94301000
☐	4	E 200101	LABRHR		10.0	HR		227.50	Labor Hour	22.75	1	94311000
☐	5	V			250	L		702.50	Red Dye New	2.81	1	51100000
☐	6	M R108	UWU2		360	L		540.00	Blue Dye	150.00	100	51100000
☐	7	M R105	UWU2		100	L		75.00	Lubricant	75.00	100	51100000
☐	8	M R106	UWU2		250	L		62.50	Surfactant	25.00	100	51100000
☐	9	M R107	UWU2		125	L		43.75	Thickener	35.00	100	51100000

Material: PURPLE INK — Purple Ink

Costing Items - Basic View

Entry: 1 from: 19 — USD: 1,934.88

Figure 2.21: Cost estimate with BOM components added in

The system returns to the main cost estimate display. Figure 2.22 shows the final itemization. This includes the text item that was copied from the cost estimate for INK MIXING.

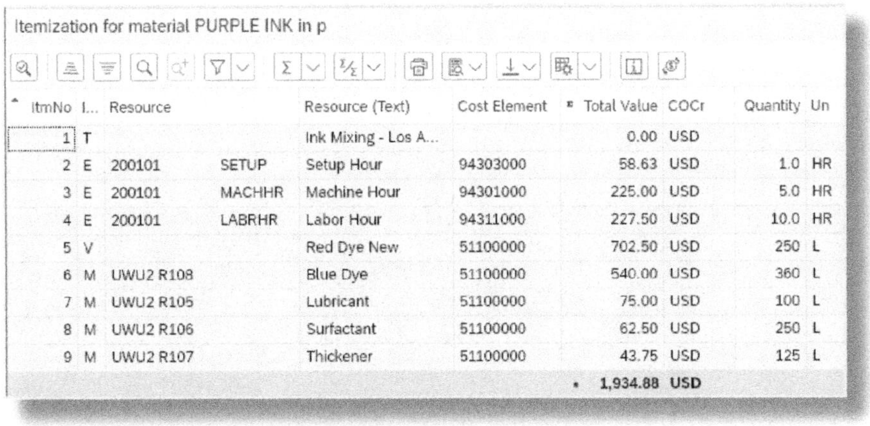

Itemization for material PURPLE INK in p

ItmNo	I...	Resource		Resource (Text)	Cost Element	¤	Total Value	COCr	Quantity	Un
1	T			Ink Mixing - Los A...			0.00	USD		
2	E	200101	SETUP	Setup Hour	94303000		58.63	USD	1.0	HR
3	E	200101	MACHHR	Machine Hour	94301000		225.00	USD	5.0	HR
4	E	200101	LABRHR	Labor Hour	94311000		227.50	USD	10.0	HR
5	V			Red Dye New	51100000		702.50	USD	250	L
6	M	UWU2 R108		Blue Dye	51100000		540.00	USD	360	L
7	M	UWU2 R105		Lubricant	51100000		75.00	USD	100	L
8	M	UWU2 R106		Surfactant	51100000		62.50	USD	250	L
9	M	UWU2 R107		Thickener	51100000		43.75	USD	125	L
						•	1,934.88	USD		

Figure 2.22: Itemization for PURPLE INK

The previous example shows some of the options that are possible when creating a unit cost estimate for a prospective product for which a material ID has not yet been assigned. Security requirements often prevent production materials from being created or changed. Usually, this is maintained based on material type. One or more simulation material types can be created to allow a company's development team to create materials as needed. These materials are not productive, so they can be used as a means of estimating manufacturing costs prior to creating the regular material.

3 Cost estimates without quantity structure

Once products get beyond the research stage of the life cycle, information concerning how a material is to be manufactured becomes clearer. However, it is still too early to create finalized BOMs and routings for the manufacturing process. Unit costing for creating cost estimates without quantity structure can be used to generate initial standard costs for these materials.

3.1 Organizational structures for cost estimates

SAP provides two methods for creating cost estimates for a material: cost estimates **without** quantity structure and cost estimates **with** quantity structure. A *quantity structure* associated with a material is a set of data that defines sources of cost external to the material, that are applied to the material based on a quantity relationship. An excellent example of a quantity structure is a bill of materials (BOM). The BOM contains the list of components that make up a product and the relative quantities of each component for a specified base quantity of the product. The cost of each component is assigned to the product based on the ratio of its quantity versus the product's base quantity. Another important quantity structure associated with manufactured materials is the routing. Routings can take several forms in SAP, including standard routes, recipes, and rate routings. Each form of routing contains operations assigned to work centers. The work centers are assigned to cost centers and activity types in order to transfer associated manufacturing costs to the product. The quantities associated with each of the operations control the quantity of activity allocated to the product based on the amount produced at that operation. Quantity structures are also associated with purchased materials because purchasing conditions, with specific prices for specific quantities of the raw material, can contribute to the calculation of the cost.

If quantity structures are not yet known for a material or the use of quantity structures to determine cost is not feasible, SAP provides a method for directly applying costs to the material through the use of cost estimates without quantity structure. When a material is created, cost estimate IDs are assigned for both a cost estimate with quantity structure and a cost estimate without quantity structure. The cost estimate ID is the link between the cost estimate and the material in the database. Both types of cost estimates can exist side by side, but only one of them can be used when updating the material master.

Figure 3.1: Costing 1 tab showing quantity structure flag

Figure 3.1 shows the WITH QTY STRUCTURE checkbox on the COSTING 1 tab of the material master. If the normal process is to cost the material without using a quantity structure, this checkbox should not be selected. However, if it is not selected, then certain features such as the costing run or mixed costing cannot be used. They require materials to have this option selected. When finding a cost estimate to update the material using Release Material Cost Estimates (covered in Chapter 7), the system first looks for the type of cost estimate specified by the WITH QTY STRUCTURE setting. If this is not set, then a cost estimate without quantity structure is used in the material master update. If no cost estimate without quantity structure exists, then the system searches for a cost estimate with quantity structure, and if it exists, it is used for the update.

Selecting this option also impacts the transfer control for cost estimate with quantity structure. If a component material is found with this checkbox not selected, the system first looks for a cost estimate without quantity structure for it, and the results of an existing cost estimate are transferred to the top-level cost estimate. If there is no cost estimate without quantity structure, then the standard price assigned to the material master of the component is used. However, if the Ignore Prod Cost Est w/o Qty Structure checkbox is selected for the costing variant, then the system does not use the results of a cost estimate without quantity structure in the cost estimate, regardless of the setting in the Costing 1 tab of the material master. Figure 3.2 shows this option not selected, indicating that cost estimates without quantity structure are to be considered.

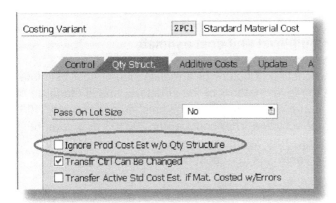

Figure 3.2: Quantity structure setting in costing variant

3.2   Single-level cost estimates

SAP provides two different methods for creating a cost estimate without quantity structure, also known as a unit cost. The first method is to create a cost estimate for a specific material at a single level. Component costs are included by defining the materials, and in which quantities, directly in the cost estimate. Manufacturing costs are generated by manually calculating quantities of activities and assigning those quantities to the cost estimate. This was covered in detail in Section 2.4 and is not repeated here. Instead of using simulation materials, actual production materials are used to generate the cost.

95

3.3   Multilevel cost estimates

Creating a unit costing can be time-consuming and labor-intensive. SAP has provided a tool to make managing unit cost estimates a bit easier. Instead of creating cost estimates material by material, the multi-level cost estimate transaction helps in its ability to create multiple cost estimates within the same costing structure. Editing tools such as drag-and-drop and worklists allow for a complete product structure to be costed within a single session. The Create Unit Cost Estimate Multi Fiori tile (SAPGUI transaction CKUC) is used for this. In addition to creating new cost estimates, existing unit cost estimates and costing structures can be changed or displayed using the same transaction.

3.3.1   Creating a multilevel unit cost estimate

Figure 3.3 shows the costing structure of a multilevel unit cost estimate. Material H107 is the top-level material of the structure, and is made up of the raw material component R101 and the semi-finished component H106. There are also internal activities from cost center 200103 that contribute to the cost. H106 in turn has two components: R101 and R100. It also includes manufacturing activities from cost center 200102.

Double-click on material H107 and the item entry window is displayed (see Figure 3.4). In this window, costs are edited and updated in the same manner as described in Section 2.4.

Material F301 (white pen with red ink) is a new material that needs to be costed. To create a new cost estimate, click on the 🗋 ∨ (🗋 🗉) button in the costing structure window. The system asks for the costing data including MATERIAL and PLANT, COSTING VARIANT, COSTING VERSION, COSTING LOT SIZE, and TRANSFER CONTROL (see Figure 3.5).

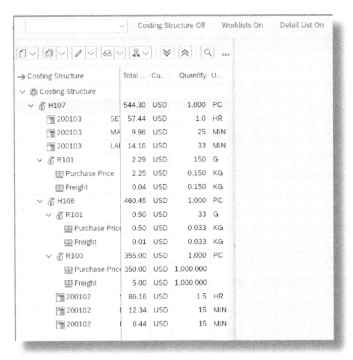

→ Costing Structure	Total ...	Cu..	Quantity	U..
∨ 🏷 Costing Structure				
∨ 🔘 H107	544.30	USD	1.000	PC
🖼 200103 SE	57.44	USD	1.0	HR
🖼 200103 MA	9.96	USD	25	MIN
🖼 200103 LA	14.16	USD	33	MIN
∨ 🔘 R101	2.29	USD	150	G
🔲 Purchase Price	2.25	USD	0.150	KG
🔲 Freight	0.04	USD	0.150	KG
∨ 🔘 H106	460.45	USD	1.000	PC
∨ 🔘 R101	0.50	USD	33	G
🔲 Purchase Price	0.50	USD	0.033	KG
🔲 Freight	0.01	USD	0.033	KG
∨ 🔘 R100	355.00	USD	1.000	PC
🔲 Purchase Price	350.00	USD	1.000.000	
🔲 Freight	5.00	USD	1.000.000	
🖼 200102	86.16	USD	1.5	HR
🖼 200102	12.34	USD	15	MIN
🖼 200102	6.44	USD	15	MIN

Figure 3.3: Costing structure for multilevel unit cost estimate

		Material:	H107					🐞 Ink Reservoir			
Costing Items - Basic View											
☐	... Item	... Resource	Plant/...	Pur...	Quantity	Un...	... Value - Total	Description	Price - Total	Price...	Cost Element
☐	1 E	200103	SETUP		1.0	HR	57.44	Setup Hour	5,743.75	100	94303000
☐	2 E	200103	MACHHR		25	MIN	9.95	Machine Hour	238.75	10	94301000
☐	3 E	200103	LABRHR		33	MIN	14.16	Labor Hour	25.75	1	94311000
☐	4 M	R101	UWU2		150	G	2.29	Brass Sheeting	1,525.35	100	51100000
☐	5 M	H106	UWU2		1,000	PC	460.50	Ballpoint	46.05	100	54300000
☐	6						0.00				

Figure 3.4: Item entry for multilevel unit cost estimate

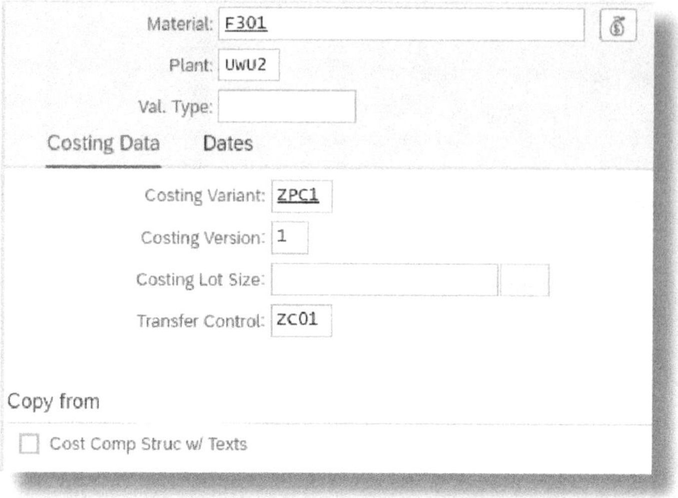

Figure 3.5: Costing data for new cost estimate

Next, the system asks for the specific dates for the cost estimate. The dates default to those that were configured in the date control definition assigned to the costing variant (see Section 1.4.11).This is shown in Figure 3.6. If configuration allows for the dates to change, this can be done here. The quantity structure date from the date control configuration is not shown because no quantity structures are referenced in the cost estimate. Sections 4.2.1 and 4.2.2 provide more detail on how to use the COSTING DATA and DATES tabs when creating a cost estimate.

After specifying the date, the costing item window is displayed. Add items as needed. If a material item is added, the system searches for an existing cost estimate for that item to add into the costing structure. It first looks for the cost estimate type that matches the WITH QTY STRUCTURE setting on the COSTING 1 tab of the material master for that component. If this flag is set, the system uses a cost estimate with quantity structure to add into the costing structure, as shown in Figure 3.7. Cost estimates with quantity structure have the ☷ (☷) icon next to them. Unit cost estimates are identified with the ☷ (☷) icon. Only cost estimates without quantity structure can be edited.

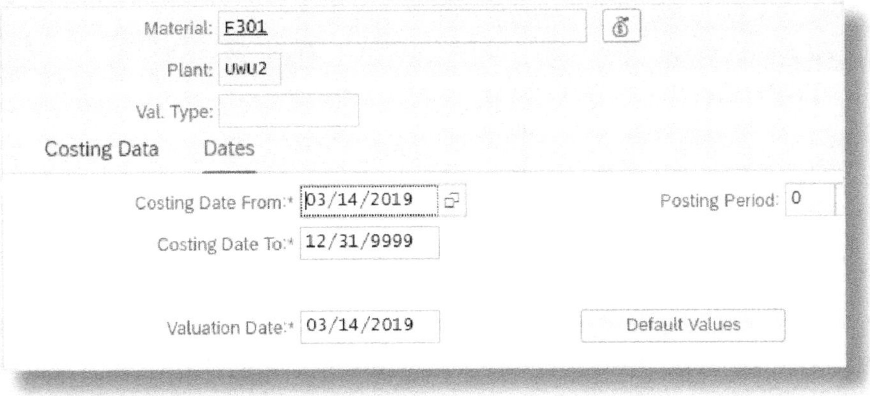

Figure 3.6: Cost estimate dates entry

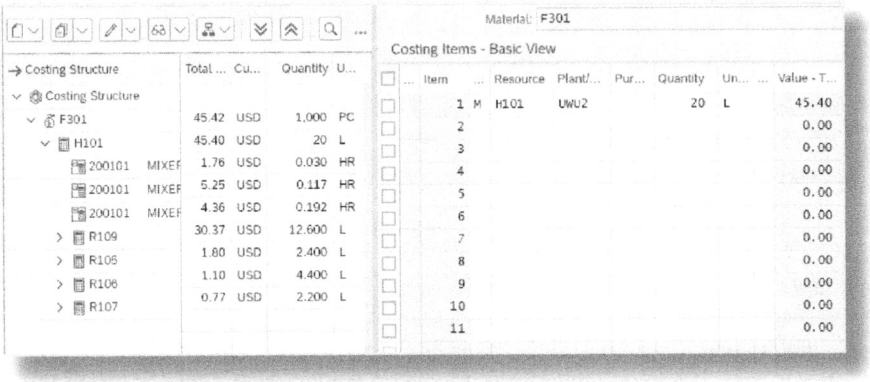

Figure 3.7: Costs transferred to costing structure

The next component to be added is material H103 (white barrel). This is a new item that does not have a cost estimate associated with it yet. To create a cost estimate that does not yet exist for a component, click on ☐ ∨ (☐ ☐) in the costing structure and enter the information for the new component. Select CREATE MATERIAL COST ESTIMATE from the dropdown menu. This is added to the costing structure at the same level as the main material. The system then requests the costing variant and date information as above. After adding the items for this cost estimate, it is ready to be included in the cost estimate for F301, as shown in Figure 3.8.

→ Costing Structure	Total ...	Cu...	Quantity	U...
∨ ⚙ Costing Structure				
∨ ⑤ F301	45.42	USD	1,000	PC
> ▦ H101	45.40	USD	20	L
> ⑤ H103	128.51	USD	1,000	PC

Figure 3.8: Additional material cost estimate at same level

At this point, the drag and drop method can be used to insert this material cost in the itemization of the top-level material F103. Figure 3.9 illustrates the procedure to follow.

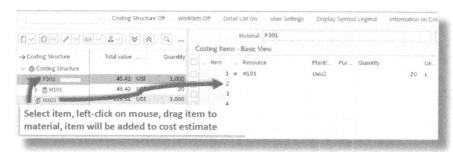

Figure 3.9: Drag and drop of cost estimate

A dialog box (see Figure 3.10) is then displayed. Choose either option shown, and the material is added as the next line in the itemization for the top-level cost.

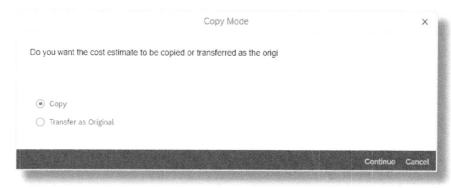

Figure 3.10: Copy cost estimate selections

Figure 3.11 shows the transferred item. Update the quantity to the desired value for the cost estimate.

Costing Items - Basic View

	...	Item	...	Resource	Plant/...	Pur...	Quantity	Un...	...	Value - Total	Description
☐		1	M	H101	UWU2		20	L		45.40	Red Ink
☐		2	M	H103	UWU2		1,000	PC		128.50	White Barrel

Figure 3.11: Transferred item

Continue adding items to the F103 cost estimate until complete. At any time during the procedure, the costs from the itemization can be transferred to the costing structure by clicking on the [⟳ Transfer] button at the bottom of the item entry window. This performs a "temporary save" of the cost estimate, enabling the updated costs to be displayed in the costing structure.

When the cost estimate for F301 is complete, there will still be two top-level cost estimates in the costing structure. The top-level cost estimate for H103 is no longer needed and can be removed from the costing structure by selecting it and then right-clicking to display a dropdown menu. Select REMOVE COST ESTIMATE (see Figure 3.12). The cost estimate is not deleted and is still accessible because it has also been inserted at the lower level.

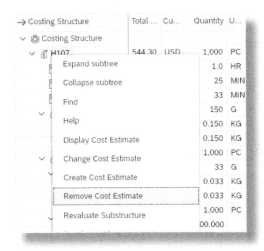

Figure 3.12: Removing a cost estimate from the costing structure

References to base planning objects

 The multilevel unit costing transaction still contains references to base planning objects. These are now considered obsolete, so they cannot be used by default. If your system still allows the use of base planning objects, they should be avoided.

The costing structure has other editing features that are found in the row of buttons at the top of the window:

- ▶ ⌧ ⌄ (🗔 🗐) **Copy**—copy from one cost estimate into another

- ▶ ✏ ⌄ (✏ 🗐) **Change**—make changes to an existing cost estimate

- ▶ 👓 ⌄ (👓 🗐) **Display**—display an existing cost estimate

- ▶ 🖳 ⌄ (🖳 🗐) **Change display settings**—change how the costing structure is displayed. The following options are available:

  - ▶ COST COMPONENT VIEW…—change which cost component view is used for the cost estimate.

  - ▶ CONVERT QUANTITIES…—change the quantity base.

  - ▶ CONTROLLING AREA CURRENCY/COMPANY CODE CURRENCY—change the currency used in the display.

  - ▶ SHOW ALL ITEMS—toggle between showing all costing items or only material items in the costing structure.

  - ▶ DISPLAY COSTING STRUCTURE ABOVE—if the costing structure is on the left side of the screen, it readjusts to appear above the costing item window. This provides more room for editing the costing items.

  - ▶ DISPLAY COSTING STRUCTURE LEFT—if the costing structure is at the top of the screen, it is moved to the left in the more traditional view.

3.3.2 Using worklists

Worklists are repositories of frequently used items to be included in unit cost estimates. These items can be dragged and dropped into a material on the costing structure and are automatically included in the cost estimate itemization. Worklists and detail lists share the same lower right-hand window area of the cost estimate. Turning on the worklist display turns off the detail list window, if it has been enabled. Click on the Worklists On button to display the worklists.

Use an existing worklist or create a new one by clicking on the ☐ button in the worklist window. If a new worklist is being created, the window in Figure 3.13 is displayed. A worklist can be declared as private or global, depending on how it should be used.

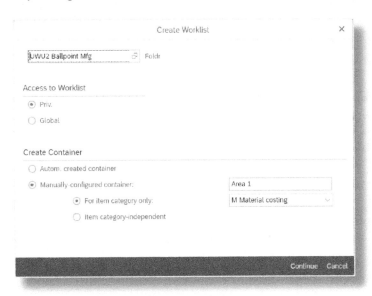

Figure 3.13: Create worklist window

Worklists are made up of containers. The containers are used to store the specific costing items. The first container is created when a worklist is defined. The container can be labelled automatically or created with a user-defined name. Containers can include costing items of just one item category, such as internal activities, or they can be set up to include items of any item category. To create a new container, select an existing one and right-click on it to show the dropdown menu. Select CREATE CONTAINER from the list. Enter the desired container definition in the window shown in Figure 3.14.

Insert Container   ✕

Name of new container: |

◉ For item category only: M Material costing   ⌄

◯ Item category-independent

Continue   Cancel

Figure 3.14: Insert container window

Costing items can be added by selecting the container and using the right-click dropdown menu to choose which type of costing items should be added to the container. If the container is set up for only one item type, then only that item type shows up in the menu. Worklists can be saved by clicking on the 🖫 button.

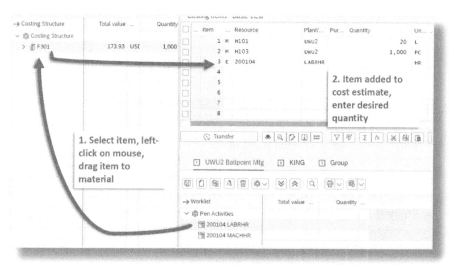

Figure 3.15: Moving item from the worklist

Figure 3.15 shows how a worklist item can be moved to the cost estimate. First, open the desired container in the work list. Next, left-click on the item and drag that item to the material in the costing structure list. The item is then added to the end of the cost estimate. The desired quantity should then be updated in the quantity field.

4 Cost estimates with quantity structure

When a material goes into regular production with repeatable production parameters, BOMs and routings are used by planning and manufacturing to describe the method of production. CO-PC-PCP uses these structures to create cost estimates which can become standard costs for these materials. Creating these types of cost estimates requires an extensive understanding of the master data involved and the procedures required for generating standard costs.

4.1 Costing master data

Cost estimates with quantity structure rely on various sources of master data to automatically calculate the costs. Unlike costing without quantity structure, no manually entered cost items are involved. When a cost estimate is created, the system looks through the master data associated with the material to automatically calculate quantities of cost objects which make up the costing sources. The value of each included cost object is multiplied by the calculated quantity to determine the costing contribution of that object. The types of quantity structures that are referenced are varied. They include obvious ones such as BOMs, routes, and recipes, but there are some others that are not so straightforward. Raw materials can be costed based on purchasing conditions associated with purchase orders or purchase information records. Overhead costs can be allocated based on the assignment of an overhead key to the material which is associated with a specific overhead costing sheet. Business process costs are allocated by using costing templates. The use of all these different sources makes material costing in SAP an extremely powerful tool in determining and understanding product values. Even better, the process is repeatable and uses data in common with other modules in the SAP suite.

4.2 Creating a cost estimate with quantity structure

To create a cost estimate for a material, execute the Create Material Cost Estimates Fiori tile. For SAPGUI users, the transaction is CK11N.

4.2.1 Selection—costing data

The initial window is shown in Figure 4.1. Material ID and plant are required entries. If multiple valuation types are configured for split valuation, then a specific valuation type can also be entered. The COSTING DATA tab is the first to be displayed.

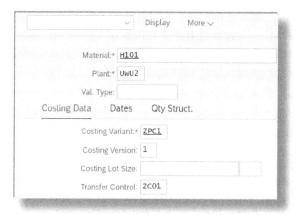

Figure 4.1: Create cost estimate costing data selection

COSTING VARIANT is a required field because it defines the purpose of the cost estimate and how the costs are assigned to the cost estimate. Select the costing variant that suits the purpose of the cost estimate.

COSTING VERSION defaults to 1, but this can be changed to another version. The costing version defines the exchange rate required for foreign purchases and transfers, the quantity structures assignments for mixed costing, and the procedure used to calculate transfer pricing when parallel valuation is used. Configuration is covered in Section 1.4.18.

Costing lot size determines the quantity of the material for which the costs are calculated. Leave this blank to use the costing lot size from the COSTING 1 tab of the material master. To see the impact of a specific lot size, enter the value and an associated unit of measure. Unit of measure defaults to the base unit of measure from the material master, but it is also possible to use an alternative unit of measure that is defined for the material, or to use one that has a set conversion to the base unit of measure within the same unit dimension (such as LB instead of KG, both of which are defined as MASS units).

The behavior of TRANSFER CONTROL depends on configuration of the costing variant and it defines how lower level costs are to be included in a multi-level cost estimate. TRANSFER CONTROL determines whether to use existing cost estimates or whether new cost estimates for the lower level materials are required. Configuration for the transfer control is covered in Section 1.4.13. When creating a costing variant, a default transfer control can be assigned (see Figure 4.2).

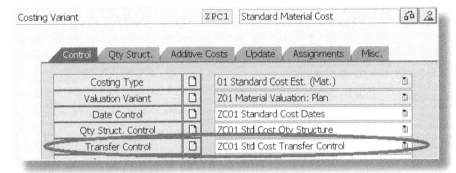

Figure 4.2: Default transfer control assignment in costing variant

If one is assigned and the transfer control key is left blank, then pressing ⌷Enter⌷ loads the default value. Press ⌷Enter⌷ again to move on. At this point, the transfer control ID can be changed if this is allowed in configuration. If left blank, all lower level costs are recalculated. The ability to change a transfer control is defined on the QTY STRUCT. tab of the costing variant configuration (see Section 1.4.15).

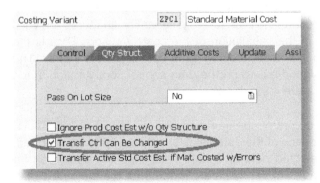

Figure 4.3: Setting to allow transfer control to be changed

109

Figure 4.3 shows that for costing variant ZPC1, transfer control can be changed. If this option is not selected, then the transfer control defined in the costing variant is always used.

4.2.2 Selection—dates

After the costing data is entered, the dates for the cost estimate must be established. Figure 4.4 shows the selections from the DATES tab.

Figure 4.4: Create cost estimate dates selection

COSTING DATE FROM defines the date from which the cost estimate is valid. COSTING DATE TO is the latest date the cost estimate is considered valid. A date of **December 31, 9999** is considered by SAP to be "the end of time". QTY STRUCTURE DATE defines the date for which quantity structures are valid and can be included in the calculation of the cost. VALUATION DATE is the date for which the values associated with the cost objects are valid. The default dates are assigned based on the date control configuration in the costing variant (see Figure 4.5).

Details regarding date control configuration are found in Section 1.4.11. Figure 4.6 shows that each of the date fields can be set up to be changed. If MANUAL ENTRY is selected next to a date field, then the dates can be manually entered. If none of the fields are marked for manual entry, then the DATES tab is skipped when creating a cost estimate. The default dates from the date control definition can be restored by clicking on the DEFAULT VALUES button (see Figure 4.4).

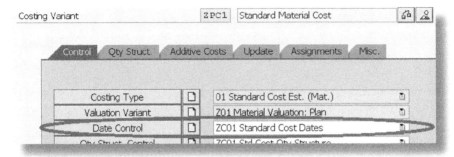

Figure 4.5: Date control definition assignment

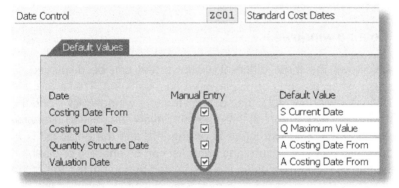

Figure 4.6: Date control manual entry configuration

4.2.3 Selection—quantity structure

The QTY STRUCT. tab, shown in Figure 4.7, is optional and must be manually selected before executing the cost estimate. BOM, routing, and production version information can be explicitly chosen, overriding the standard quantity structure selection logic. This enables a view of costs using a specific BOM or routing.

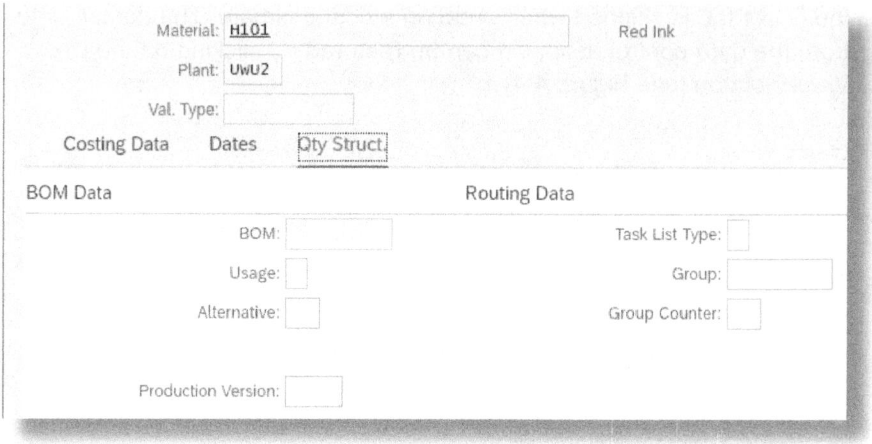

Material:	H101		Red Ink
Plant:	UwU2		
Val. Type:			

Costing Data   Dates   Qty Struct.

BOM Data   Routing Data

BOM:		Task List Type:	
Usage:		Group:	
Alternative:		Group Counter:	

Production Version:	

Figure 4.7: Quantity structure override

4.2.4 Costing windows

Figure 4.8 shows the three different windows that can be displayed simultaneously when creating or displaying a cost estimate. These are: the costing overview window (❶), the costing structure window (❷), and the detail list window (❸). When all three are displayed, the costing overview is on the right, the costing structure is on the left, and the detail list is at the bottom. The costing structure and detail list can be enabled or disabled from within the cost estimate using the associated buttons at the top of the window. COSTING STRUCTURE ON / COSTING STRUCTURE OFF controls the display of the left-hand window and DETAIL LIST ON / DETAIL LIST OFF controls the bottom window. The description on each button changes depending on whether the specific window is enabled.

The costing overview window is always enabled. There are six tabs associated with it. Each tab shows different information about the cost estimate and how it was created.

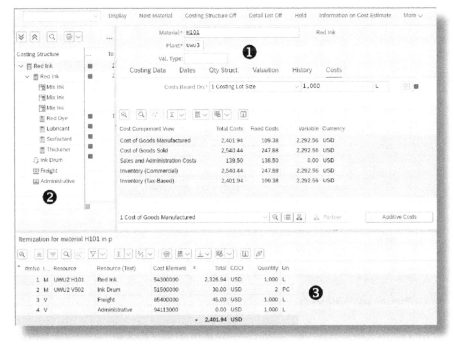

Figure 4.8: Cost estimate windows

4.2.5   Costing overview window—costs

One of the most compelling features of the SAP cost estimate is the ability to create multiple views of a product cost simultaneously by using cost component views. The power of the cost component views is seen in the costing overview window. The COSTS tab is the first tab displayed in this window when creating or displaying a cost estimate. Up to five different cost component views are displayed simultaneously, showing the impact of the different aspects of the material's cost (see area ❶ in Figure 4.9).

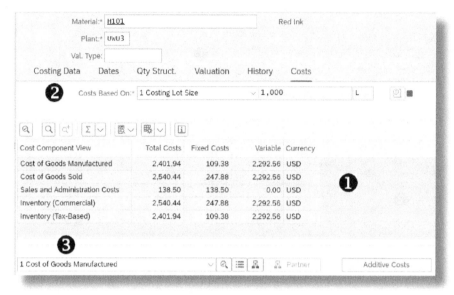

Figure 4.9: Costing overview window

The COST OF GOODS MANUFACTURED view is normally thought of as the standard cost of a product. However, the INVENTORY VALUATION view (not shown here) actually represents the valuation of inventory and goods movements and is the view that is updated in the material master. Other views show the impact of different types of costs, such as sales and administration costs, or the costs associated with raw material purchasing. The definition of the cost components that are included in each view is part of the cost component view configuration, which is covered in Section 1.3.2. Proper setup of the cost component views is paramount for understanding material costs. Cost elements and costs associated with origin groups are assigned to specific cost components and are based on the cost component definition. Each cost component is associated with one or more of the views. Cost component configuration and its assignment to one or more views is covered in Section 1.3.5. The total value of the cost component view is the cumulative costs of all cost components assigned to the view. If none of the cost components assigned to a view have costs calculated in the cost estimate, then the value for that view is 0. Eight views come pre-defined with the system, but additional views can be created if desired, each containing its own set of cost component attributes to determine which costs are included in the new view.

Users can configure which of the views to display via the Create Cost Estimate Fiori app (transaction CK11N). Select the COST DISPLAY… option from the SETTINGS dropdown menu (accessible from the More ∨ button in Fiori) to display the cost display setting window (see Figure 4.10).

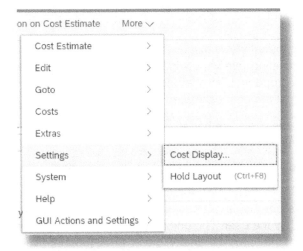

Figure 4.10: Cost display dropdown selection

The COSTS FOR VIEW section defines which views are to be displayed. To display fewer than five views, delete the number from the specific line. To change a line, enter the new view ID for that line. To change the last view from TAX-BASED INVENTORY (5) to EXTERNAL PROCUREMENT (7), enter 7 for that line (see Figure 4.11).

Costs for View

1	Cost of Goods Manufactured
2	Cost of Goods Sold
3	Sales and Administration Costs
4	Inventory (Commercial)
7	External Procurement

Select View

Figure 4.11: Changing default costing views

Press ⌊Enter⌋ to temporarily change the view. To save the setting to be used each time that cost estimates are created or viewed, click on Hold (⌊Hold⌋). The system then asks whether the setting should be defined for all costing variants or just for the currently selected costing variant. Settings for a specific costing variant take precedence over settings that are independent of costing variant.

In addition to the cost component views display, cost estimate display controls are also part of the costing overview window (see Figure 4.9, area ❷). The COSTS BASED ON dropdown list offers four cost base options that can be used when looking at the cost estimate:

► COSTING LOT SIZE—the costs are based on the costing lot size used by the cost estimate.

► PRICE UNIT—the costs are based on the price unit assigned in the material master.

► USER ENTRY—costs are displayed based on a quantity and unit of measure assigned by the user. The unit of measure must be either a unit of measure of the same dimension, such as LB (pounds) versus a base unit of KG (kilograms), or an alternative unit of measure defined for the material.

► INPUT QUANTITIES FROM MULTILEVEL BOM—this pertains to multilevel cost estimates. The top level uses the costing lot size, and the next lower level uses a size that is equivalent to the quantity of that material in the BOM based on the costing lot size. If the costing lot size is 1,000 and the quantity of component A is 25 units per 100 units of the product, then when drilling down to the cost estimate of component A, the costing lot size is adjusted to 250 (25 divided by 100 multiplied by 1,000). This ensures that the lower level costs in the costing overview and list display windows match the costs in the costing structure window.

The delivered setting is COSTING LOT SIZE. However, this can also be changed in the SETTINGS dropdown menu. The definition is found in the COST BASE section of the COST DISPLAY... option (see Figure 4.12). Select the desired option to be used temporarily or saved in the same manner, as discussed above.

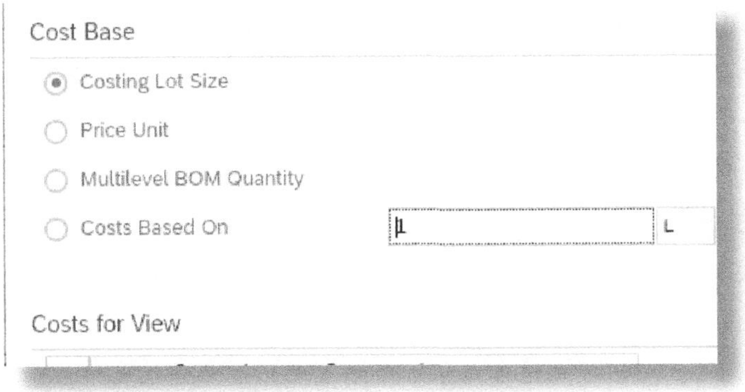

Cost Base

- (●) Costing Lot Size
- ( ) Price Unit
- ( ) Multilevel BOM Quantity
- ( ) Costs Based On ___ [μ] ___ L

Costs for View

Figure 4.12: Changing cost base defaults

At the bottom of the costing overview window, there is a set of selections for the detail list and costing structure windows (see Figure 4.9, area ❸). The dropdown menu selects the cost component view that is used for the detail list window and costing structure window. Each configured cost component view is included in the selection list, and not just those in the COSTS tab. Only those costs associated with the specific cost component view are displayed in the costing structure, itemization detail list, and the cost component detail list.

A set of buttons are used to switch between different displays:

▶ 🔍 (🔍)—select the itemization report for the detail list window. This can also be selected by pressing function key F6.

▶ ☰ (▦)—select the cost component split report for the detail list window. This can also be selected by pressing function key F5.

▶ 🔠 (🔠)—display the costing structure window if not displayed.

▶ 🔠 Partner (🔠 Partner)—use the partner cost component split for the display if configured.

If costs from an additive cost estimate were included at this level, the ADDITIVE COSTS button is displayed. Click on that button to see only the additive costs for the cost estimate. To return to the normal display, click on the specific button to display either the itemization or cost component report.

4.2.6 Costing overview window—costing data

Click on the COSTING DATA tab to view how the cost estimate was created. COSTING VARIANT, COSTING VERSION, COSTING LOT SIZE, and TRANSFER CONTROL are displayed, as shown in Figure 4.13.

Figure 4.13: Costing data tab of the costing view

Double click on the costing variant to display the costing variant configuration, assuming security allows access to this transaction. This tab, like the COSTS tab, has access to the message logs. The number of messages generated when creating the cost estimate is displayed with a message log button (🖉 or 🔊) next to it. The button is enabled if there are messages. Click on the button to see the list of messages in the detail list window. Next to this button is a traffic light icon which displays the highest severity level of all the messages. Green indicates an informational level, yellow indicates warning, and red indicates error.

The cost estimate status is also displayed. This shows the latest status of the cost estimate and not just the status based on creating it. This includes status changes that occur when processing the material master update. The following list contains the possible statuses:

▶ ER OPENED—opened

▶ FF RELEASED WITH ERRORS—released with errors

▶ FM RELEASE THROUGH MATERIAL LEDGER SETTLEMENT—released as a part of the material ledger settlement

▶ FR RELEASED WITHOUT ERRORS—released

▶ KA COSTED WITHOUT ERRORS—costed without errors

▶ KF COSTED WITH ERRORS—costed with errors

▶ SE SELECTED WITHOUT ERRORS—selected for a costing run without errors

▶ SF SELECTED WITH ERRORS—selected for a costing run with errors

▶ VF MARKED WITH ERRORS—marked with errors

▶ VO MARKED WITHOUT ERRORS—marked without errors

4.2.7 Costing overview window—Dates

Figure 4.14 shows the information on the DATES tab. The dates assigned when creating the cost estimate (see Section 4.2.2) are displayed.

Figure 4.14: Dates tab of the costing view

4.2.8 Costing overview window—quantity structure

The information from on the COSTING DATA and DATES tabs display what was entered in the cost estimate selection process. The QTY STRUCT. tab shows the quantity structures that were referenced when generating the cost estimate. Although the quantity structure can be specified, this is usually determined by the configuration of the costing variant. Figure 4.15 shows the structures used for a manufactured material. This includes the BOM, routing or task list, and production version. Double click on underlined information to jump to the display of that information. If any of the information is left blank, it means that the cost estimate did not find that type of structure. For example, purchased materials do not have BOMs or routings, and those fields are blank. If the itemization of a cost estimate for a manufactured product does not look correct, check this tab to help determine what is missing. If the BOM information is displayed, but the routing information is missing, this likely points to a problem with the cost estimate, even if the status is set to KA (costed without errors).

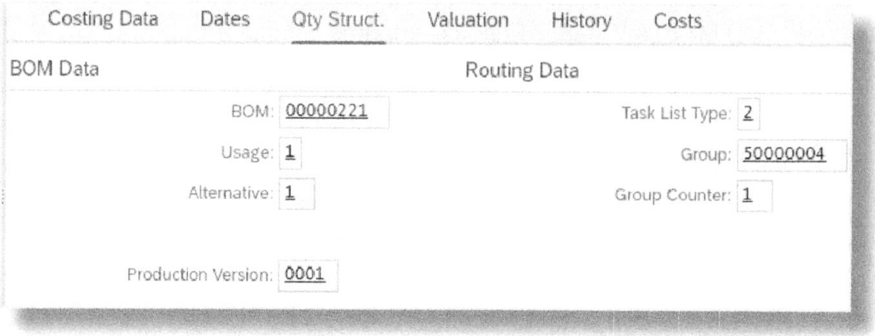

Costing Data	Dates	Qty Struct.	Valuation	History	Costs

BOM Data   **Routing Data**

BOM: 00000221   Task List Type: 2

Usage: 1   Group: 50000004

Alternative: 1   Group Counter: 1

Production Version: 0001

Figure 4.15: Manufacturing quantity structures

The version of information shown in Figure 4.16 shows a material that was transferred from another plant. In this case, a SPECIAL PROCUREMENT DATA section is added to the display. This section is included when a special procurement key is assigned, indicating one of the following: plant to plant stock transfer, manufacturing in another plant, or subcontracting.

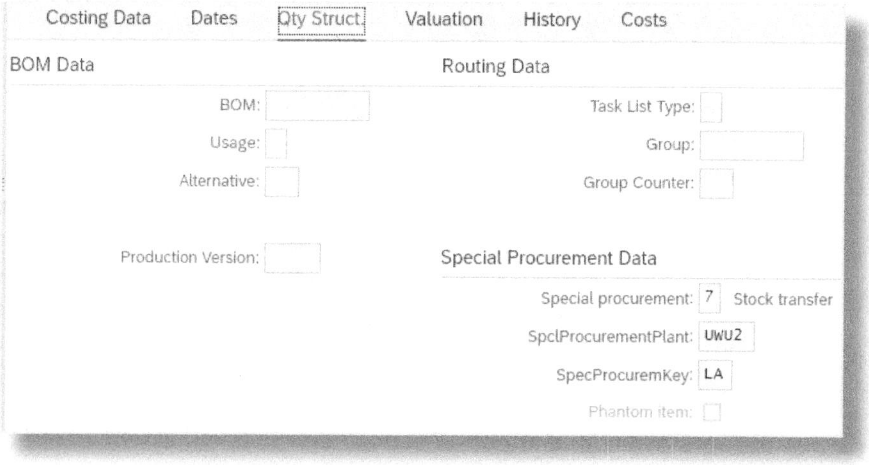

Costing Data	Dates	Qty Struct.	Valuation	History	Costs

BOM Data   **Routing Data**

BOM: Task List Type:

Usage: Group:

Alternative: Group Counter:

Production Version: **Special Procurement Data**

Special procurement: 7   Stock transfer

SpclProcurementPlant: UWU2

SpecProcuremKey: LA

Phantom item: ☐

Figure 4.16: Qty Struct. tab of the costing view

4.2.9 Costing overview window—valuation

The Valuation tab gives information on how the values were determined in the cost estimate. In Figure 4.17, the valuation view is defined with the costing type (see Section 1.4.2). Currency is determined according to the plant's company code. The overhead Costing Sheet that is referenced is assigned to the valuation variant (see Section 1.4.8). This configuration is found on the Overhead tab of the valuation variant configuration. For all materials that are not directly purchased from a vendor, the costing sheet defined for Overhead for Finished and Semifinished Materials is used. The overhead key can be used to allocate certain types of overhead to the cost estimate. The overhead key is associated with the overhead group based on configuring that overhead group for a specific plant. When the overhead group is assigned to the Costing 1 tab of the material master, the overhead key is associated with the material. If a costing template is used as part of the cost estimate, this is also displayed. The template that is assigned is based on configuration that associates a template with an overhead costing sheet/overhead key combination. Adding overhead to cost estimates, and the corresponding configuration required, is covered in "SAP® S/4HANA Product Cost Planning—Costing with Quantity Structure".

Figure 4.17: Valuation tab of the costing view

Figure 4.18 shows the Valuation tab for the cost estimate of a purchased material. The method for determining the purchase price is also included. The Material Valuation line is added, which shows the strategy used for determining the source of the price. If strategy L (Price from Purchasing Info Record) is displayed, another line is added showing the sub-strategy used to find the cost. The strategy sequence is described in Section 1.4.4.

The valuation variant allows for two different costing sheets to be defined (see Section 1.4.8). The costing sheet used for directly purchased materials on the OVERHEAD tab of the valuation variant configuration is the one defined for OVERHEAD ON MATERIAL COMPONENTS. If a material is defined in two plants and is purchased in one and then transferred to the other, the costing sheet used when costing the material at the second plant is the one defined for OVERHEAD FOR FINISHED AND SEMIFINISHED MATERIALS.

Figure 4.18: Valuation tab for purchased materials

4.2.10 Costing overview window—history

Figure 4.19 shows the HISTORY tab. This displays the user responsible for the cost estimate and the date that it occurred. Marking and release dates are displayed if either of those actions occurred. If the cost estimate was created as part of a costing run, the costing run ID and date are shown.

Figure 4.19: History tab of the costing view

4.2.11 Costing structure window

The costing structure window displays the multi-level BOM explosion of the cost estimate. If the window is not visible when the cost estimate is displayed, click on the COSTING STRUCTURE ON button on the menu bar. If the window displayed is too narrow to see all the pertinent information, click on the right edge of the window and drag to the right.

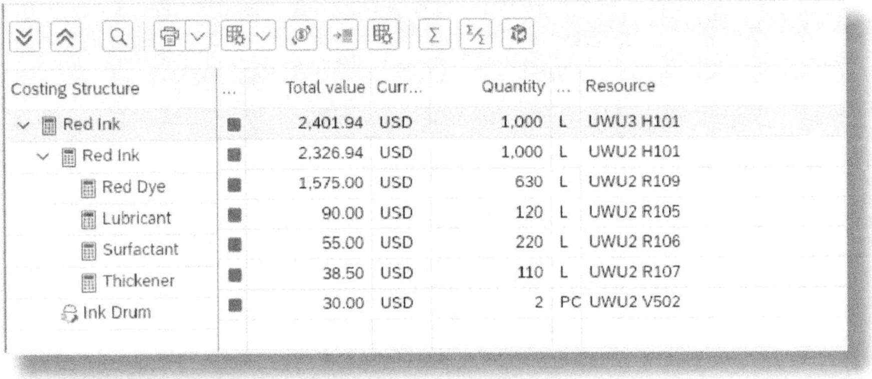

Costing Structure	...		Total value	Curr...	Quantity	...	Resource
∨ Red Ink		■	2,401.94	USD	1,000	L	UWU3 H101
∨ Red Ink		■	2,326.94	USD	1,000	L	UWU2 H101
Red Dye		■	1,575.00	USD	630	L	UWU2 R109
Lubricant		■	90.00	USD	120	L	UWU2 R105
Surfactant		■	55.00	USD	220	L	UWU2 R106
Thickener		■	38.50	USD	110	L	UWU2 R107
Ink Drum		■	30.00	USD	2	PC	UWU2 V502

Figure 4.20: Costing structure showing materials only

Figure 4.20 shows the structure for the cost estimate for material H101 at plant UWU3. This material is manufactured in plant UWU2 and transferred to UWU3. The structure of the report is hierarchical. The top line shows the total cost for the material at the top level of the cost estimate. In this case, it is material H101 (RED INK) at plant UWU3. The next line is indented and shows the first "component" of the multi-level BOM. In this case it is material H101 at plant UWU2. Next on the list are the components for the material at that level. H101 is manufactured at UWU2 and the individual components are indented under it. The packaging material V502 (INK DRUM) is part of the shipment from UWU2 to UWU3 and shows up at the same level as H101 at UWU2. The cost and quantity shown for each of the material components is the relative quantity of that material used based on the costing lot size of the top-level cost. 1,000 L of H101 at UWU2 are included in the transfer to become H101 at UWU3, but only 630 L of R109 at UWU2 are included in that cost.

Material costs usually make up only part of a product's costs. In addition, there can be costs associated with the manufacturing process, freight, overhead costs, and other costs. Figure 4.21 shows the full set of costs at each level for material H101 at plant UWU3. Processing costs for plant UWU2, freight, and administrative costs are also displayed. The administrative costs show up as 0 in this example because the cost component view chosen does not include administrative costs. Like the other cost estimate windows, the costing structure window data reflects the cost component view chosen. To switch between materials only and full reports, click on the ⇥ (📊) button. The display toggles between the two views.

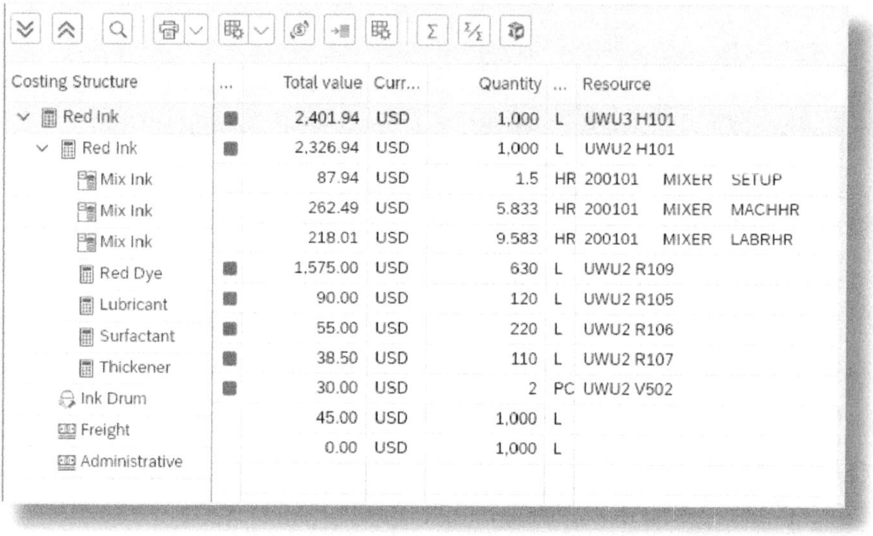

Costing Structure	...	Total value	Curr...	Quantity	...	Resource		
∨ ▦ Red Ink	■	2,401.94	USD	1,000	L	UWU3 H101		
∨ ▦ Red Ink	■	2,326.94	USD	1,000	L	UWU2 H101		
▦ Mix Ink		87.94	USD	1.5	HR	200101	MIXER	SETUP
▦ Mix Ink		262.49	USD	5.833	HR	200101	MIXER	MACHHR
▦ Mix Ink		218.01	USD	9.583	HR	200101	MIXER	LABRHR
▦ Red Dye	■	1,575.00	USD	630	L	UWU2 R109		
▦ Lubricant	■	90.00	USD	120	L	UWU2 R105		
▦ Surfactant	■	55.00	USD	220	L	UWU2 R106		
▦ Thickener	■	38.50	USD	110	L	UWU2 R107		
▦ Ink Drum	■	30.00	USD	2	PC	UWU2 V502		
▦ Freight		45.00	USD	1,000	L			
▦ Administrative		0.00	USD	1,000	L			

Figure 4.21: Costing structure showing all costs

Lower level items can be hidden or revealed using the arrow buttons. If an item has the ⟩ symbol next to it, this means that there are lower level costs that can be displayed. Select the item by clicking on the line. Then click on ⟱ (📥) to reveal all lower level items that belong to the selected item. If the item has the ⌄ symbol next to it, this means that the lower level items are showing. These can be hidden by selecting the item and clicking on ⟰ (📤) to hide the lower level details.

Click on ⌨ (📟) to change the currency used in the window. The system displays the window shown in Figure 4.22. Select the desired currency to be used.

Select an item and click on 📊 (🖥) to see information about that item. If the item is a cost object such as a material or activity type, the system brings up the master data display for that object. A message is then generated if the selected item does not have master data associated with it. These types of items include text items, variable items, operation items, and totals items.

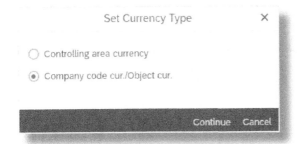

Figure 4.22: Select currency window

Each item in the list has an icon associated with it. To see what the icons represent, click on the legend button (). The window in Figure 4.23 is displayed.

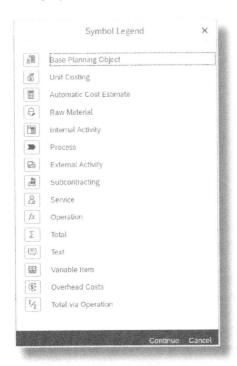

Figure 4.23: Cost structure legend

Double click on a material in the costing structure window, and the context for the costing overview and detail list windows in the cost estimate switches to the material selected. This is a way of viewing cost estimates for lower level costs in the costing structure. If the transfer control is set so that an existing cost estimate is being used, the cost estimate must first be saved before the lower level costs can be viewed.

Cost component costs can be pulled into the costing structure report based on the assignment of a unique cost component group for each cost component. The available fields are highlighted in Figure 4.24.

Figure 4.24: Costing structure report cost component group fields

Instead of being the actual cost components, these fields are made up of the primary groups that are assigned to the cost components. To get this level of detail, there must be one group assigned uniquely to each cost component. The cost component group definitions corresponding to the costing structure report fields are shown in Figure 4.25. The cost component configuration is found under IMG menu path CONTROLLING • PRODUCT

Cost Controlling • Product Cost Planning • Basic Settings for Material Costing • Define Cost Component Structure or via transaction OKTZ.

Dialog Structure	Cost comp. grp	Name
▽ ☐ Cost Component Struct	A0	Direct Material
▽ ☐ Cost Components w	A1	Ink
☐ Assignment: Cost	A2	Packaging
☐ Update of Additive	A3	Labor
☐ Transfer Structur	A4	Utilities
☐ Cost Component Views	A5	3rd Party Costs
☐ Assignment: Organiz. L	A6	Supplies
🗐 Cost Component Group	A7	Depreciation
	A8	Freight
	A9	Transfer Surcharge
	AA	Sales / Admin
	AB	Inventory Overhead
	AC	Other

Figure 4.25: Cost component group definitions

These groups are directly associated with the cost components by assigning each group to a specific cost component (see Figure 4.26). A full description of the cost component configuration is found in Section 1.3.

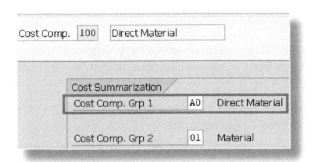

Figure 4.26: Cost component group assignment

4.2.12 Detail list window—itemization

If the detail list window is enabled, the itemization report is the default display. If the itemization report is not currently displayed, press ⌴F6⌴ or click on the [🔍] ([🖥]) button in the costing overview window. Figure 4.27 shows an itemization report. Each line item on the report is a separate source of cost for the specific level of the cost estimate.

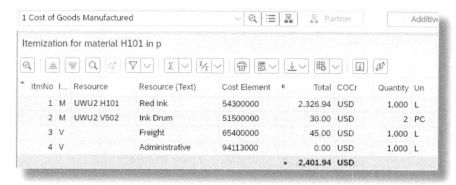

Figure 4.27: Itemization view in the detail list window

Each line item has a type identifier to specify the cost object representing a specific cost included in the report. Item types that can appear in the report are as follows:

▶ A—co-product. This indicates costs associated with a co-product that is manufactured with this material.

▶ B—base planning object. Base planning objects are not intended to be used in S/4HANA.

▶ E—internal activity. This specifies an activity type/cost center combination derived from a manufacturing operation or template allocation.

▶ F—external activity. This is the cost associated with paying a vendor for an external processing operation.

▶ G—overhead allocation. This indicates the costs calculated from an overhead costing sheet.

▶ I—delivery costs. This is the cost for purchasing a material from a vendor.

▶ L—subcontracting. This is the expected cost paid to a vendor for subcontracting services.

▶ M—material. This indicates the standard cost of a material.

- ▶ N—external service. This specifies the cost of an external service. This is not the same as external processing for a route operation.

- ▶ O—arithmetical operation. This can only come from an additive cost estimate.

- ▶ P—process (manual). This indicates the costs associated with manually assigning a business process to an additive cost estimate.

- ▶ V—variable item. This is a manually specified cost that is part of additive costs.

- ▶ X—process (automatic). This specifies the costs associated with template allocation of a business process.

4.2.13 Detail list window—cost components

The cost component list is the alternative costing report available in the detail list window. Press the $\boxed{F5}$ key to see the report. This is also available by clicking on the $\boxed{\equiv}$ (🎛) button in the costing overview window. Each line in the report represents a different cost component. However, only those cost components associated with the selected cost component view are displayed. Figure 4.28 shows the COST OF GOODS MANUFACTURED view. The report can also display both cost component groups assigned to each cost component, and the report can be subtotaled by group.

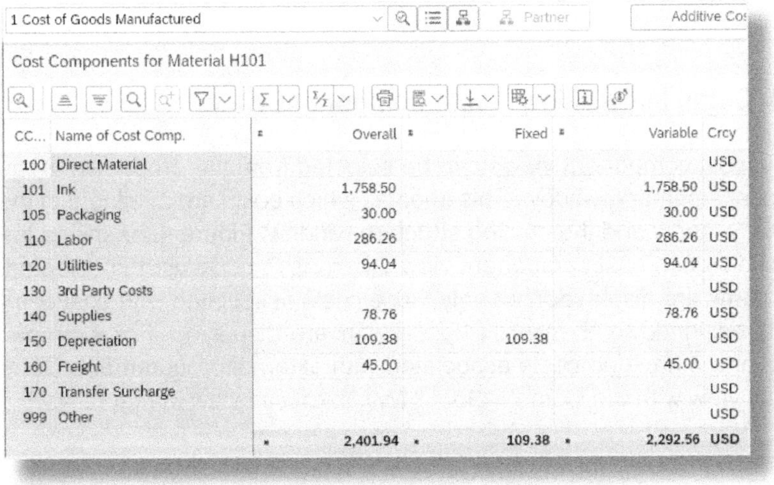

CC...	Name of Cost Comp.	Overall	Fixed	Variable	Crcy
100	Direct Material				USD
101	Ink	1,758.50		1,758.50	USD
105	Packaging	30.00		30.00	USD
110	Labor	286.26		286.26	USD
120	Utilities	94.04		94.04	USD
130	3rd Party Costs				USD
140	Supplies	78.76		78.76	USD
150	Depreciation	109.38	109.38		USD
160	Freight	45.00		45.00	USD
170	Transfer Surcharge				USD
999	Other				USD
		2,401.94	109.38	2,292.56	USD

1 Cost of Goods Manufactured — Additive Cos — Cost Components for Material H101

Figure 4.28: Cost component report in detail list window

129

Two different levels of the cost component split are maintained for cost estimates. The top level includes the cost component split for only those costs that were incurred to manufacture or purchase the cost estimate material. The lower level breaks down the costs for all materials in the exploded multi-level BOM. The delivered report layout 1SAP03 shows the level split. In Figure 4.29, the top-level costs (LEVEL) are low because this is a manufactured material that was transferred between plants. The LOWER LEVEL costs account for the bulk of the value of material H101 at plant UWU3.

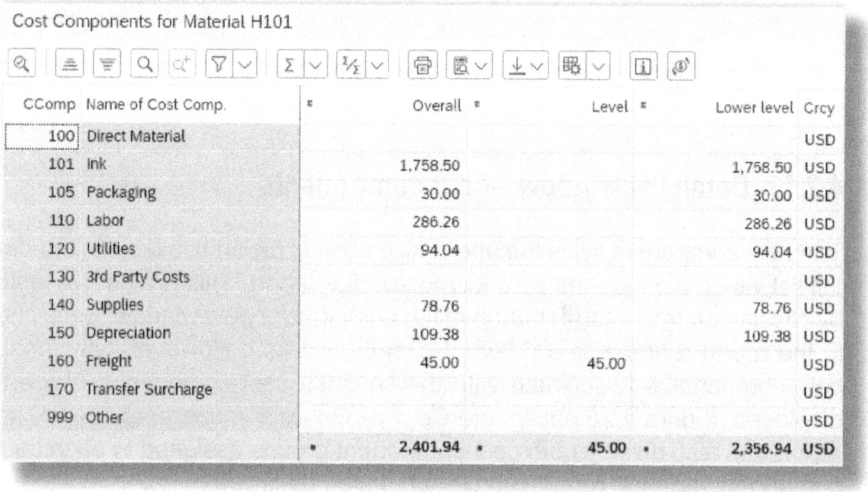

Cost Components for Material H101

CComp	Name of Cost Comp.		Overall	Level	Lower level	Crcy
100	Direct Material					USD
101	Ink		1,758.50		1,758.50	USD
105	Packaging		30.00		30.00	USD
110	Labor		286.26		286.26	USD
120	Utilities		94.04		94.04	USD
130	3rd Party Costs					USD
140	Supplies		78.76		78.76	USD
150	Depreciation		109.38		109.38	USD
160	Freight		45.00	45.00		USD
170	Transfer Surcharge					USD
999	Other					USD
			2,401.94	45.00	2,356.94	USD

Figure 4.29: Cost component level/lower level view

4.2.14 Detail list window—cost component view

Specific cost component views can be selected from the dropdown menu in the cost summary window. This impacts which costs are available in the detail list window and the costing structure window. Figure 4.30 shows the itemization when cost component view EXTERNAL PROCUREMENT is selected. All the items are displayed, but only those costs associated with cost components assigned to EXTERNAL PROCUREMENT are displayed. For example, items 2 and 3 have no costs associated with external procurement. Compare this view with the COST OF GOODS MANUFACTURED view in Figure 4.27.

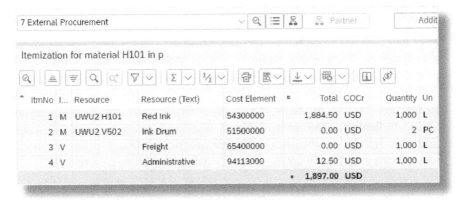

ItmNo	I...	Resource	Resource (Text)	Cost Element	≡	Total	COCr	Quantity	Un
1	M	UWU2 H101	Red Ink	54300000		1,884.50	USD	1,000	L
2	M	UWU2 V502	Ink Drum	51500000		0.00	USD	2	PC
3	V		Freight	65400000		0.00	USD	1,000	L
4	V		Administrative	94113000		12.50	USD	1,000	L
					■	1,897.00	USD		

Figure 4.30: External procurement view itemization

Figure 4.31 shows the cost component report for the External Procurement cost component view. In contrast to what was seen in Figure 4.29, only a few of the cost components are displayed. This is because only those cost components associated with a specific cost component view are displayed when that cost component view is selected. As an example, cost components 180 (Sales / Admin) and 190 (Inventory Overhead) are seen in this report but are not part of the Cost of Goods Manufactured view report.

CComp	Name of Cost Comp.	≡	Overall	≡	Level	≡	Lower level	Crcy
100	Direct Material							USD
101	Ink		1,758.50				1,758.50	USD
130	3rd Party Costs							USD
180	Sales / Admin		138.50		12.50		126.00	USD
190	Inventory Overhead							USD
		■	1,897.00	■	12.50	■	1,884.50	USD

Figure 4.31: External procurement view cost component

131

4.2.15 Detail list window—message log

Costing messages can be selected for viewing in the detail list window by clicking on the message log button (💬 or 🖼) in either the COSTING DATA or COSTS tab in the cost summary window. If the button is not highlighted, then there are no messages to display. Next to the button is a traffic light icon which displays the highest severity level of all the messages. A green square indicates an informational level, a yellow triangle indicates warning, and a red circle signifies error. The messages displayed in the detail list window are specifically for the current costing level (see Figure 4.32).

Log for cost est material H102 in plant UWU2

Light	...	Material	Plant	AppAr	MsgNo	Message Text	Vari
■	I	H102	UWU2	CK	229	No routing could be determined for material H102	
■	I	H102	UWU2	CK	424	Material H102 in plant UWU2 has no BOM	
✹	E	H102	UWU2	CK	060	Object was not costed	
✹	E	H102	UWU2	CK	240	Cost component split costed with value of zero	

Figure 4.32: Message log view in detail list window

To view costing messages for all materials in the costing structure, select the multilevel log option when defining settings for the costing display. Select MULTILEVEL LOG from the COST DISPLAY... option window to see these messages in the detail list window (see Figure 4.33).

Figure 4.33: Costing message log default setting

Another way to access message logs is by clicking on the LOG WITH ALL MESSAGES button on the menu bar (see Figure 4.34). On SAPGUI screens this shows up as the 🖼 button at the top of the main window.

Figure 4.34: Menu bar message log button

Instead of being displayed in the detail list window, a separate window shows the messages (see Figure 4.35). This log shows all messages associated with the cost estimate; if costing was performed as part of a costing run, it shows the costing run messages as well.

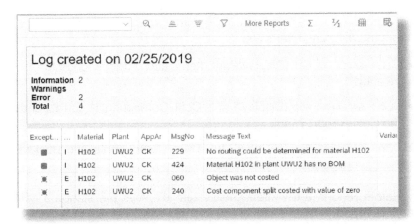

Figure 4.35: Full message log

4.2.16 Cost estimate display options

Custom cost reports can be displayed in the detail list window in place of the cost component list. To change the report displayed, select the COST DISPLAY... option from the SETTINGS dropdown menu (accessible from the More ⌄ button in Fiori) which displays the cost display setting window (see Figure 4.10). The SELECT VIEW section of the window contains radio buttons to select which cost report to display (see Figure 4.36).

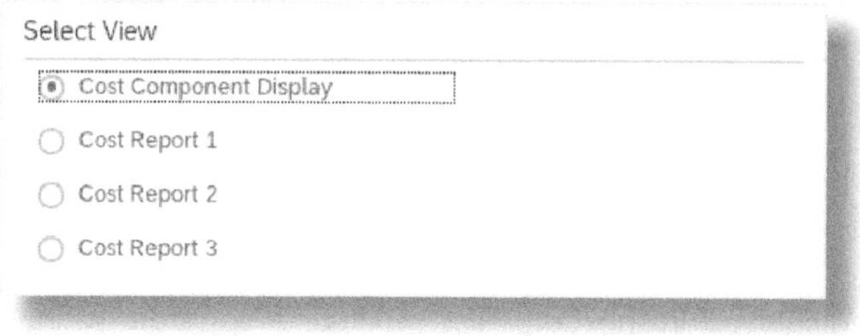

Figure 4.36: Selection of costing report

The delivered report is the COST COMPONENT DISPLAY. This is the default display when clicking on the ☰ button or when pressing F5. Three other custom reports can also be selected. Customer-written reports are accessible from the following user exits:

▶ EXIT_SAPLCKAZ_001 (Display/Print: Itemization) corresponds to Cost Report 1.

▶ EXIT_SAPLCKAZ_002 (Display/Print: Cost Components) corresponds to Cost Report 2, and

▶ EXIT_SAPLCKAZ_003 (Display/Print: Cost Components and Itemization) corresponds to Cost Report 3.

If no custom reports are written, the system displays the standard cost component report.

4.2.17 Displaying costing master data

Master data used for costing a material can be viewed from the cost estimate. There are three methods which can be used. First, if the value of a field is underlined, then double-click on that field to go to the master data. As an example, let's look at the QTY STRUCT. tab for the cost estimate of material H101 at plant UWU2 in Figure 4.37.

Double-click on the material ID in ❶ to display the material master. Double-click on any of the BOM information fields in section ❷ to view the BOM. Double-click on the production version in ❸ to see the production version definition. Finally, double-click on any of the routing data fields in ❹ to switch to the display of the recipe or routing. The task list type determines which master data is displayed. Type 2 indicates a recipe, type N is for a routing, and type R is for a rate routing.

Figure 4.37: Displaying master data

Some of the master data is not directly available using the above method. An alternative way to view the data is to use the costing information drop-down list. There are two ways to access this. The first method is to use the EXTRAS • INFORMATION menu option, accessible in Fiori through the More ⌄ button (see Figure 4.38). The highlighted items are available to select.

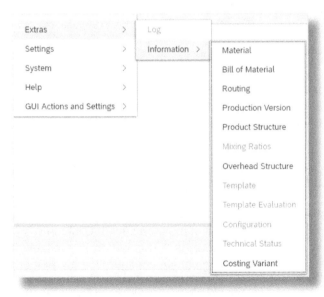

Figure 4.38: Information dropdown menu

The second way is to click on the INFORMATION ON COST ESTIMATE button (SAPGUI [ℹ️]). A window is displayed, giving a selection of which master data to view. Only master data views active for the cost estimate are shown (see Figure 4.39). Click on a specific option to view the master data.

Figure 4.39: Information selection window

The third method for accessing cost estimate master data is to double-click on an item line in the itemization list. The master data that is displayed depends on the item type of the line selected.

4.2.18 Exiting and saving the cost estimate

To allow the cost estimate to be used for updating the material master or for comparisons to other cost estimates, it must be saved. Click on Save (💾) to save the cost estimate for further use. This button is available if SAVING ALLOWED is selected in the costing variant configuration (see Figure 4.40).

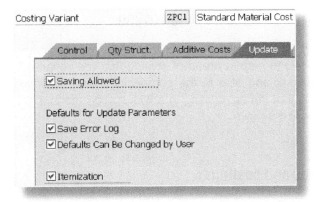

Figure 4.40: Costing variant update configuration

The cost component split is always saved when a cost estimate is saved. The itemization detail and the message log can be saved via selections in the costing variant. It is usually best to save both if saving is allowed. In configuration, the DEFAULTS CAN BE CHANGED BY USER selection determines if the predefined selections allow for changes. The window in Figure 4.41 is displayed if this option is selected. Note that the cost component split selection cannot be changed, but ITEMIZATION and the error log selections can be changed. The UPDATE PARAMETERS window does not show the error log selection here, because no messages were raised when creating the cost estimate. If messages were generated, the ERROR LOG selection would also be displayed for update. Normally, there should not be a reason to make a change in this selection, so DEFAULTS CAN BE CHANGED BY USER should be deselected in configuration.

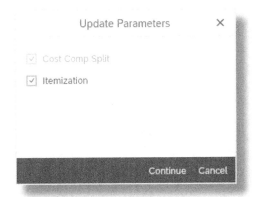

Figure 4.41: Update parameters window

137

4.3 General material settings affecting costing

There are many settings in the material master that affect cost estimates. Most of these are specific to certain areas of costing that are covered in other chapters of this book and also in the companion book. However, there are a few settings that impact costing in a widespread manner and don't warrant a chapter of their own.

4.3.1 Material status and costing

Statuses are assigned to materials to affect how they are used in the system. The status can define whether the material can be planned, produced, or even costed. Statuses can change over the span of the product life cycle. A status can be assigned to a material at two different levels. The cross-plant status is found on the BASIC DATA 1 tab of the material master, and it directs the material's behavior on a global basis. Figure 4.42 shows the BASIC DATA 1 tab of the material master with a status set in section ❶. If a future date for the status change is required, section ❷ allows for the entry of this effective date. If the cost estimate costing date is prior to that date, then the status does not affect the costing. The status only becomes effective for the date entered, or later.

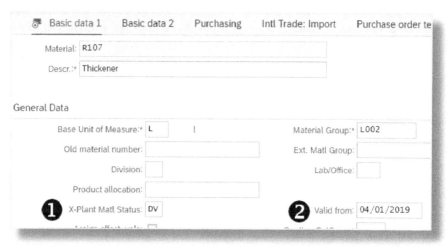

Figure 4.42: Cross plant material status

The plant-specific status is found on the Purchasing tab, the MRP 1 tab, and the Costing 1 tab of the material master. This is the same field which can be maintained in several places. Figure 4.43 shows the assignment of the plant status on the Costing 1 tab of the material master. In area ❶, the status is assigned. In area ❷ the validity date for the plant-based status is entered.

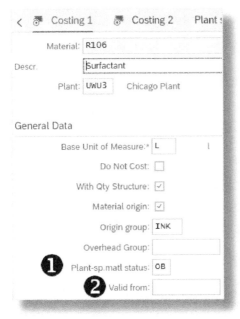

Figure 4.43: Assignment of plant-based material status

The plant-specific status affects the material only at the plant level. However, if a status is assigned to both the global level and the plant level, both statuses are processed together. If the plant-based status allows for costing and the global status does not allow for costing, a cost estimate cannot be created for the material at the plant.

Material status configuration is found under IMG menu path Controlling • Product Cost Controlling • Product Cost Planning • Material Cost Estimate with Quantity Structure • Settings for Quantity Structure Control • Material Data • Check Material Status or by executing transaction OMS4. Figure 4.44 shows the configuration of status OB.

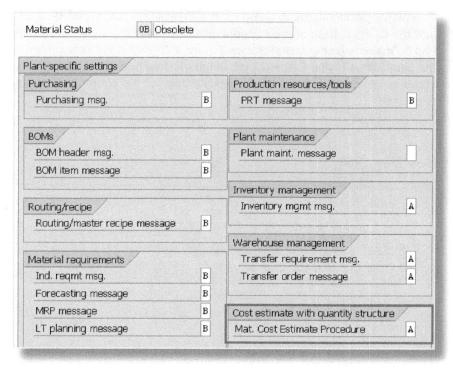

Figure 4.44: Status configuration for costing

There are five possible entries to define the impact of the status on costing a material:

▶ Blank—COST MATERIAL

▶ A—COST MATERIAL; ISSUE WARNING IF MATERIAL COMPONENT

▶ B—COST MATERIAL; ISSUE ERROR IF MATERIAL COMPONENT

▶ C—DO NOT COST MATERIAL; ISSUE WARNING IF MATERIAL COMPONENT

▶ D—DO NOT COST MATERIAL; ISSUE ERROR IF MATERIAL COMPONENT

Material R106 has the status OB assigned at the plant level. The costing configuration for OB is set to A (cost material, but issue warning if used in a BOM). Material R107 has the status DV assigned at the cross-plant level to become active on April 1. Costing configuration for the status is set to D (do not cost the material and issue an error if used in a BOM).

Both materials are in the BOM for material H100. Figure 4.45 shows the resulting status and warning message for a cost estimate with a costing date prior to April 1. There is a warning issued but the costing status is set to KA (costed without errors). If material R106 is costed separately, no messages are generated because the OB status has costing procedure A assigned to it.

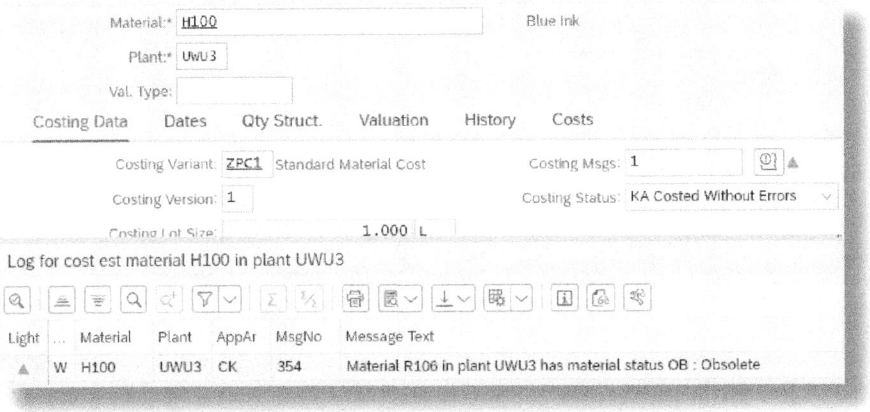

Figure 4.45: Cost estimate message for obsolete component

Starting from April 1, material R107 is no longer able to cost based on the status assigned to it at the global level. When trying to cost material R107, the system does not allow it and generates message CK399 to indicate the reason (see Figure 4.46)

Costing is not allowed for material/PPS status

Message no. CK399

Diagnosis

Material R107 in plant UWU3 has material status DV. The setting for this status is such that costing cannot be carried out.

Figure 4.46: Error message for status DV

When trying to cost a material that uses R107 in the BOM, there is also an error generated. Figure 4.47 shows a status of KF for material H100 which is trying to use component R107. There is also a warning generated because component R106 is still considered obsolete.

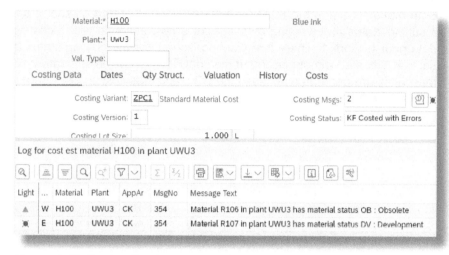

Figure 4.47: Cost estimate message for development component

4.3.2   Bulk materials

Bulk materials are materials that are readily available at a work center for use in the manufacturing process. The value of such a material is usually expensed and should not figure into the cost of a product. Examples of bulk materials include grease and water. Because they are readily available at the work center, there is no need to generate a procurement plan for them even though they are included in the BOM for the manufactured material. The bulk material setting is on the MRP 2 tab of the material master.

Figure 4.48 shows a material with the BULK MATERIAL checkbox selected. Bulk materials can be costed by themselves so that a valuation can be assigned. However, when a material marked as bulk is included in the BOM of another material, its cost is not included in the cost of the other material. A user exit is available to enable inclusion of the cost of bulk materials found in a BOM: EXIT_SAPLKKEX_001 in enhancement COPCC004 (see SAP Note 1642424[4]).

---

4   SAP Note 1642424—"CO Bulk material is not costed"

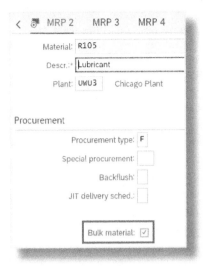

Figure 4.48: Bulk material setting in material master

4.3.3 Do not cost flag

The DO NOT COST setting is found on the COSTING 1 tab of the material master. If set, no cost estimate is created for this material. Figure 4.49 shows material R106 at plant UWU3 with the DO NOT COST flag set. This flag is plant dependent.

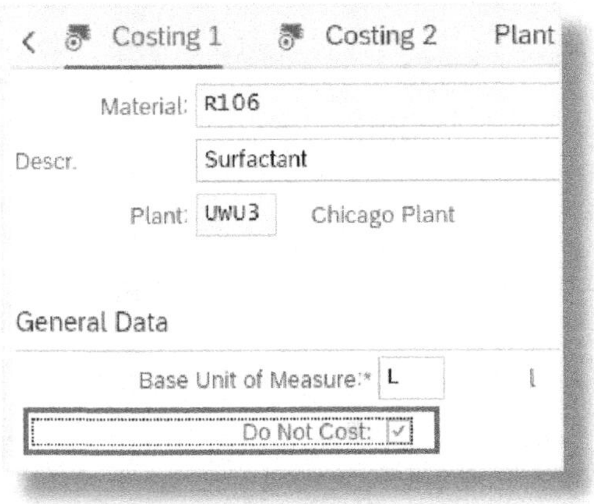

Figure 4.49: Material R106 set to do not cost

The system does not allow material R106 to be costed. When costing is attempted, message CKCC026 is displayed, as shown in Figure 4.50.

Material R106 in plant UWU3 cannot be costed

Message no. CKCC026

Diagnosis

The costing view for material R106 in plant UWU3 specifies that the material cannot be costed.

System Response

You cannot create a cost estimate for material R106.

Procedure

Check the indicator No costing in the costing view for material R106 in plant UWU3.
Change Material

Figure 4.50: Error message for material with "do not cost"

Material R106 is included in the BOM of material H100. The system allows for H100 to be costed, but it does not trigger a new cost estimate for R106. If a cost estimate for R106 exists, this cost estimate is not used to determine the cost of the material in the BOM. A cost is included for R106 and comes from the standard cost assigned to the material. The material is treated as a "raw material" using icon 🔄 (🔳). This is highlighted in Figure 4.51. The materials with cost estimate are indicated by a calculator icon 🔲 (🔳).

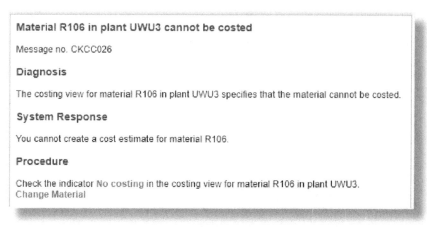

Figure 4.51: Costing structure for material H100

4.3.4 With quantity structure flag

The WITH QTY STRUCTURE flag on the COSTING 1 tab of the material master indicates the method that should be used to cost the material. Material H100 in Figure 4.52 does not have WITH QTY STRUCTURE selected.

Figure 4.52: With quantity structure not selected

When attempting to create a cost estimate with quantity structure, the message in Figure 4.53 is displayed.

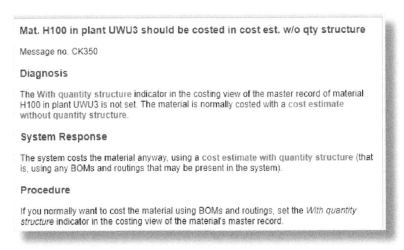

Figure 4.53: Warning when "with quantity structure" is missing

145

The message is just a warning, and a cost estimate with quantity structure can be created for the material. However, if this is to be used as a standard, it cannot be marked and released. Only a cost estimate without quantity structure (unit cost) can be marked and released for a material defined this way. Always select the checkbox if the cost estimate to be used for the standard is generated using the Create Cost Estimate app, transaction CK11N, or the costing run.

5 Raw material cost estimates

Materials purchased from a vendor are treated differently than materials that are manufactured. Special purchasing master data and material master data are used to determine the costs of raw materials. There are many methods provided for generating raw material cost estimates, and it is important to understand how these methods work.

5.1 Purchased materials

A company that sells a product to a customer must obtain that product by some means. The item can be purchased from another company and then resold to a customer, or, a more common approach is for a company to purchase components that are then used to make a different product. In either case, the company providing the product to the customer buys materials to be used as part of the product. Purchasing is part of the MM (Materials Management) module of SAP. This module involves the identification of business partners who sell materials, and the conditions under which the materials are purchased. These conditions determine the cost of the materials and are used as the basis for creating purchase orders that are submitted to the vendor business partner.

Understanding the cost of the purchased items is important in determining the overall cost of the outgoing product. In addition, a standard cost for a purchased item sets a benchmark that can be used to evaluate the purchasing process and to determine variances associated with that process.

A value can be directly assigned to the purchased material using a transaction such as MR21 (Change Material Prices). This does not require a purchased item to have a cost estimate associated with it. However, this is a very manual process, and this is not a recommended approach. Another method is to generate a cost estimate for the material. This requires the ability to determine a cost based on master data that is available in the system. This is a more repeatable method for assigning cost to purchased materials.

Purchased items are usually considered to be raw materials, but that does not always have to be the case. Purchased materials can also include packaging, semi-finished goods, and finished goods, that are either used for conversion into other products or are sold directly to the customer. The CO-PC-PCP module distinguishes between materials that are purchased externally and those that are manufactured or transferred from another location within the same company, regardless of material type. The valuation variant defines the rules used for determining the cost associated with purchasing.

5.2   Purchased material cost estimate

The Los Angeles plant (UWU2) purchases several raw materials that are used in the manufacture of ink. A cost estimate is created for material R108 (BLUE DYE). The itemization is shown in Figure 5.1.

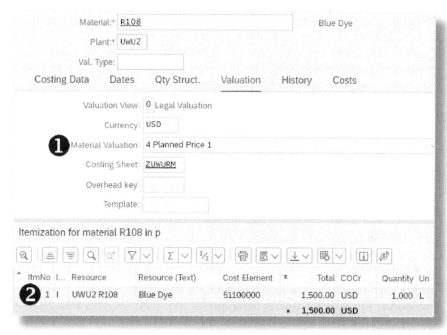

Figure 5.1: Cost estimate for material R108 at plant UWU2

The VALUATION tab has been selected to show the source of the cost for the raw material. PLANNED PRICE 1 is found in section ❶, indicating that the source of the cost came from the PLANNED PRICE 1 field of the COSTING 2 tab of the material master. Drilling down into the material shows a value of 150.00 (see Figure 5.2) for the base quantity of 100 L, which corresponds to the 1,500.00 USD shown in the cost estimate using a costing lot size of 1,000 L.

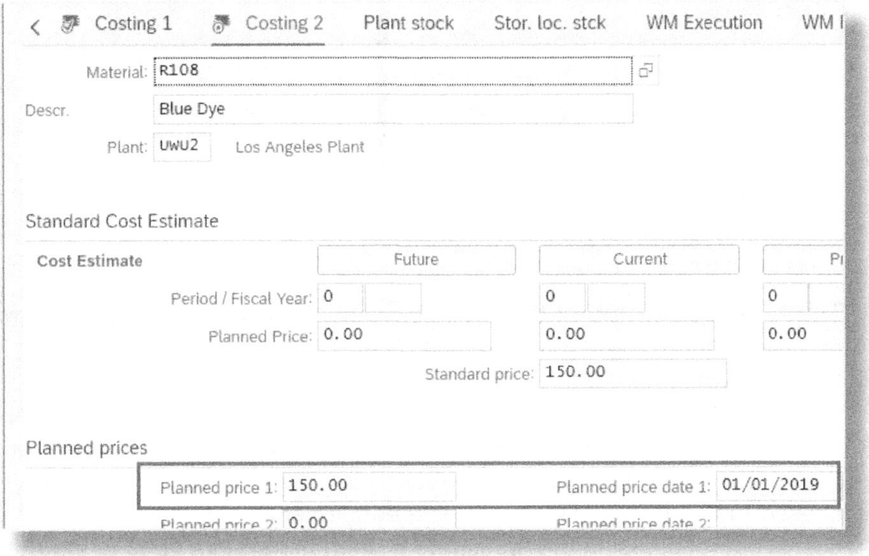

Figure 5.2: Planned price 1 assignment for R108

To understand why the system selected to create a raw material cost estimate for this material requires looking at the COSTING 1 and MRP 2 tabs of the material master. Figure 5.3 shows that the special procurement key for costing on the COSTING 1 tab is left blank, indicating that the procurement defined in the MRP 2 tab has been used. In the MRP 2 tab, the PROCUREMENT TYPE is F and SPECIAL PROCUREMENT is left blank. This indicates that the material comes from an outside source, and the cost should be derived from one of the raw material costing strategies in the valuation variant.

Section ❷ of Figure 5.1 shows the itemization for the cost estimate. Item type I (delivery costs) is used. This item type is used to represent the purchase price, regardless of the source of the cost.

149

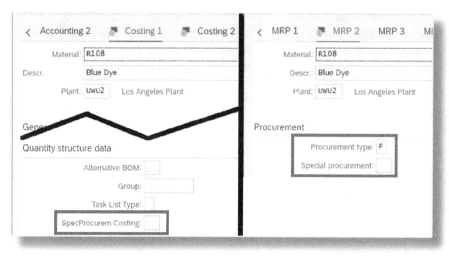

Figure 5.3: Procurement check for costing

The Material Val. tab of the valuation variant configuration defines how raw material costing is processed. Follow IMG menu path Controlling • Product Cost Controlling • Product Cost Planning • Material Cost Estimate with Quantity Structure • Costing Variant: Components • Define Valuation Variants, or use transaction OKK4, to maintain the configuration. Figure 5.4 shows the strategy sequence for determining the cost of purchased raw materials. Up to five different strategies can be selected. If a cost is not found using the first strategy, then the system goes to the next strategy, and so on, until a cost is found or the last strategy is reached. This is shown in section ❶ of Figure 5.4. For each strategy selected, there is a corresponding checkbox indicating whether additive cost estimates should be included in the cost estimate with this strategy.

Section ❷ is only displayed if one of the strategies defined in section ❶ is Price from Purchasing Info Record. If this strategy is selected, another set of strategies is defined to determine how the cost is pulled from the purchasing information record master data for the material. A Delivery Costs link is also provided as part of the configuration in order to assign origin groups to specific purchasing conditions. This is used to define which cost components are to be used to represent the purchase costs for the material.

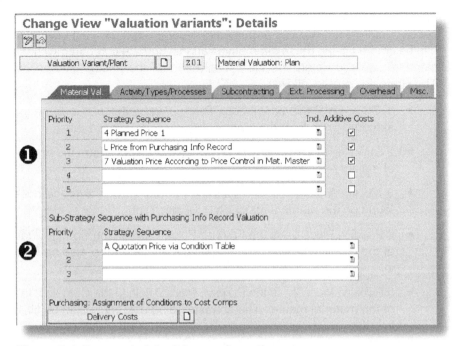

Figure 5.4: Raw material pricing configuration

PLANNED PRICE 1 is the number 1 priority in the strategy sequences of valuation variant Z01. A value with a valid date was found in the material master, so this has been selected for costing material R108. If no value is found in PLANNED PRICE 1 or the PLANNED PRICE 1 date is blank or is later than the valuation date of the cost estimate, then the next strategy in the sequence is used. If no valid cost is found for that, then the next strategy in the sequence is tried. If no valid cost is found after the last defined strategy, then error CK465 (No PRICE COULD BE DETERMINED FOR MATERIAL/BATCH X PLANT Y) is displayed, and the cost estimate fails.

5.2.1 Main costing strategies

There are 22 main costing strategies that can be used to find the cost of a purchased material. All but one of them involve using data directly associated with the material master. Many of those require that the cost be updated manually or via an alternative cost estimate. A few of the items look at the standard or moving average price at some point in time. Another method is to calculate the cost based on purchasing conditions from purchasing information records or purchase orders. Separate cost estimates can be created using these alternative variants and are compared with the standard costs to determine the overall effect of the pricing differences. The strategies are as follows:

► 1 Standard Price in Previous Period—uses the previous period standard price from the material master Accounting 1 tab.

► 2 Standard Price—uses the current standard price form the material master Accounting 1 tab.

► 3 Moving Average Price—uses the current moving average price found on the material master Accounting 1 tab.

► 4 Planned Price 1—is the Planned Price 1 field in the Costing 2 tab of the material master. The corresponding date must also be filled in.

► 5 Planned Price 2—is the Planned Price 2 field in the Costing 2 tab of the material master. The corresponding date must also be filled in.

► 6 Planned Price 3—is the Planned Price 3 field in the Costing 2 tab of the material master. The corresponding date must also be filled in.

► 7 Valuation Price According to Price Control in Mat. Master—uses the standard price if the price control is S and the moving average price if the price control is V.

► 8 Valuation with Additive Cost Component Split—uses an additive cost estimate for the material and can only be used in costing with quantity structure.

► 9 Future Standard Price—is the future price from the Accounting 1 tab of the material master.

► A Valuation Price 1 Based on Tax Law—is from the Accounting 2 tab of the material master.

► B Valuation Price 1 Based on Commercial Law—comes from the Accounting 2 tab of the material master.

► C Valuation Price 2 Based on Tax Law—is from the Accounting 2 tab of the material master.

- ▶ D Valuation Price 2 Based on Commercial Law—comes from the Accounting 2 tab of the material master.

- ▶ E Valuation Price 3 Based on Tax Law—is from the Accounting 2 tab of the material master.

- ▶ F Valuation Price 3 Based on Commercial Law—comes from the Accounting 2 tab of the material master.

- ▶ G Future Price from Accounting—uses the Future Price field of the Accounting 1 tab of the material master.

- ▶ H Planned Price Whose Date is Closest to the Valuation Date—selects the planned price from the Costing 2 tab of the material master with the date that is closest to the valuation date selected for the cost estimate.

- ▶ I Current Planned Price—uses current planned price from the Costing 2 tab of the material master.

- ▶ J Time-Based Valuation Price According to Price Control—comes from the standard price (price control S) or moving average price (price control V) for the material as of the valuation date used when creating the cost estimate.

- ▶ K Price from Preliminary Order Cost Est (Goods Receipts Only)—is from the raw material portion of a production order cost estimate used to calculate the price for valuated sales order stock.

- ▶ L Price from Purchasing Info Record—derives cost from pricing conditions associated with the purchasing information record as defined in the sub-strategy sequence.

- ▶ U Valuation Price with User Exit—is the user exit enhancement COPCP005 component EXIT_SAPLCK21_002.

- ▶ Z Price from Last Valid Alternative Valuation Run –takes the cost from the latest alternative valuation run for actual costing.

Not all strategies are applicable to every costing situation, and care must be taken to select the proper strategies based on the use of the cost estimate. Error CK485 should be avoided by making sure that the last strategy in the sequence provides a cost. Strategies such as Standard Price, Moving Average Price, or Valuation Price According to Price Control in Mat. Master should be selected because they are most likely to provide a non-zero value to the cost estimate.

5.2.2   Purchasing information record strategies

If strategy L (PRICE FROM PURCHASING INFO RECORD) is chosen as a strategy for determining raw material valuation, another set of strategies is required to generate the cost. The sub-strategy sequence is then made available for selecting the methods to be used.

Pricing Schema RM0000 (Partial)					
Step	Counter	Condition	Name	Subtotal	Calculation
1	1	PB00	Gross Price	9	Quantity
1	2	PBXX	Gross Price	9	Quantity
2	0	VA00	Variants/Quantity		Quantity
10	1	RB00	Absolute discount		Fixed
10	2	RC00	Discount/Quantity		Quantity
17	0	EDI1	Confirmed Price	D	Quantity
19	0	EDI2	Value variance		Fixed
20	0			7	
21	1	NAVS	Non-Deductible Tax		Fixed
21	2	NAVM	Non-Deductible Tax		Fixed
22	0				
31	1	FRA1	Freight %		Percentage
31	2	FRB1	Freight (Value)		Fixed
31	3	FRC1	Freight/Quantity		Quantity
35	1	SKTO	Cash Discount		Percentage
37	0	A001	Rebate		Percentage
38	0	A002	Material Rebate		Quantity
40	0			S	
60	0	WOTB	OTB Procurement		Quantity
79	0			C	

Figure 5.5: Purchasing pricing schema RM0000 (partial)

To understand how the sub-strategies work, a brief introduction to pricing is required. Figure 5.5 represents the list of pricing conditions that make up a pricing procedure or calculation schema for determining purchase order prices. The calculation schema is a series of steps and sub-steps that are processed when the system determines a price. Some of the conditions are statistical and don't figure into the actual price. Some conditions represent delivery costs that are incurred but are paid to a third party. The conditions represent costs such as vendor price, rebates, discounts, surcharges, freight, and duty. Not all conditions are active for a given purchasing situation. This depends on whether values are assigned to the conditions either manually or automatically, determined by the system based on configuration requirements. The actual RM0000 pricing procedure contains many conditions, but for illustrative purposes, Figure 5.5 shows a subset of these, and does not include many of the conditions that are not used in the following examples. The table is divided into four sections. The top light gray section contains the conditions that are used to calculate gross price. They are also represented by subtotal type 9. The second slightly darker section contains the conditions that are also included when calculating net price. This includes all steps through to the one that defines subtotal type 7. The third and darker gray section contains additional conditions that make up the effective price. This includes all steps through to subtotal type S. The final unshaded section contains additional conditions that are not used in costing.

Configuring pricing procedures

 The configuration of the calculation schema or pricing procedure is found in the IMG menu MATERIALS MANAGEMENT • PURCHASING • CONDITIONS • DEFINE PRICE DETERMINATION PROCESS • SET CALCULATION SCHEMA—PURCHASING. Work with your MM team to make any necessary changes to the configuration. Additional conditions can be added, and new schemas can be created and assigned to purchasing.

The sub-strategies used for strategy L are assigned to one of two sources of information. Half of the strategies use purchasing information records as the source of the conditions to use in costing. The other half use the latest purchase order information as the source. Up to three sub-strategies can be assigned. If the first sub-strategy does not succeed in finding a cost, then the system looks to the next strategy until the last strategy is reached. If no cost is found at that point, the system looks to the next main strategy in its sequence (see Figure 5.4).

Strategies based on purchasing information records are:

▶ A QUOTATION PRICE VIA CONDITION TABLE—based on conditions defined in the PIR that are configured for DELIVERY COSTS in the valuation variant. Each condition that is found has a separate itemization line.

▶ 3 NET QUOTATION PRICE—based on active conditions from the pricing procedure (calculation schema) up to subtotal type 7 (rebate basis 1). The values of all active conditions are added together and displayed on one line of the itemization.

▶ 4 GROSS QUOTATION PRICE—based on active conditions from the pricing procedure up to and including the first subtotal type 9 (gross value). Only one gross value condition should be active at any time.

▶ 5 EFFECTIVE PRICE FROM QUOTATION—based on active conditions from the pricing procedure up to subtotal type S (effective value). The values of all active conditions are added together and displayed on one line of the itemization.

▶ 2 EFFECTIVE PRICE FROM QUOTATION WITHOUT FIXED COST—same as EFFECTIVE PRICE FROM QUOTATION, but no fixed condition values are included except tax. The values of all active conditions are added together and displayed on one line of the itemization.

Strategies based on the latest purchase order information:

▶ B PURCHASE ORDER PRICE VIA CONDITION TABLE—based on conditions used in the purchase order that are configured for DELIVERY COSTS in the valuation variant. Each condition that is found has a separate itemization line.

▶ 7 NET PURCHASE ORDER PRICE—based on active conditions from the pricing procedure (calculation schema) up to subtotal type 7 (rebate basis 1). The values of all active conditions are added together and displayed on one line of the itemization.

▶ 8 GROSS PURCHASE ORDER PRICE—based on active conditions from the pricing procedure up to and including the first subtotal type 9 (gross value). Only one gross value condition should be active at any time.

▶ 9 EFFECTIVE PRICE FROM PURCHASE ORDER—based on active conditions from the pricing procedure up to subtotal type S (effective value). The values of all active conditions are added together and displayed on one line of the itemization.

▶ 6 EFFECTIVE PRICE FROM PURCHASE ORDER WITHOUT FIXED COST—same as EFFECTIVE PRICE FROM PURCHASE ORDER, but no fixed condition values are included except tax. The values of all active conditions are added together and displayed on one line of the itemization.

Using a purchase order sub-strategy

 If a purchase order sub-strategy is the primary source of finding the cost, use a purchasing information record sub-strategy as the next in line to return a cost in case the purchase order information is missing.

Figure 5.6 shows the purchasing conditions for a purchasing information record for material R109 (red dye) at the Los Angeles plant UWU2. Four different conditions have been assigned. PB00 defines the purchase price from the vendor. PB00 is assigned subtotal type 9 in the calculation schema (see Figure 5.5). RC00 is a discount available from the supplier. This is in the section associated with subtotal type 7 in the calculation schema. There are also two freight conditions, FRB1 and FRC1, which are used in the calculation of freight cost. FRB1 is a fixed value which accounts for the base charge for the freight at 50.00 USD per load. FRC1 is a variable charge based on the quantity shipped. Both conditions are in the subtotal type S section of the schema.

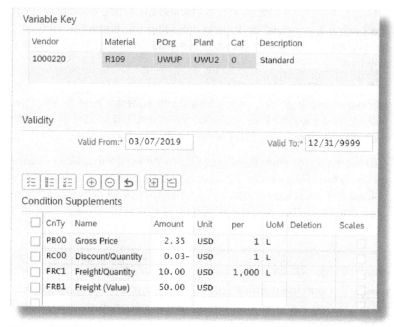

Figure 5.6: Purchasing information record conditions for R109

Because the source of the cost is derived from a purchasing information record, the valuation variant should use one of the purchasing information sub-strategies to provide the value.

Purchasing condition selection

 Purchasing conditions do not have to be explicitly assigned to a purchasing information record. Conditions can be triggered in a pricing procedure based on master data definitions. Condition values can be maintained separately and associated with material, profit center, plant, or other master data.

Raw material cost using gross price

Costing using gross price uses the cost from the PB00 condition in this case. This represents the price originally charged by the vendor. When multiple conditions are assigned to subtotal type 9, only one of the conditions should be active at a time. The gross price strategies are: 4 GROSS QUOTATION PRICE, which uses the purchasing information record as the source, or 8 GROSS PURCHASE ORDER PRICE, which uses purchase order information. If the valuation variant sub-strategy is set to 4 GROSS QUOTATION PRICE, the cost estimate only uses the PB00 condition from the purchasing information record for the cost (2.35 USD per L). Figure 5.7 shows the line item for the cost of 1,000 L of material R109 based on gross price.

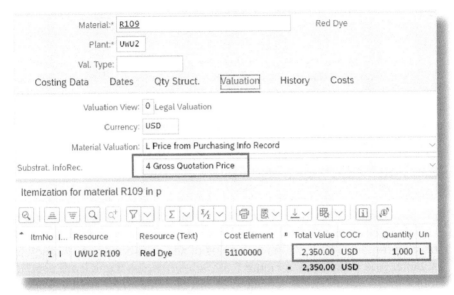

Figure 5.7: Cost estimate using gross quotation price

Raw material cost using net price

Sub-strategies 3 and 7 use the net price method to determine cost. This includes all active conditions up to subtotal type 7, which are the first two shaded sections in Figure 5.5. In the case of the purchasing information record from Figure 5.6, the conditions for PB00 (2.35 per 1 L) and RC00 (-0.03 per 1 L) are added together to determine the cost. Figure 5.8 shows the result at 2,320 USD per 1,000 L (or 2.32 USD per L), as expected.

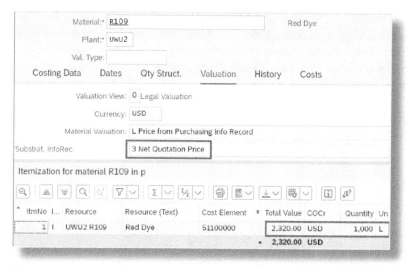

Figure 5.8: Cost estimate using net quotation price

Raw material cost using effective cost

Effective cost includes costs such as freight, that are incurred as part of the procurement process but are not necessarily paid to the specific vendor. Using effective cost gives a much clearer understanding of the actual cost of procurement. This includes the values of all active conditions through to subtotal type S (as seen in Figure 5.5). Sub-strategies 5 and 9 are used to make this calculation. All conditions in the purchasing information record in Figure 5.6 are included in the cost. Condition FRB1 is what is known as a *fixed condition*—its value remains the same regardless of the costing lot size. The cost estimate uses a costing lot size of 1,000 L, so the 50.00 USD associated with it is associated with that quantity. If a lot size of 100 is used for the cost estimate, the value would still be 50.00 USD. The value of condition FRC1 is based on quantity and so its effect on the cost estimate varies with the lot size chosen. Because a lot size of 1,000 is used for the cost estimate, the resulting value should become 2,350.00—30.00 + 10.00 + 50.00, or 2,380.00 USD per 1,000 L. This is shown in Figure 5.9.

Raw material cost—effective price no fixed conditions

Sub-strategies 2 and 6 use the same procedure as sub-strategies 5 and 9 to calculate the cost; however, any fixed price conditions such as FRB1 are excluded. This ban on fixed price conditions does not include any condition associated with tax, such as NAVS or NAVM. Tax is always included if it is associated with an active condition. Figure 5.10 shows the result with a costing lot size of 1,000 L. Compare this with Figure 5.9.

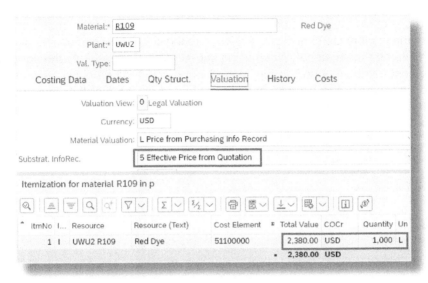

Figure 5.9: Cost estimate using effective price

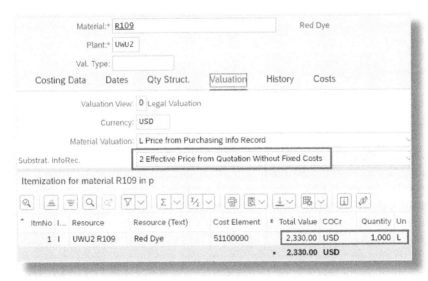

Figure 5.10: Cost estimate using effective price no fixed conditions

5.2.3 Segregating delivery costs

One of the results of using sub-strategies 2 through 9 is that all of the costs associated with each of the active purchasing conditions are added together into one lump sum. There is no way to separate out individual portions of cost to get a clear understanding of what makes the cost. This also means that the total cost is assigned to the single cost component determined for the material. When using sub-strategy 2 to generate the cost, the cost component split in Figure 5.11 is obtained. All purchasing costs are assigned to the INK cost component based on the fact that material R109 is defined with origin group INK in the COSTING 1 tab of the material master.

CC...	Name of Cost Comp.	Overall	Fixed	Variable	Crcy
100	Direct Material				USD
101	Ink	2,330.00		2,330.00	USD
105	Packaging				USD
110	Labor				USD
120	Utilities				USD
130	3rd Party Costs				USD
140	Supplies				USD
150	Depreciation				USD
160	Freight				USD
170	Transfer Surcharge				USD
999	Other				USD
		2,330.00		**2,330.00**	**USD**

Cost Components for Material R109

Figure 5.11: Cost component split for sub-strategy 2

Another effect of using sub-strategies 2 through 9 is that all active conditions are included in the cost. Sub-strategies A (QUOTATION PRICE VIA CONDITION TABLE) and B (PURCHASE ORDER PRICE VIA CONDITION TABLE) enable the use of selected conditions from the calculation schema. Additionally, the value of each condition can be explicitly assigned to its own cost component.

Configuration for this can be found in the valuation variant (MATERIAL VAL.) tab by clicking on the DELIVERY COSTS button to assign purchasing information costs to cost components via origin groups (see Figure 5.12). To create new assignments, click on the 🗋 button.

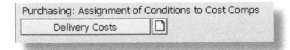

Figure 5.12: Delivery costs button in the valuation variant

This can also be configured using transaction OKYO or IMG menu path CONTROLLING • PRODUCT COST CONTROLLING • PRODUCT COST PLANNING • SELECTED FUNCTIONS IN MATERIAL COSTING • RAW MATERIAL COST ESTIMATE • ASSIGN CONDITION TYPES TO ORIGIN GROUPS. When using strategy A or B, the delivery cost definition dictates that any purchasing condition found in the pricing schema will have a separate item created in the cost estimate. The example in Figure 5.13 shows two condition types defined: PB00 (gross price) is assigned to the MATL origin group and conditions FRB1 and FRC1 (freight conditions) are assigned to the FRT origin group. PB00 normally has a condition value based on the purchasing information and generates a costing item for the purchase price assigned to the material cost component. If either or both of the freight conditions have been assigned values, then a separate line item appears on the cost estimate for each one, with its value assigned to the freight cost component. The cost component assignments for these origin groups are maintained in the cost component configuration (see Section 1.3.6).

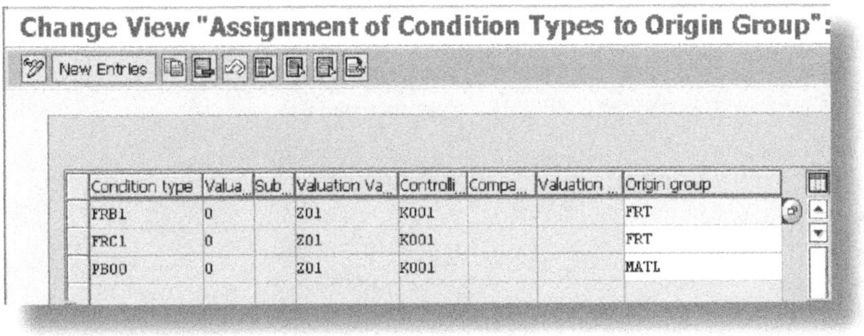

Change View "Assignment of Condition Types to Origin Group":

Condition type	Valua	Sub	Valuation Va	Controll	Compa	Valuation	Origin group
FRB1	0		Z01	K001			FRT
FRC1	0		Z01	K001			FRT
PB00	0		Z01	K001			MATL

Figure 5.13: Delivery costs configuration

The resulting cost estimate is shown in Figure 5.14. Note that there are now three line items of type I (delivery costs) in the itemization view of the cost estimate. The origin group for each line item has been included in the report display to highlight the impact of the delivery cost configuration.

Figure 5.14: Cost estimate using sub-strategy A

Figure 5.15 shows the resulting cost component split for this cost estimate. Note that instead of using the INK cost component for the gross price cost, the DIRECT MATERIAL cost component is used instead. The delivery cost configuration overrides the normal procedure for determining the cost component used. In addition, note that the values of the two freight conditions FRB1 and FRC1 are added together and assigned to the FREIGHT cost component. This is based on the association of the origin groups with specific cost components in the cost component split configuration.

Cost Components for Material R109				
CC...	Name of Cost Comp.	Overall	Fixed	Variable	Crcy
100	Direct Material	2,350.00		2,350.00	USD
101	Ink				USD
105	Packaging				USD
110	Labor				USD
120	Utilities				USD
130	3rd Party Costs				USD
140	Supplies				USD
150	Depreciation				USD
160	Freight	60.00		60.00	USD
170	Transfer Surcharge				USD
999	Other				USD
		▪ 2,410.00		▪ 2,410.00	USD

Figure 5.15: Cost component split for sub-strategy A

5.2.4 Finding the vendor

Raw materials can be purchased from multiple alternative suppliers. SAP uses a hierarchical approach to identify which vendor to use when creating cost estimates using valuation strategy L- PRICE FROM PURCHASING INFORMATION RECORD.

Step 1—check if source list is required

The system first searches to see if there is a source list requirement in place. A source list requirement can be defined at the plant level using configuration via IMG menu path MATERIALS MANAGEMENT • PURCHASING • SOURCE LIST • DEFINE SOURCE LIST REQUIREMENT AT PLANT LEVEL, or it can be assigned directly to the material in the PURCHASING tab of the material master. The source list defines the valid suppliers for a material. If the source list is required and no source list is found, then the process for determining the vendor stops with message CK776—NO VALID SOURCE OF SUPPLY FOR MATERIAL X IN PLANT Y. This message is usually displayed as an informational message but indicates that the valuation strategy for finding the cost has failed, thereby allowing the system to search for a cost using the next configured strategy.

Step 2—check for a quota arrangement

If the source list is not required or the source list was found, the system next checks to see if there is a quota arrangement defined for sourcing the material. A quota arrangement specifies that a certain percentage of the material is purchased from one vendor and other percentages are assigned to other vendors. If a valid quota arrangement is found, the system checks for permitted vendors in the list. The vendor with the highest plan quota, or lowest actual quota, is chosen. The purchasing information for that vendor is used in the cost estimate. If neither a quota arrangement nor a permitted vendor is found, the system goes to step 3 of the process.

Step 3—check for vendors from the source list

This step looks for a source list associated with the plant and material. If the source list exists, then the system checks if one of the vendors has been set as a fixed source of supply. If such a vendor is found, the system uses the purchasing information for that vendor. If no fixed source of supply is found, the next check is to see if the plant uses a regular vendor. If the regular vendor is found in the source list for the material, the purchasing information for that vendor is used for the cost. If a regular vendor is not permitted or one is not found in the source list, the system goes through the purchasing information for all vendors on the list and determines the cheapest vendor using all active conditions through to subtotal type 7. This includes any discounts and surcharges that are defined. If, after these checks, a vendor is found, the system makes one last set of checks in step 4.

Step 4—check for regular vendor allowed

If a regular vendor is allowed at the plant level, the system searches through all the purchasing information records for the plant to see if a match is found for the regular vendor. If such a match is found, the purchasing information record is used for the cost. If a regular vendor is not allowed or the above search has failed, then a general search of the purchasing information records for that plant and material is performed. The record for the cheapest vendor, including discounts and surcharges, provides the values for the cost estimate.

If a complete search is done and no valid purchasing information record is found, the main valuation strategy will have failed, and the system tries to find a cost using the next available valuation strategy.

Material R110 (black dye) can be supplied by two separate vendors. The Ink Supply company has a list price of 1.53 USD per L for this material. However, this company is currently offering a 0.05 USD discount per L. This is reflected in the purchasing information record conditions in Figure 5.16.

SC Chemical Corporation supplies the same material with a list price of 1.49 USD per L. However, there are no discounts associated with the sale, as shown in Figure 5.17.

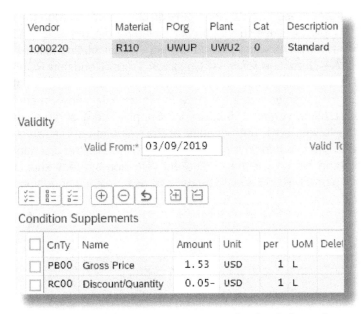

Figure 5.16: Ink Supply company purchasing information conditions

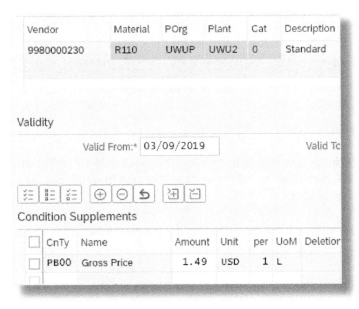

Figure 5.17: SC Chemical purchasing information conditions

The cheapest vendor, based on list price plus discounts and surcharges, should be Ink Supply because the total cost including discounts is 1.48 USD per L (1.53—0.05). The valuation sub-strategy for calculating the cost estimate cost is A—QUOTATION PRICE VIA CONDITION TABLE. Condition RC00 is not included in the resulting cost based on the delivery cost assignment to origin groups. The resulting cost estimate in Figure 5.18 shows a cost of 1.53 USD per L using vendor 1000220—Ink Supply. The cost does not appear to be the lowest cost, but because of the valuation sub-strategy selected, the discount is not included in the final cost. To see the discount and fully understand the cost, either a different valuation strategy should be used in costing or the RC00 should be defined as a delivery condition.

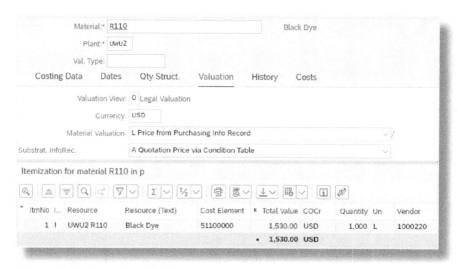

Figure 5.18: Resulting R110 cost estimate

If the RC00 condition is changed from 0.05 USD per L to 0.03 USD per L (see Figure 5.19), the selection of the vendor changes from Ink Supply to SC Chemical Corporation.

The cost and the vendor have now changed for the cost estimate in Figure 5.20.

Vendor	Material	POrg	Plant	Cat	Description
1000220	R110	UWUP	UWU2	0	Standard

Validity

Valid From:* 03/09/2019   Valid T

Condition Supplements

	CnTy	Name	Amount	Unit	per	UoM	Dele
☐	PB00	Gross Price	1.53	USD	1	L	
☐	RC00	Discount/Quantity	0.03-	USD	1	L	

Figure 5.19: Discount changed to 0.03 USD per L

Material:* R110	Black Dye
Plant:* UWU2	
Val. Type:	

Costing Data   Dates   Qty Struct.   Valuation   History   Costs

Valuation View: 0 Legal Valuation

Currency: USD

Material Valuation: L Price from Purchasing Info Record

Substrat. InfoRec.   A Quotation Price via Condition Table

Itemization for material R110 in p

ItmNo	I...	Resource	Resource (Text)	Cost Element	Total Value	COCr	Quantity	Un	Vendor
1	I	UWU2 R110	Black Dye	51100000	1,490.00	USD	1.000	L	9980000230
					1,490.00	USD			

Figure 5.20: Updated cost estimate with new low-cost vendor

Understanding how the cost was determined requires an understanding of two different concepts. First, we need to know which valuation sub-strategy is used for the cost estimate. This is important in order to know which conditions are included in the cost estimate. Second, the determination of the low-cost vendor includes not only the gross price conditions, but also any additional conditions associated with discounts and surcharges.

5.2.5 Pricing scales and costing

Many vendors offer price breaks for purchasing items at different quantity levels. The vendor of material R109 (red dye) offers price breaks at levels of 100, 1,000, and 10,000 L. This is represented in the purchasing information record as a scale assignment to a specific purchasing condition. Figure 5.21 shows the scales associated with the gross price condition PB00 for material R109.

Scales								
Scale Type	Scale quantity		UoM	Amount		Unit	per	UoM
From		1	L		3.00	USD	1	L
		100			2.75			
		1,000			2.35			
		10,000			2.10			

Figure 5.21: Scales for condition PB00

When a scale exists for a specific condition, it is noted in the purchasing information. A checkmark is placed in the SCALES column for that specific condition (see Figure 5.22). Double-click on the condition to see the scale definition.

	CnTy	Name	Amount	Unit	per	UoM	Deletion	Scales
☐	PB00	Gross Price	3.00	USD	1	L		☑
☐	RC00	Discount/Quantity	0.03-	USD	1	L		
☐	FRC1	Freight/Quantity	10.00	USD	1,000	L		
☐	FRB1	Freight (Value)	50.00	USD				

Condition Supplements

Figure 5.22: Indicator for scales for a condition

Scales can exist for any condition, and multiple conditions can have scales assigned to them. Understanding the purchasing scale levels when setting a costing lot size for the cost estimate is important. The costing lot size that was chosen for material R109 is 1,000 L. The cost estimate is created using valuation sub-strategy A QUOTATION PRICE VIA CONDITION TABLE using the cost component configuration from Figure 5.13. The resulting cost estimate in Figure 5.23 picks up the 2.35 USD per L cost from the scales for condition PB00. Adjusting according to the costing lot size provides a value of 2,350.00 USD per 1,000 L. Condition FRC1 accounts for the 10.00 USD cost. Condition FRB1 is a fixed price condition and the value is 50.00 USD regardless of lot size. The overall cost is 2,410.00 USD for the costing lot size, or 2.41 USD per L. Condition RC00 does not figure into the cost estimate because it was not assigned to an origin group in configuration. Had a different valuation sub-strategy been used, its value would have been included.

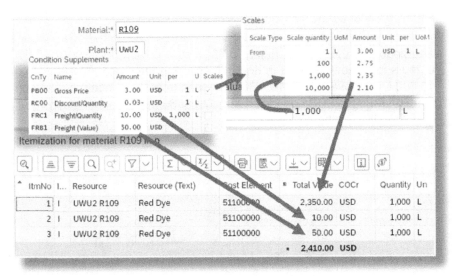

Figure 5.23: Scale with costing lot size 1,000

Figure 5.24 shows a cost estimate for the same material with a costing lot size of 100. This lot size fits into the 100 to 999 L scale level and uses 2.75 USD per L for the PB00 cost. For item 3 in the cost estimate, the 50.00 USD is taken directly from the FRB1 condition value as it is lot-size independent. The value of FRC1 is adjusted by the costing lot size. The overall cost at this lot size level is 3.26 USD per L.

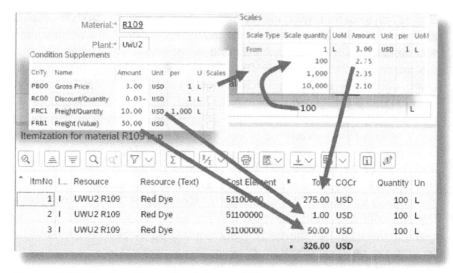

Figure 5.24: Scale with costing lot size 100

The final cost estimate in Figure 5.25 uses a costing lot size of 10,000 L and shows how the cost is determined using the scale. Any lot size of 10,000 L or above uses 2.10 USD (the price from the condition). The contribution from the FRB1 condition remains at 50.00 and has a much smaller contribution to the cost per L.

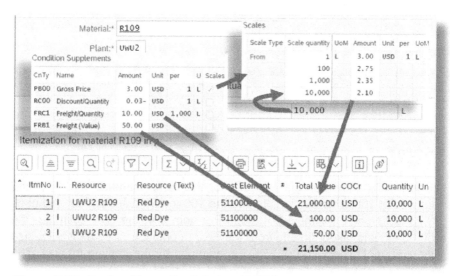

Figure 5.25: Scale with costing lot size 10,000

When using purchasing information with scales in cost estimates, it is important to understand the price breakdowns. Scales don't have to start at 1 as they did in this example. If the lowest scale value is greater than the costing lot size of the cost estimate, the purchasing information cannot be found, and this purchasing valuation strategy fails.

6 Costing manufactured materials

Manufactured materials are normally produced in a plant that is owned by the company. Data that is used in the planning and manufacturing processes is also used in the creation of product cost estimates. Knowing how this data fits together is important in order to understand and explain manufactured material cost estimates.

6.1 Manufactured materials

A company purchases materials from external vendors. The materials are then made into products to be sold to customers. These products are manufactured in a plant; the cost to make the products (i.e. turn the components into something else) includes both the costs for the purchased components and the costs of utilizing equipment and labor. Costing the manufactured materials is simplified with the use of cost estimates with quantity structure. Planning and production require structures to describe the manufacturing process. Bills of materials (BOMs) define the components, and the relative quantities of each, that are used to make a product. Manufacturing routings contain one or more operations that describe the steps to be taken in the production process. These operations are assigned to various work centers so that capacity can be measured, and work scheduling can be performed. These same quantity structures can be used for costing purposes as well. This eliminates the need to manually build up the costs for each product, saving a great deal of time and effort.

6.2 Bills of materials

BOMs are the structures that are perhaps the easiest to understand for costing. They are assigned a list of materials (component items), with specific quantities, that are used to make a pre-determined quantity of a product. The standard price of each component is then multiplied by its quantity and divided by the base quantity of the product. The total component cost is the sum of all of these individual costs. The BOM that is used for manufacturing and planning purposes can also be used in the calculation of these costs.

There are two methods to maintain BOMs in S/4HANA. The first method is to use the classic SAPGUI transactions CS01 (create), CS02 (change), and CS03 (display). The structure of the item entry window of these transactions does not include all possible parameters associated with each item, and to update some fields that are used in costing requires the need to drill down into specific items to get to those fields. The Maintain Bill of Materials Fiori tile combines the features of all the SAPGUI BOM transactions with the ability to customize the item entry window to include those fields that are necessary for costing. BOM illustrations use the Fiori application.

6.2.1   Selecting the BOM for the cost estimate

Each BOM has a header that contains general information about the BOM. This includes how the BOM is used and the base quantity to which each of the component items relates.

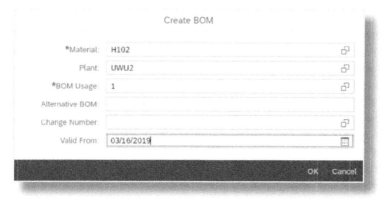

Figure 6.1: Create BOM window

When a BOM is created, a usage type must be assigned to it (see Figure 6.1). The usage type indicates the primary purpose for creating the BOM. For example, a production BOM is primarily used in planning and manufacturing but could also be used for costing. Special BOMs can be created for costing purposes only and shouldn't be used for manufacturing at all. The selection ID defines the order for the BOM types for a material to be searched to determine the BOM to use. In this case, the BOM is used for material cost estimates. BOM usage is maintained as part of the Production Planning (PP) module. This is done using transaction OS20 or via IMG menu path PRODUCTION • BASIC DATA • BILL OF MATERIAL • GENERAL DATA • BOM USAGE • DEFINE BOM USAGES.

BOM Usg	Prod.	Eng/des.	Spare	PM	Sales	CostRel	Usage text
1	+	.	.	-	-	.	Production
2	.	+	.	-	-	.	Engineering/Design
3	.	.	.	-	.	.	Universal
4	-	-	.	+	-	.	Plant Maintenance
5	.	.	.	-	+	.	Sales and Distribution
6	.	.	.	-	.	+	Costing
7	.	-	-	-	.	.	Empties

Figure 6.2: BOM usage configuration

Figure 6.2 shows the configuration parameters. There are six different categories for BOM usage. A symbol is assigned under each category for specific uses. The symbol "+" indicates that usage must be associated with that category. For example, BOM usage 1 (PRODUCTION) is intended for the PROD. category. The symbol "." indicates that the usage is possible for that category, and the symbol "-" means that usage is not available for that category of BOM. The COSTREL category defines the uses that are relevant for costing purposes. Any usage which is assigned "+" or "." for COSTREL can be used for costing. These designations come into play when defining the BOM application and the search strategies used for determining which BOM is relevant for that application.

Configuration for the BOM application is processed using transaction OPJM or via IMG menu path CONTROLLING • PRODUCT COST CONTROLLING • PRODUCT COST PLANNING • MATERIAL COST ESTIMATE WITH QUANTITY STRUCTURE • SETTINGS FOR QUANTITY STRUCTURE CONTROL • BOM SELECTION • CHECK BOM APPLICATION. This is also accessible from the CONTROL tab of the costing variant configuration described in Section 1.4.15.

Configuring BOM applications

Be careful making changes to BOM applications and selection IDs because these can also be used for planning and manufacturing. Make sure that only items applicable to costing are changed.

Applic	SelID	AltSel	ProdVers	Application description	ExplMRP	PIndOr	RelCstg	RelWkSch	RelOrd.	ColWith	SalesOr
❶	Y1	☑	**❷** ☐	Inventory Management	☑	☑	☐	☐	☐	☐	☐
	CC	☐	☐	Configuration Control	☐	☐	☐ **❸**	☐	☐	☐	☐
INST	03	☐	☐	Plant Maintenance	☐	☐	☐	☐	☐	☐	☐
PC01	Y5	☑	☑	Costing	☐	☐	☑	☐	☐	☐	☐
PI01	T4	☑	☑	Process Manufacturing	☑	☑	☑	☑	☑	☐	☐
PP01	Y1	☑	☑	Production - General	☑	☑	☑	☑	☑	☐	☐
SD01	04	☑	☐	Sales and Distribution	☐	☐	☐	☐	☐	☐	☑
TQ01	98	☑	☑	Process manufacturing Rework	☑	☑	☑	☑	☑	☐	☐

Figure 6.3: BOM selection criteria

Definition of the application is divided into three parts, as shown in Figure 6.3. The BOM application meant for costing is highlighted. Section ❶ assigns a selection ID to the application. The selection ID defines a search strategy to be used to choose a BOM.

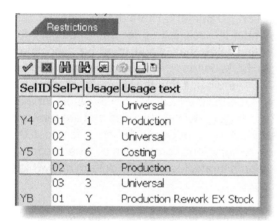

Figure 6.4: BOM selection ID

Figure 6.4 shows the configuration of the BOM selection criteria. This can be processed by using transaction OPJI or via IMG menu path CONTROL-LING • PRODUCT COST CONTROLLING • PRODUCT COST PLANNING • MATERIAL COST ESTIMATE WITH QUANTITY STRUCTURE • SETTINGS FOR QUANTITY STRUCTURE CONTROL • BOM SELECTION • CHECK BOM SELECTION. Selection ID Y5 was chosen for BOM application PC01. The search strategy for Y5 is to first look for a BOM with usage 6 (COSTING). If a BOM with that usage is not found, the next type to look for is a BOM with usage 1 (PRODUCTION). If neither is available, then a UNIVERSAL BOM (usage 3) is chosen, if one exists. The search strategy can be extended to include more types of BOMs if desired.

BOM selection IDs for costing

Make sure that the selection ID chosen for costing contains only BOM usages that are valid for costing purposes. See Figure 6.2.

Production versions and costing in S/4HANA

Although production versions are now required in Production Planning in S/4HANA, they are not necessary for costing as of on-premise release 1809. The search strategy for both BOMs and routings is still in force as long as a production version has not yet been created for the material, or if the production version parameters do not match the costing dates or lot size.

Section ❷ of Figure 6.3 defines if a BOM selection can be overridden based on material master settings. As of S/4HANA on-premise release 1511, this configuration has lost much of its meaning. The use of the ALT-SEL and PRODVERS checkboxes were dependent on the setting of the SELECTION METHOD field on the MRP 4 tab of the material master. This setting is not supported in S/4HANA, and only production versions are supported for planning and production (see SAP Note 2267880[5]). PRODVERS should probably still be selected, but ALTSEL can no longer be used because it was based on a specific setting of SELECTION METHOD which is no longer available.

Another attribute of the BOM header is the status. When a BOM is created, a status is assigned to it. Each status has indicators that determine how the BOM can be used. Section ❸ of Figure 6.3 defines which statuses are supported by the specific BOM application. BOM status is configured using transaction OS23 or via IMG menu path PRODUCTION • BASIC DATA • BILL OF MATERIAL • GENERAL DATA • DEFINE BOM STATUS. Figure 6.5 shows three different statuses defined for BOMs.

---

[5] SAP Note 2267880—"S4TWL—BOM, Routing, Production Version"

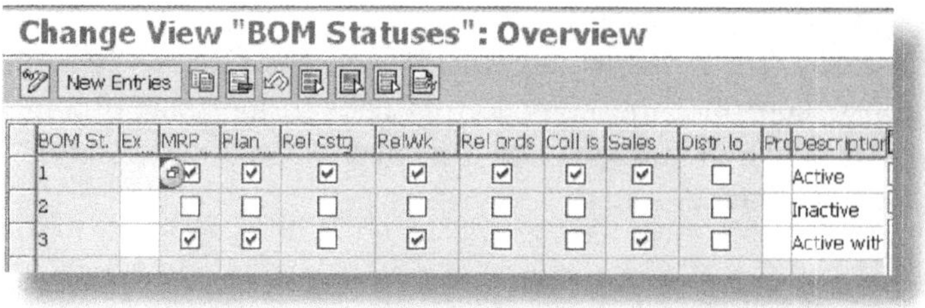

Figure 6.5: BOM status configuration

In this case, only status 1 (ACTIVE) has REL CSTG (relevant for costing) selected. Looking back at the definition of PC01 in Figure 6.3, only the RELCSTG box has a checkmark. This means that only BOMs with status 1 in this implementation can be used for costing purposes. Other statuses can be assigned to be costing-relevant as the need arises.

After the BOM application is configured, it can be assigned to the quantity structure control configured for the costing variant. This provides the means to select the BOM used for costing in a manufacturing cost estimate. Quantity structure control is configured using transaction OKK5 or via IMG menu path CONTROLLING • PRODUCT COST CONTROLLING • PRODUCT COST PLANNING • MATERIAL COST ESTIMATE WITH QUANTITY STRUCTURE • COSTING VARIANT: COMPONENTS • DEFINE QUANTITY STRUCTURE CONTROL. Figure 6.6 shows the selection of BOM application for BOM determination on the BOM tab of the quantity structure control configuration. Quantity structure control can be configured in general, as outlined here, or specific BOM applications can be defined dependent on the plant. Click on QTY STRUCT. CONTROL/PLANT to make changes to the plant-specific definition. Click on the ☐ button next to it to add a new plant-specific definition.

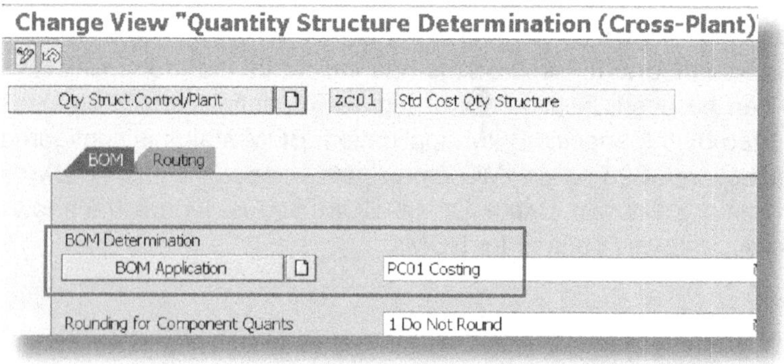

Figure 6.6: BOM application setting in quantity structure control

The quantity structure control ID is assigned to the costing variant on the CONTROL tab. See Sections 1.4.1 and 1.4.12 for more details.

6.2.2 BOM header

The default window that is selected when maintaining a BOM is the item window. To get to the header window, click on the HEADER ATTRIBUTES tab. Use the 🔲 button in the SAPGUI transactions. Figure 6.7 shows the BOM header window.

Figure 6.7: BOM header

181

The following list of items on the header are important for costing purposes:

❶ BASE QUANTITY—this is the divisor that is used to convert component quantities to a quantity per unit. This is usually configured to default to 100.

❷ FROM LOT SIZE/TO LOT SIZE—these define the valid order size range when using this BOM for a material. This affects the selection of the BOM for a production version as well as dictating a specific costing lot size to be able to select this BOM.

❸ BOM USAGE—this is defined when the BOM is created. Configuration around BOM usage, as discussed earlier, helps determine if the BOM can be selected for costing.

❹ ALTERNATIVE BOM—when first creating a BOM for a material, alternative 1 is selected. New BOMs can be created for the same material representing different methods for manufacturing. Each of these BOMs is assigned an alternative. These alternatives can be assigned to production versions, or lot size information for different alternatives can be used for selection. If there is no production version and there is no differentiation between the lot size ranges for the BOMs, the lowest alternative is selected.

❺ BOM STATUS—configuration of the status determines if the BOM can be used for costing.

6.2.3   BOM components

The BOM components are viewed by clicking on the COMPONENTS tab. Use ⌂ Item for the SAPGUI transactions.

Figure 6.8 shows a listing of the components for material H102 at plant UWU2. The component quantities are determined with respect to the base quantity defined in the BOM header. In this case, the quantities are the expected quantities to be consumed in order to manufacture 240 L of the product. The standard display for the component window has been adjusted slightly to show some additional information. If the FIXED QUANTITY checkbox is selected for an item, it means that the quantity is independent of the costing lot size. The same quantity is included in the cost estimate regardless of the costing lot size used.

H102	Plant: UWU2, BOM Usage: Production, Alternative: 1											

Timeline　　Components　　Header Attributes　　Header Attachments

Standard * ∨　Select by Date　03/18/2019 　　　　Search 　　　　Q　+　☐　☐　Assign Change Number　Maintain Software　Software Const

Item... △	Item Category	Component	Component Description	Component Quantity		Valid From	Valid To	Fixed...	Releva..	Speci..	
☐ 0010	L(Stock Item) ...	R110 ☐	Black Dye	132.000	L ☐	03/16/2019	12/31/9999	☐	X ☐	☐ >
☐ 0020	L(Stock Item) ...	R105 ☐	Lubricant	25.000	L ☐	03/16/2019	12/31/9999	☐	X ☐	☐ >
☐ 0030	L(Stock Item) ...	R108 ☐	Surfactant	48.000	L ☐	03/16/2019	12/31/9999	☐	X ☐	☐ >
☐ 0040	L(Stock Item) ...	R107 ☐	Thickener	23.000	L ☐	03/16/2019	12/31/9999	☐	X ☐	☐ >
☐ 0050	L(Stock Item) ...	V502 ☐	Ink Drum	1.000	PC ☐	03/16/2019	12/31/9999	☐	B ☐	☐ >
☐ 0060	L(Stock Item) ∨	☐		0.000	☐	03/18/2019	12/31/9999	☐	☐	☐ >
☐ 0070	L(Stock Item) ∨	☐		0.000	☐	03/18/2019	12/31/9999	☐	☐	☐ >

Figure 6.8: BOM components

RELEVANCY TO COSTING is in the column to the right of FIXED QUANTITY in Figure 6.8. Normally, this is found in the item details under the STATUS/LONG TEXT tab. This can be reached by clicking on the ⟩ button at the end of the line in the Fiori app or by double-clicking on the item number in the SAPGUI transaction. The relevancy for costing indicator specifies how much of the value of the costing item is included in the cost. Two of the IDs are fixed by SAP. Leaving the field blank indicates that no cost is determined for that component. "X" indicates that the item is 100% cost relevant, meaning that the full cost is included in the cost estimate. Other IDs can be created which represent different percentages. The creation of these IDs is part of the valuation variant configuration that is covered in Section 1.4.9. Pricing factors other than blank and X are configured for each valuation variant they are to be used in. The factor values are assigned at that time. As long as a factor is defined, it can be used in a BOM or routing operation. If a non-blank factor does not pertain to the specific valuation variant used in the cost estimate, it is treated as an X. For any cost estimate that is intended to be used to update the standard cost (costing type 01), a costing item must be either 100% relevant or 0% relevant. Any non-blank factor is treated as an X. Item 0050 for material V502, shown in Figure 6.8, has its relevancy to costing factor set to B. This is treated as if it is an X for a standard cost estimate. Only costing variants used for inventory costing can take advantage of pricing factors that are not set to 100% relevant.

Certain units of measure should normally not be expressed as a fraction. An example if this is the unit PC (piece). The idea of a fractional portion of a piece does not make sense in the physical world. However, when a material with this unit of measure is assigned as a BOM component and used in a cost estimate, the combination of the base quantity of the BOM and the costing lot size used can result in a fractional calculation of the quantity of that component. This result can be reasonable depending on the purpose of the cost estimate. The quantity structure control configuration is able to control whether the quantity calculated should be rounded up to the next whole number or left as a fraction. This is handled as part of the Quantity Structure Control configuration of the costing variant, which is processed using transaction OKK5 or via IMG menu path CONTROLLING • PRODUCT COST CONTROLLING • PRODUCT COST PLANNING • MATERIAL COST ESTIMATE WITH QUANTITY STRUCTURE • COSTING VARIANT: COMPONENTS • DEFINE QUANTITY STRUCTURE CONTROL. Figure 6.9 depicts the BOM tab.

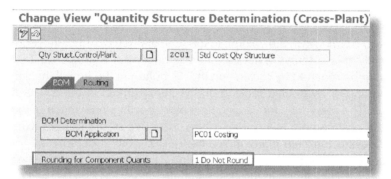

Figure 6.9: Quantity structure determination—BOMs

ROUNDING FOR COMPONENT QUANTS is highlighted. Select DO NOT ROUND to retain the fractional units in the cost estimate. Select ROUND UP WITH NON-DIMENSIONAL UNITS OF MEASURE to have the quantity rounded up to the next whole number. There is no option for rounding down as this does not make sense in this context. Once a fractional part of such a component is calculated, the whole component is required.

The BOM for material H102 at plant UWU2 in Figure 6.10 has a base quantity of 240 L. It also has material V502 (INK DRUM) as a component with a non-dimensional unit of measure (PC). The other components use L as the unit of measure.

Figure 6.11 shows the itemization portion of the cost estimate for H102 using a costing lot size of 1,000. ROUNDING FOR COMPONENT QUANTS is set to

Do Not Round. Notice that several components have fractional quantities including V502.

Material	H102		
Plant/Usage/Alt.	UWU2 / 1 / 01		
Description	Black Ink		
Segmentation			
Char. Value	/ /		
Char. description	/ /		
Base Qty (L)	240.000		
Reqd Qty (L)	240		

Obj...	Object ID	Description	Comp. Qty (BUn)	Unit
⊖	R105	Lubricant	25	L
⊖	R106	Surfactant	48	L
⊖	R107	Thickener	23	L
⊖	R110	Black Dye	132	L
⊖	V502	Ink Drum	1	PC

Figure 6.10: BOM for material H102 for base quantity 240

ItmNo	I...	Resource	Resource (Text)	Cost Element	◌	Total	COCr	Quantity	Un
1	M	UWU2 R110	Black Dye	51100000		819.50	USD	550	L
2	M	UWU2 R105	Lubricant	51100000		78.13	USD	104.167	L
3	M	UWU2 R106	Surfactant	51100000		50.00	USD	200	L
4	M	UWU2 R107	Thickener	51100000		33.54	USD	95.833	L
5	M	UWU2 V502	Ink Drum	51500000		62.51	USD	4.167	PC

Figure 6.11: Itemization for H102 with no rounding selected.

With Rounding for Component Quants set to Round Up with Nondimensional Units of Measure, the cost estimate changes, as shown in Figure 6.12. The contribution for material V502 has now been rounded up to the next whole number—from 4.167 to 5. Rounding up has also impacted the items with unit of measure L, but this only occurs at the third decimal place and is almost unnoticeable (see item 4 in both cost estimates). The difference here is that the unit of measure L rounds to the third decimal place and PC rounds to the whole number.

ItmNo	I...	Resource	Resource (Text)	Cost Element	ᴱ	Total	COCr	Quantity	Un
1	M	UWU2 R110	Black Dye	51100000		819.50	USD	550	L
2	M	UWU2 R105	Lubricant	51100000		78.13	USD	104.167	L
3	M	UWU2 R106	Surfactant	51100000		50.00	USD	200	L
4	M	UWU2 R107	Thickener	51100000		33.54	USD	95.834	L
5	M	UWU2 V502	Ink Drum	51500000		75.00	USD	5	PC

Figure 6.12: Itemization for H102 with rounding selected

The rounding decision should depend on the purpose of the cost estimate. If the costing lot size represents a standard manufacturing quantity, then the use of rounding gives a more accurate picture of the cost.

6.3 Routings and recipes

SAP uses the term *task list* to describe the operations necessary to manufacture a product. Routes and recipes are two forms of task lists that are used in production based on the type of manufacturing that is being performed. Routes are used in the discrete manufacturing and mill products industries. A special form of routing known as the rate routing is used in repetitive manufacturing situations. Repetitive manufacturing uses product cost collectors instead of orders for managing production. Recipes are used in the process industry, such as chemical manufacturing. Regardless of the type of task list that is used, the structures that link cost center activity types to a cost estimate are the same.

6.3.1 Routing and recipe header

The task list header contains information that is used to determine if that routing or recipe can be selected. The header information required for each is slightly different. Figure 6.13 shows a route header.

Figure 6.14 shows a recipe header.

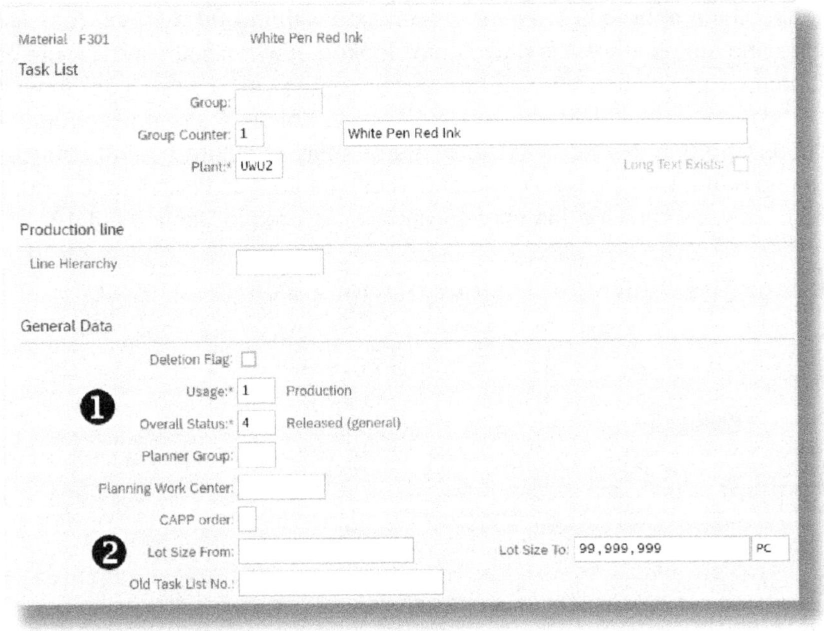

Material F301   White Pen Red Ink

Task List

Group:

Group Counter: 1   White Pen Red Ink

Plant:* UWU2   Long Text Exists: ☐

Production line

Line Hierarchy

General Data

Deletion Flag: ☐

❶ Usage:* 1   Production

Overall Status:* 4   Released (general)

Planner Group:

Planning Work Center:

CAPP order:

❷ Lot Size From: Lot Size To: 99,999,999   PC

Old Task List No.:

Figure 6.13: Header information for a route

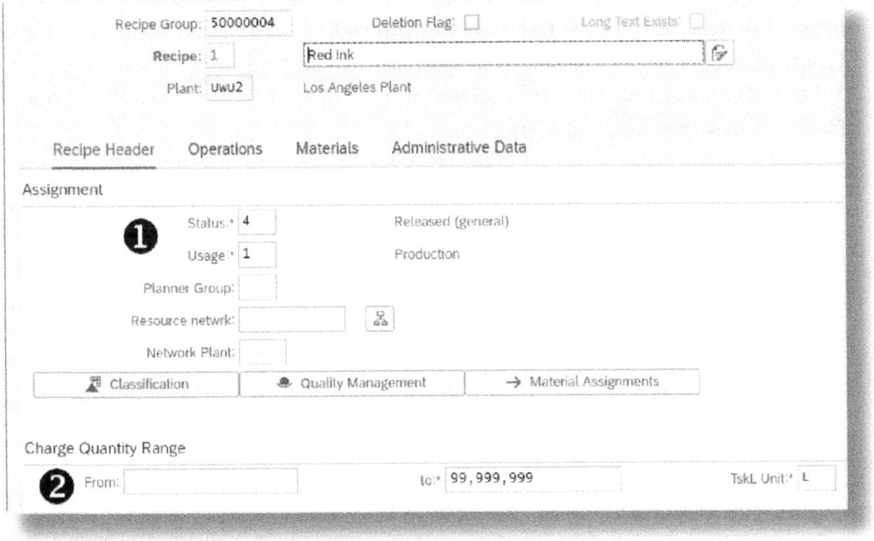

Recipe Group: 50000004   Deletion Flag: ☐   Long Text Exists: ☐

Recipe: 1   Red Ink

Plant: UWU2   Los Angeles Plant

Recipe Header   Operations   Materials   Administrative Data

Assignment

❶ Status:* 4   Released (general)

Usage:* 1   Production

Planner Group:

Resource netwrk:

Network Plant:

🜨 Classification   ⚫ Quality Management   → Material Assignments

Charge Quantity Range

❷ From: to:* 99,999,999   TskL Unit:* L

Figure 6.14: Header information for a recipe

The first thing to note is in the area identified with the ❶ symbol. Task list usage and status are the first two items looked at when selecting a route or recipe if no production version has been created yet. A search strategy is defined in the quantity structure control configuration. A strategy sequence ID is assigned in the ROUTING tab of the quantity structure control configuration to determine the type of routing to use for cost estimates (see Figure 6.15). The overview for this configuration is covered in Section 1.4.12.

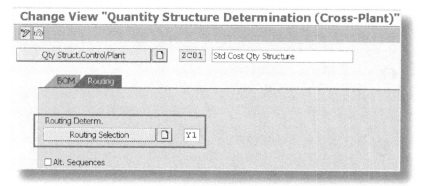

Figure 6.15: Routing tab of the quantity structure control definition

Figure 6.16 shows the configuration for a strategy sequence ID for routings. Use transaction OPJF or IMG menu path CONTROLLING • PRODUCT COST CONTROLLING • PRODUCT COST PLANNING • COST ESTIMATE WITH QUANTITY STRUCTURE • SETTINGS FOR QUANTITY STRUCTURE CONTROL • ROUTING SELECTION • CHECK AUTOMATIC ROUTING SELECTION.

Task list type N corresponds to routes in production, 2 corresponds to recipes, and R corresponds to rate routings for repetitive manufacturing. The S task list type is for reference operation sets which refer to lists of common operations that can be included in multiple other task lists. The PLAN USAGE field is used to define how the task list is used in production and has no costing relevance other than as a selection criterion. The STATUS field is used to control the current level of use that the task list or routing may be eligible for. This field does have a costing connotation. Status is defined under IMG menu path PRODUCTION • BASIC DATA • ROUTING • GENERAL DATA • DEFINE ROUTING STATUSES, or by using transaction OP46 (see Figure 6.17).

Change View "Automatic Selection": Overview

ID	SP	Task L...	Plan...	Description	Status	Description of the Status
Y1	1	N	1	Production	4	Released (general)
Y1	2	N	1	Production	2	Released for order
Y1	3	2	1	Production	4	Released (general)
Y1	4	2	1	Production	2	Released for order
Y1	5	R	1	Production	4	Released (general)
Y1	6	R	1	Production	2	Released for order
Y1	7	S	1	Production	4	Released (general)

Figure 6.16: Routing search strategy Y1

Change View "Task list status": Overview

Status	Description of the Status	RelInd	Cstng	Cons.chk.
1	Created	☐	☐	☐
2	Released for order	☑	☐	☑
3	Released for costing	☐	☑	☑
4	Released (general)	☑	☑	☑

Figure 6.17: Routing status configuration

Only those task lists with statuses that have been enabled for costing (CSTNG column) can be used to cost a material. Selection strategy Y1 includes items with status 2. Because this status is not enabled for costing purpose, a routing with this status is skipped when checked for the cost estimate.

Section ❷ in Figure 6.13 and Figure 6.14 points to a range of quantities for which the route or recipe is valid. This is important when selecting the task list for a production version. However, if the production version does not yet exist when the material is costed, the costing lot size must fall within that range for the task list to be selected.

6.3.2 Calculation of activity quantities

Resources and work centers

 A *resource* describes an area where production is performed in process industries. Resources are assigned to operations in recipes for planning, manufacturing, and costing purposes. The analogous piece of master data for discrete manufacturing is the work center. Work centers are assigned to operations in routings and rate routings. These two entities perform identical functions when it comes to costing, and when the term *work center* is used in the text it refers to either a resource or a work center depending on the context.

The main purpose served by manufacturing routings in costing is to allocate activity type costs from cost centers to the material cost estimate. These costs represent the added value of the cost associated with production processes. One of the attributes of an activity type is a unit of measure. During cost center planning, the quantity of each activity type associated with a cost center is assigned to that cost center for a specific time range, either for a single period or for an entire fiscal year. Once activity type quantities are planned, costs associated with that activity can be planned in the cost center using cost elements. A price per unit can then be calculated for the activity type. Alternatively, a price per unit can be assigned to an activity type; however, the method of calculating activity prices gives a much richer view of the cost component split of the resulting cost estimates. Refer to Section 1.3 for more details on the cost component split.

A mechanism is required for allocating a quantity of each activity type, including its attendant costs, to the cost estimate. Figure 6.18 shows a schematic representation of how the activity type is associated with the cost estimate. Starting in the upper right-hand corner, we see the operation from the task list. In this case, the task list is a recipe. Arrow ❶ indicates the connection between the work center assigned to the operation and the work center's master data. Arrow ❷ connects the cost center to the cost center activity plan to determine the available activity types that can be associated with the work center. Arrow ❸ shows that all three planned activity types have been defined to be used for this work center.

Arrow ❹ indicates an indirect connection between the activity types in the work center and the activity types that show up in the cost estimate at the bottom of the figure.

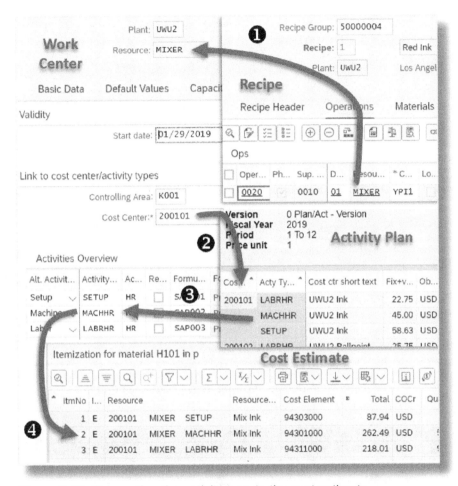

Figure 6.18: Connecting the activity type to the cost estimate

The connection at ❹ is indirect because the activity type assignment is copied into the operation when the work center is used for the operation. Figure 6.19 shows the details of the operation depicted in the upper right-hand corner of Figure 6.18. The highlighted area shows the activity types that were copied from the work center when the operation was created. These can be changed, but this is not recommended. The activity types that are used in the cost estimate come from this definition rather than directly from the work center definition.

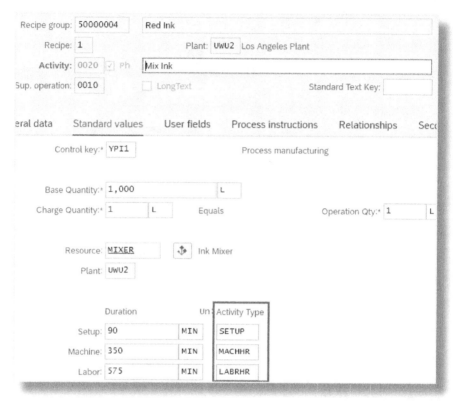

Figure 6.19: Operation details showing activity type assignment

Changing activity types for a work center

If the activity types are changed in the definition of a work center, the operation activity types do not automatically change. These must be manually updated, or incorrect costing results can occur. The order of the activity type assignments in the operation must match the order in the work center definition so that the formula in the work center is properly paired up with the activity type.

Formula parameters

The calculation of activity quantity involves the use of formulas that are assigned to the work center. Formulas use special parameters which must be configured. These parameters refer to specific constants or fields in the tables that are used in the operation. Transaction OP51 is used to define the parameters. There is also the IMG menu path CONTROLLING • PRODUCT COST CONTROLLING • PRODUCT COST PLANNING • MATERIAL COST ESTIMATE WITH QUANTITY STRUCTURE • SETTINGS FOR QUANTITY STRUCTURE CONTROL • ROUTING SELECTIONS • CHECK SETTINGS FOR FORMULAS.

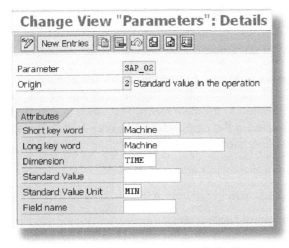

Figure 6.20: Formula parameter definition

Figure 6.20 shows the definition of a formula parameter. Each parameter has several attributes that define the source of the data and how the parameter can be used in formulas:

▶ PARAMETER—a 6-character ID for the parameter

▶ ORIGIN—identifies the data source of the parameter

▶ SHORT KEY WORD—the name of the parameter used when looking at formulas

▶ LONG KEY WORD—the longer name of the parameter

▶ DIMENSION—the unit-of-measure dimension for the parameter (e.g. time, mass, or length)

▶ STANDARD VALUE—the value assigned to a constant or a value that can be used to test mathematical errors when creating formulas

▶ STANDARD VALUE UNIT—the unit of measure for the parameter that must match the dimension

▶ FIELD NAME—the name of a field that the parameter represents for general operation parameters (origin 0) or values from PRT allocations (origin 5)

The parameter origin dictates what attributes are required for a parameter, as well as indicating the general source of the data.

Origin 0—general operation parameter

These parameters are directly assigned to specific fields associated with the operation. An example of this is the SAP-supplied parameter SAP_08 (base quantity), which is assigned to the field BMSCH. The value in that field for the specific operation is used in the calculation. The only fields allowed for assignment to a general operation parameter are:

▶ ANZMA—number of employees in network activity

▶ ANZZL—number of capacities in network activity

▶ ARBEI—work element in network activity

▶ BMSCH—base quantity

▶ DAUNO—length of network activity

▶ MGVRG—operation quantity

▶ QRASTMENG—QM: quantity between two inspections

▶ QRASTZFAK—QM: time factor

▶ SPLIM—number of splits

▶ ZLMAX—maximum wait time

▶ ZLPRO—minimum wait time

▶ ZMERH—break time

▶ ZWNOR—queue time

The dimension and unit of measure are derived from the field and are not required in the parameter definition. Field name must be assigned.

Origin 1—work center constant

These are values defined directly in the work center definition. An example of this is the number of people assigned to the work center. If this doesn't vary based on the operation that uses the work center, setting this value directly in the work center can be the best solution when considering data maintenance. ZWCLBR has been defined as a formula parameter to assign a specific number of people to a particular work center. At the bottom of the Costing tab of the work center definition is a button labeled Formula constnts. Click on this button to assign work center constants along with their values. Figure 6.21 shows the assignment of a constant at the work center level. Up to six parameters can be assigned to a work center. The values assigned to the parameters are dependent on the work center and can be different for different work centers. The assignment of parameters can also vary from work center to work center.

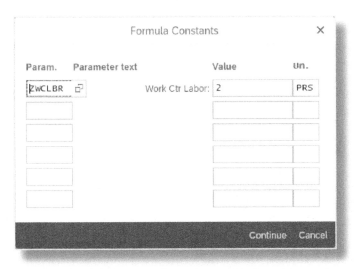

Figure 6.21: Work center formula constant assignment

Origin 2—standard value in the operation

Each operation has six special fields called *standard values*. Each standard value field has a separate unit of measure field associated with it.

195

Standard value parameters are assigned to a route operation when the work center is defined for that operation. Figure 6.22 shows the BASIC DATA tab of the work center definition. The STANDARD VALUE KEY that is highlighted has a set of standard value parameters configured for it. These standard values are then associated with the work center.

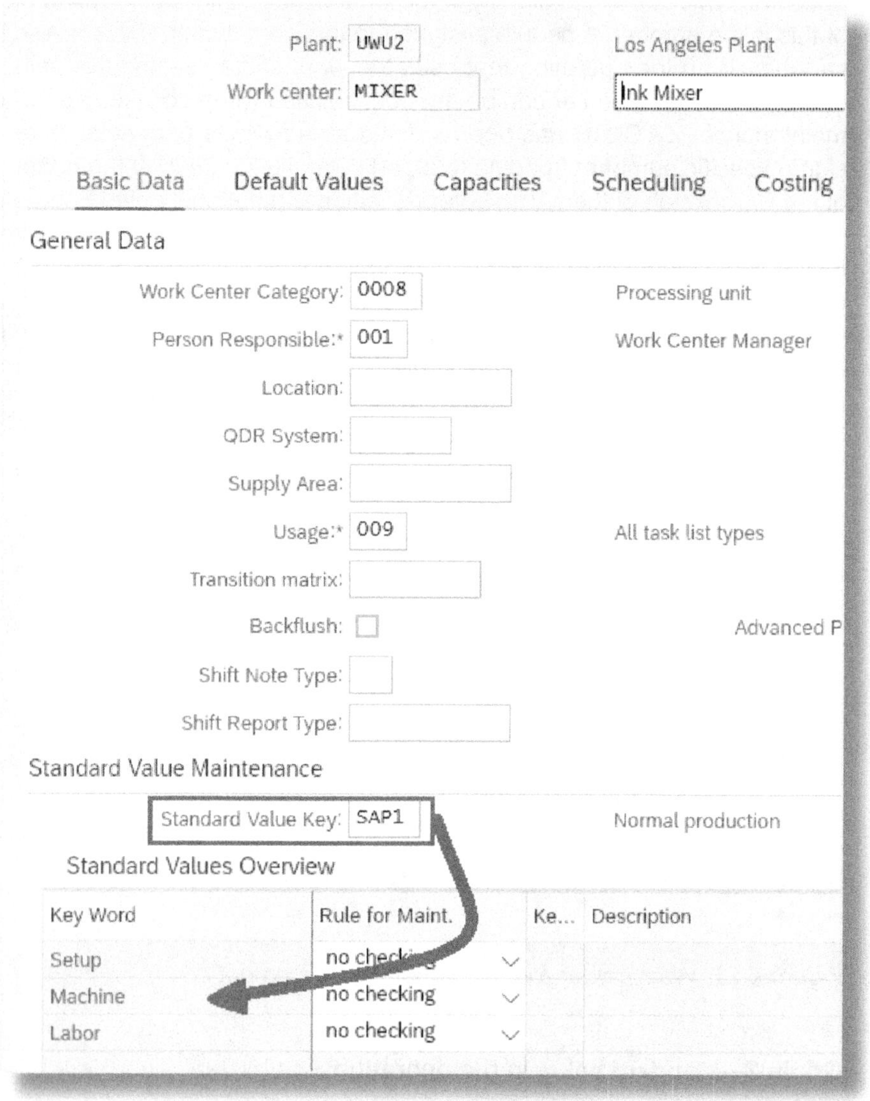

Plant:	UWU2	Los Angeles Plant
Work center:	MIXER	Ink Mixer

Basic Data   Default Values   Capacities   Scheduling   Costing

General Data

Work Center Category:	0008	Processing unit
Person Responsible:*	001	Work Center Manager
Location:		
QDR System:		
Supply Area:		
Usage:*	009	All task list types
Transition matrix:		
Backflush:	☐	Advanced P
Shift Note Type:		
Shift Report Type:		

Standard Value Maintenance

Standard Value Key:	SAP1	Normal production

Standard Values Overview

Key Word	Rule for Maint.	Ke...	Description
Setup	no checking	⌄	
Machine	no checking	⌄	
Labor	no checking	⌄	

Figure 6.22: Standard value key assignment in work center

196

The configuration of the standard value key determines both the order and number of parameters defined to be used in up to six standard values. This is processed using transaction OP19 or via IMG menu option Production • Basic Data • Work Center • Standard Value • Define Standard Value Keys (see Figure 6.23).

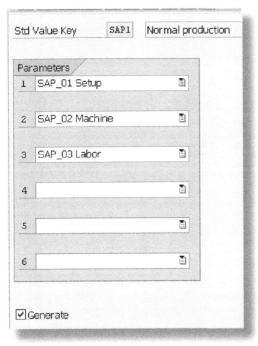

Figure 6.23: Standard value key configuration

Any parameter defined for origin 2 can be assigned to the key. In this case, three parameters have been assigned to the first 3 standard values. When a work center using this standard value key is used in an operation, the first three standard values are available to be used. In addition, if the formulas assigned to the work center use standard value parameters, they can only use the parameters assigned to the standard value key. Different work centers can have different key assignments, and the association of a particular set of parameters is operation dependent. Standard value 1 can mean one thing for one operation and have a totally different meaning for another operation.

The DEFAULT VALUES tab of the work center (see Figure 6.24) is used to define default units of measure for each standard value to be used in the operation. If no unit of measure is entered when the operation is defined, the default unit of measure is used. This unit of measure must be one that is associated with the dimension assigned to the parameter for that standard value.

Figure 6.24: Default units of measure for standard values

Standard values can be assigned to the routing or recipe when entering the operation. The location of the standard values for the operation is shown in Figure 6.25, in areas ❶, ❷, and ❸. They are also accessible by drilling into the operation details.

Figure 6.25: Standard values for an operation

Origin 4—user-defined field from operation

SAP provides the capability to create user-defined fields that can be assigned to the operation in a routing or recipe. Ten user-defined fields can
be defined for a field key. The field key is assigned to the operation, which
allows the fields associated with the field key to be updated in the operation. There are two 20-character text fields, two 10-character text fields,
two quantity fields, two value fields, two date fields, and two checkbox
fields. Only the two quantity fields can be referenced for use in formulas,
because formulas are used to calculate quantity and not value. Figure 6.26
shows two parameters that are set up with origin 4. These parameters
are intended to account for the time required to gather the materials used
in mixing. The left side is used to define the time, and the right side determines the number of employees required to gather the materials.

Parameter	ZPMMIN		Parameter	ZPMPRS
Origin	4 User-defined field from operation		Origin	4 User-defined field from operation
Attributes			**Attributes**	
Short key word	Premix Min		Short key word	Premix Prs
Long key word	Premix Minutes		Long key word	Premix Persons
Dimension	TIME		Dimension	AAAADL
Standard Value			Standard Value	
Standard Value Unit	MIN		Standard Value Unit	PRS
Field name			Field name	

Figure 6.26: User-defined field parameters

199

Figure 6.27 shows how the quantity fields in the definition of the field key are assigned to the parameters. This can be configured via IMG menu path PRODUCTION • BASIC DATA • ROUTING • OPERATION DATA • DEFINE USER-DEFINED FIELDS, or by using transaction OPEC. The quantity fields have an optional link to origin 4 parameters. If this link exists, the user quantity fields can be used in work center formulas.

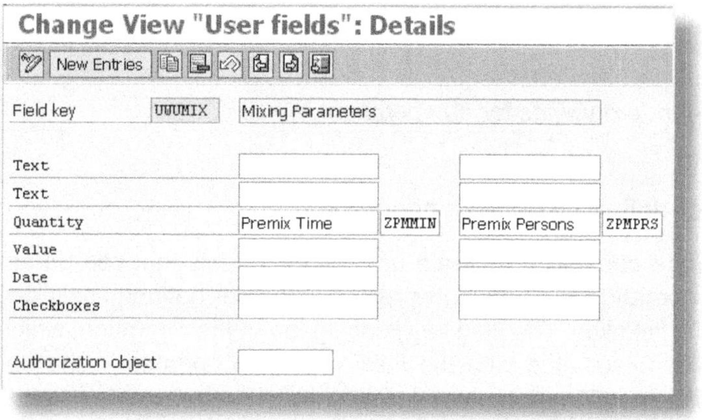

Figure 6.27: User defined fields

Different user-defined field keys can be assigned to different operations. This allows additional flexibility in how these fields can be used. When assigning a field key to a routing or recipe, only the fields defined in the configuration are displayed.

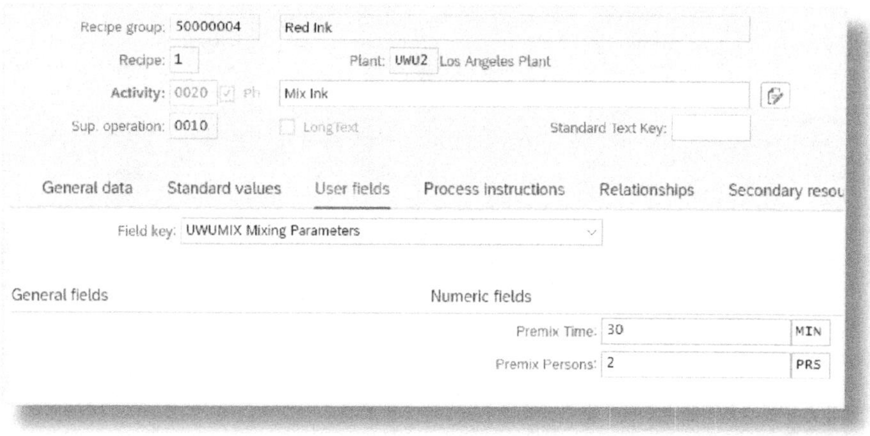

Figure 6.28: User fields in a recipe

200

Figure 6.28 shows the USER FIELDS tab of a recipe after drilling into the operation. The field key UWUMIX was selected and the two quantity fields are displayed under the NUMERIC FIELDS area of the window.

Material F301	White Pen Red Ink Grp.Count1

Operation

Activity:* 0010	Suboperation:

Work center / Plant: INJECT /* UwU2 Ink Injector

Control key:* PI01 Process Manufacturing

Standard Text Key: Ink Injection

☐ Long Text Exists

Standard Values

Conversion of Units of Measure

	Header	Unit	Operat.	Un
Base Quantity:* 1,000				
Operation unit:* PC	1	PC	<=>:* 1	PC
Break Time:				

	Std Value	Un	Act. Type	Efficiency
Setup:	30	MIN	SETUP	
Machine:	10	MIN	MACHHR	
Labor:	10	MIN	LABRHR	

Recording view: Single values and summarized ... (default view) ∨

User-Specific Fields

Field key: UWUCLN			
Cleaning type: Injector cleaning			
Clean Time: 50	MIN	ZPMMIN	
Clean Persons: 1	PRS	ZPMPRS	

Figure 6.29: User fields in a routing

The routing user fields are also displayed after drilling into the operation in the route (see Figure 6.29). If a field key has been selected, these appear in the USER-SPECIFIC FIELDS section of the window. In this case, the parameters are also displayed. The same parameters are selected for FIELD KEY UWUCLN and UWUMIX, but they have different values assigned. The values are operation specific. UWUCLN also uses one of the text fields (CLEANING TYPE) for description.

201

Origin 5—value from PRT allocation

These values originate from the assignment of production resources and tools (PRT) to an operation. These cannot be used for costing purposes. One of two PRT fields can be assigned to these parameters. These are EWVGW (standard value for the usage value) and MGVGW (standard value for quantity).

Origin 6—PRT constant

These are constant values to be assigned for use with PRT formulas. They are not available for use in costing.

Origin 7—general formula constant

Work center formulas return a value that represents a quantity with a unit of measure. The general formula constants are defined with a dimension, a unit of measure for that dimension, and a value in the field STANDARD VALUE. The value is used in the formula, and the dimension/unit of measure combination is used to ensure that the result is returned with a proper unit of measure.

Formulas

Formulas intended for costing are made up of parameters and arithmetic operators. They are used to calculate a quantity for an activity type so that quantity of activity can be allocated to the cost estimate. Only four arithmetic operators are allowed. These are + for addition,—for subtraction, * for multiplication, and / for division. If-then-else logic is not supported. Care must be taken when using the division operator because there is no protection against a divide-by-zero error. If the result of a formula is a divide-by-zero error, the cost estimate fails with a costing error. The order of operations is multiply, divide, add, subtract. Operations that are grouped together within parentheses are processed first. Numeric constants can be used along with the configured parameters. A space is required between formula parameters, constants, and operators.

Using numeric constants in formulas

! The use of numeric constants in formulas can give unexpected results. Because numeric constants don't have dimension or unit of measure, the system can only make assumptions as to the meaning. For example, in a time calculation, a numeric constant is assumed to refer to seconds. A much better approach is to define a constant as a parameter with origin type 7.

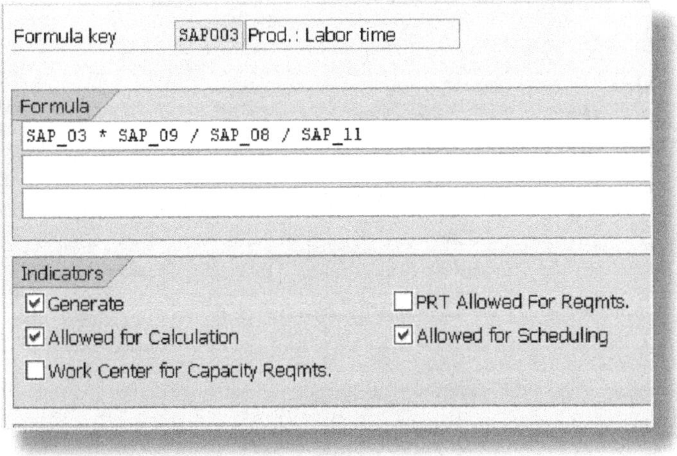

Formula key   SAP003 Prod.: Labor time

Formula

SAP_03 * SAP_09 / SAP_08 / SAP_11

Indicators

☑ Generate   ☐ PRT Allowed For Reqmts.
☑ Allowed for Calculation   ☑ Allowed for Scheduling
☐ Work Center for Capacity Reqmts.

Figure 6.30: Formula SAP003 to calculate labor time

Figure 6.30 shows the formula that is used to calculate labor time. SAP_03 is a standard value parameter referring to labor time. SAP_09 is a general operation parameter referring to operation quantity. This corresponds to the costing lot size for a cost estimate. SAP_08 is a general operation parameter referring to base quantity defined for the operation. SAP_11 is a general operation parameter referring to the number of operation splits. Splitting is a feature of routings which is used to denote that the operation is being processed in parallel on different machinery. If splitting is not enabled, a value of 1 is used in the formula. Splitting is not a feature of recipes, and the default is used.

Formulas are assigned to work centers in the COSTING tab of the definition. Figure 6.31 shows the assignment of formulas to the activity types used for allocating the manufacturing costs from the work center's cost center. Each activity type used for allocation has its own formula.

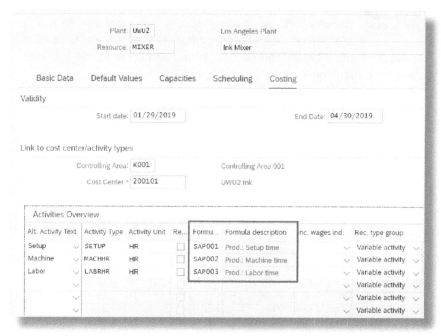

Figure 6.31: Costing tab of the work center definition

Work center costing validity dates

The COSTING tab definitions in the work center are date dependent. A new definition can be set for the future by entering a new start date and changing the settings. When the changes are saved, the original settings then have an END DATE set to the day before the START DATE just saved. Looking at Figure 6.31, the end date of the validity period is set to 04/30/2019, which means that a new costing definition becomes available on 05/01/2019. Cost estimates with a quantity structure date of 05/01/2019 or later will use the new settings. There is a VALIDITIES button at the bottom of the COSTING tab window. Click on the button to select a specific time period to view the work center definition.

Figure 6.32 shows the details from the mixing operation. Highlighted at area ❶ is the base quantity of 1,000 L. Area ❷ shows the number of minutes of labor time associated with the 1,000 L of mixing.

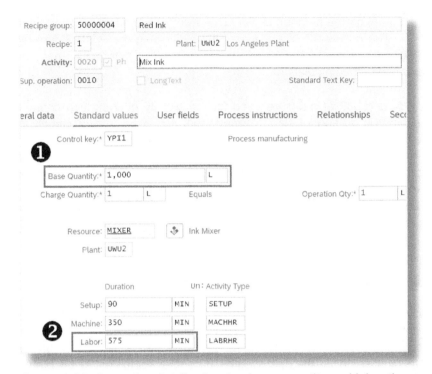

Figure 6.32: Operation details showing base quantity and labor time

Item number 3 in Figure 6.33 represents the labor costs for mixing in the itemization of the resulting cost estimate. The quantity is calculated using the formula in Figure 6.30.

Itemization for material H101 in p

ItmNo	I...	Resource			Resource...	Cost Element		Total	COCr	Quantity	Un
1	E	200101	MIXER	SETUP	Mix Ink	94303000		87.94	USD	1.5	HR
2	E	200101	MIXER	MACHHR	Mix Ink	94301000		262.49	USD	5.833	HR
3	E	200101	MIXER	LABRHR	Mix Ink	94311000		218.01	USD	9.583	HR

Figure 6.33: Itemization of activity costs for mixing

The costing lot size is 1,000. The quantity calculation is 575 MIN (from the standard value) multiplied by 1,000 L (from the costing lot size) divided by 1,000 L (from the base quantity) divided by 1 (number of splits). This results in a value of 575 minutes, or 9.583 hours. The value assigned to that is based on the planned activity type rate for LABRHR in cost center 200101. The rate is 22.75 USD per HR. Multiplying the 9.583 hours by 22.75 gives a value of 218.01 USD. Refer to Figure 6.18 for a pictorial representation of the calculations.

The resulting unit of measure used for the activity quantity can change depending on costing lot size. Normally, the unit of measure assigned to the activity type is used. In this case, the unit of measure is HR. However, if this results in a field size overflow, the next higher unit of measure for the dimension is used instead (DAY in this case). If rounding errors cause the value to be incorrectly displayed, then the next lower unit of measure for the dimension is used. Please refer to SAP Note 72442[6] for a full explanation.

6.3.3   Operation fields affecting costing

Two fields in the operation have an impact on the calculation of costs. The first is the costing relevancy factor. This works in the same manner as the costing relevancy factor for BOMs, covered in Section 6.2.3. If the costing relevancy is set to "X" the operation is 100% relevant to cost. If it is blank, then no costs are calculated for that operation. If other costing relevancy percentages are defined, then these are only applicable for inventory cost estimates and not standard cost estimates. Any non-blank value for costing relevancy in the operation is treated as 100% for standard cost estimates. For cost estimates with a costing type that is defined for non-standard usage, the percentage assigned to the factor is used in the calculation of the cost associated with the activity. Costing relevancy is updated for both recipes and routings by drilling into the operation. Figure 6.34 shows the location of the costing relevancy (COSTINGRELEVNCY) in the GENERAL DATA section of the operation details of a routing.

---

[6] SAP Note 72442—"Unit conversion in product costing for the display of unit of measure for activity allocation"

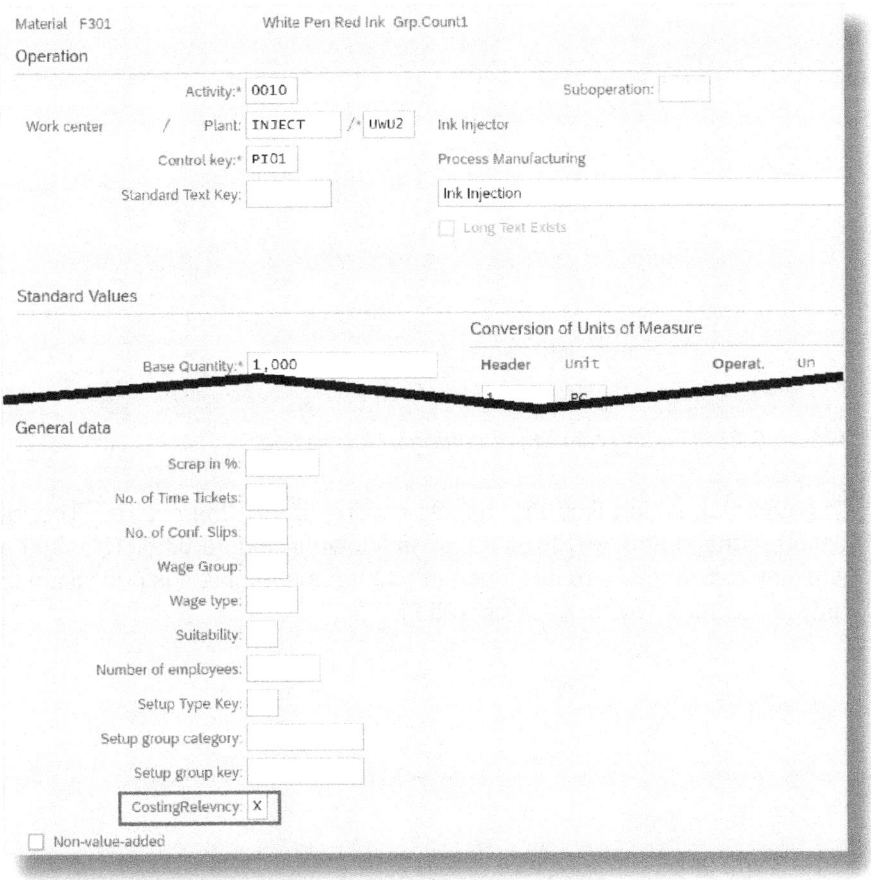

Material   F301   White Pen Red Ink Grp.Count1

Operation

Activity:* 0010   Suboperation:

Work center   /   Plant: INJECT   /* UwU2   Ink Injector

Control key:* PI01   Process Manufacturing

Standard Text Key: Ink Injection

☐ Long Text Exists

Standard Values

Conversion of Units of Measure

Base Quantity:* 1,000   Header   Unit   Operat.   Un

General data

Scrap in %:

No. of Time Tickets:

No. of Conf. Slips:

Wage Group:

Wage type:

Suitability:

Number of employees:

Setup Type Key:

Setup group category:

Setup group key:

CostingRelevncy: X

☐ Non-value-added

Figure 6.34: Costing relevancy setting in the routing

Figure 6.35 shows the location of the costing relevancy setting for an operation in the recipe, shown as CostRel. This is on the GENERAL DATA tab after drilling into the operation.

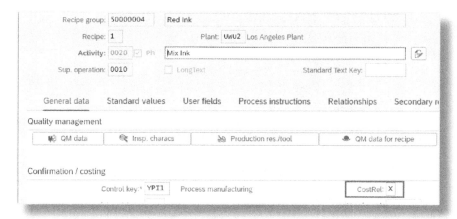

Figure 6.35: Costing relevancy setting in the recipe

The other operation field that affects costing is the CONTROL KEY. The location of the control key for a recipe is shown in Figure 6.36. This is in a similar location to where it is found in routing operations. It is necessary to assign a control key for each operation.

Recipe Group:	50000004	Deletion Fla.
Recipe:	1	Red Ink
Plant:	UWU2	Los Angeles Plant

Recipe Header   Operations   Materials   Adminis

Ops

Operat...	Ph...	Sup. ...	Des...	Resource	* Control key
0010				MIXER	YPI1
0020		0010	01	MIXER	YPI1
0030					YPI1

Figure 6.36: Control key of a recipe operation

The control key is important in determining which business functions are processed for that operation. This includes behavior in planning, capacity calculations, document printing, processing goods receipts, and costing. An operation may be excluded from costing if the control key does not allow for costing to occur. In addition, a control key can be set up to make the operation useable only for costing, enabling special costing-only operations to be defined, if so required. Configuration for this is found via IMG menu path Production • Basic Data • Routing • Operation Data • Define Control Key or by using transaction OP67.

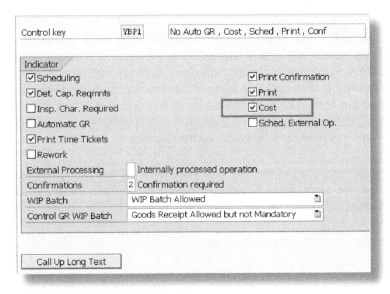

Figure 6.37: Control key configuration

Figure 6.37 shows the configuration of a control key. The Cost checkbox must be selected for the control key to allow costing to occur. The control key definition for costing supersedes the costing relevancy setting. If the control key is defined for no costing and the costing relevancy is set to X for 100%, no costs are calculated for the operation.

Operations in routings and recipes

 Regarding costing, each operation and sub-operation defined in a routing stands by itself. Each can have an impact on the assignment of costs from activity type. Recipes have operations and phases associated with the operation. Phases are similar to sub-operations in routings, and they can be used for costing purposes. However, the main operation is just a placeholder for the phases, and is not cost-relevant.

6.4 Production versions

A *production version* is a method for manufacturing a product. It links together a specific BOM with a specific manufacturing routing. Prior to the introduction of S/4HANA, the use of production versions was optional in many cases and depended on settings in the SELECTION METHOD field on the MRP 4 tab of the material master. This is no longer available because only the use of production versions is supported in the material master. Refer again to SAP Note 2267880. Costing still does not have that requirement, but when costing a material, the system looks for a production version that matches the cost estimate parameters. If no version is found, then it uses the logic defined in Sections 6.2 and 6.3 to find a BOM and a manufacturing routing to generate the costs for the product.

Production versions are maintained in several different transactions. One application is the standalone Manage Production Versions Fiori tile, as shown in Figure 6.38.

Figure 6.38: Manage Production Versions Fiori application

Maintenance is also accessible when editing a recipe (but not a routing) or from the MRP 4 and COSTING 1 tabs of the material master. Click on the [🗋 Versions] button on the COSTING 1 tab to access the production versions for the material.

Figure 6.39: Material master production version details window

Figure 6.39 shows the maintenance window for production versions in the material master. Area ❶ shows the PRODUCTION VERSION ID and the name. The ID is four characters long. In area ❷, the validities for the production version are defined. The lot size range defines the manufacturing lot quantities for which this combination of BOM and routing are valid. The BOM and the routing must have lot size ranges that are compatible with this range. For this production version to be selected for cost estimates, the costing lot size must fit within the range. The quantity structure date used for costing must also fit in the range for the validity dates. A production version can be locked from use. If it is locked, it cannot be used for costing purposes. In area ❸, the routing is assigned to the production version. TASK LIST TYPE, GROUP ID and GROUP COUNTER specifically identify a specific routing. Master recipes use task list type 2, routings use N, and rate routings use R. Area ❹ defines which specific BOM is associated with the routing. BOM USAGE and ALTERNATIVE BOM define the specific BOM. The apportionment structure is used to define how co-products interact with each other in the cost estimate. Area ❺ shows the CHECK button. To ensure that the BOM and routing validity criteria (lot size, dates, and deletion flag status) allow them to be assigned to the production version, click on the CHECK button. If both the routing and the BOM are valid for the production version, the check indicators in area ❻ change to green. A yellow triangle is initially displayed, indicating that the check has yet to be done. A red indicator means that the routing or BOM either does not exist or that the validity criteria do not match.

Although production versions are mandatory for use in manufacturing and planning in S/4HANA, as of on-premise release 1809, they are not required in product costing. The automatic strategy for selecting the production version, BOM, and routing is as follows:

1. Search for the production version by checking production version validity using costing lot size and the quantity structure date used for the cost estimate on the DATES tab. The first production version that is found to be valid is selected for the cost estimate.

2. If no production version is found that matches the costing criteria, the system checks for a valid BOM. This includes checking the deletion flag, BOM usage, lot sizes, and validity dates. The search strategy for BOM usage follows the configuration in Section 1.4.12 and the first valid BOM with the highest priority usage is selected. The BOM selection is independent of the routing selection. If a BOM is not found that matches the selection criteria, informational message CK424 (MATERIAL X IN PLANT Y HAS NO BOM) is logged. This does not cause the cost estimate to fail.

3. Again, if no valid production version is found, the system then checks for a valid routing. Validity checks include task list type, deletion flag, usage, status, lot sizes, and dates. The strategy is defined in the quantity structure configuration from Section 1.4.12. The first valid routing that matches the search criteria is used for the cost estimate. If no routing is found, informational message CK229 (NO ROUTING COULD BE DETERMINED FOR MATERIAL X) is logged. This does not cause the cost estimate to fail.

4. If none of the above checks returns a valid quantity structure, message CK219 (NO ITEMIZATION EXISTS FOR MATERIAL X IN PLANT Y) is displayed. Because no itemization is created, the cost estimate generates a KF costed with error status. Error messages CK060 (OBJECT WAS NOT COSTED) and CK240 (COST COMPONENT SPLIT COSTED WITH VALUE OF 0) are written to the message log.

7 Updating the material master

After a cost estimate is saved, it can be used to update the material master. Several fields in the material master can be modified using the result of certain cost estimates. The definition of the costing type assigned to the costing variant determines which fields can be updated. A primary purpose of cost estimates is to determine the standard for a material, and this is one of the fields that can be written to. There are several other fields representing special inventory costs and other planned costs that are also used to store the results of cost estimates.

7.1 Updating standard prices

To update a standard cost in the material master, Costing Type 01 must be assigned to the costing variant (see Figure 7.1). Only one costing type is allowed when updating the standard costs. Costing type 01 is delivered with the system and its Price Update is set to Standard Price.

Figure 7.1: Costing type for updating standard price

After a cost estimate is created, it must be saved prior to making any price updates in the material master. Updating a standard price requires a two-step process: cost estimate *marking* and *releasing*. First, the cost estimate must be "marked" or made ready to update the material master. The actual release of a standard cost estimate is time-dependent and must take place during the fiscal period associated with the costing date used in the cost estimate. Usually, the standard price should be updated at the beginning of a period, and if Material Ledger actual costing is turned on, this is a requirement.

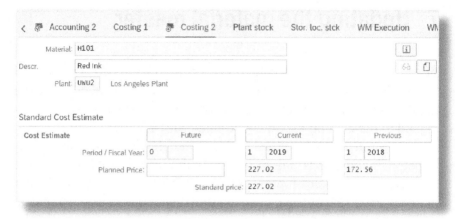

Figure 7.2: Standard cost estimate fields in Costing 2

Figure 7.2 shows the fields associated with the standard price update in the COSTING 2 tab of the material master. The STANDARD COST ESTIMATE section shows three different prices associated with cost estimates. Under the FUTURE button is the next cost to be released. PERIOD / FISCAL YEAR shows the period and year that the cost estimate will be released to become the standard cost estimate. Under the CURRENT button, we see the price and effective date for the cost estimate that is used for the standard cost for the material. The price associated with the cost estimate that was previously used for the standard is under the PREVIOUS button. If the period and year are filled in under this button, then clicking on the button displays the cost estimate.

A new standard cost estimate for material H101 at plant UWU2 has been created using a costing date of 04/01/2019 (see Figure 7.4), which corresponds to period 4, 2019. This cost estimate will be used to set a new standard for the material beginning in period 4. Figure 7.3 shows the cost estimate based on the price unit of 100 L. The highlighted cost component view INVENTORY VALUATION has been selected to be displayed in the COSTS tab. This is the one used for updating standard costs. This view matches the COST OF GOODS MANUFACTURED view in this example, but it does not necessarily have to do this, and it can have a different value.

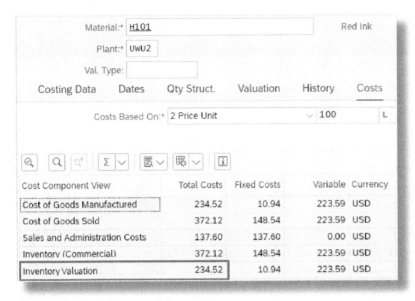

Cost Component View	Total Costs	Fixed Costs	Variable	Currency
Cost of Goods Manufactured	234.52	10.94	223.59	USD
Cost of Goods Sold	372.12	148.54	223.59	USD
Sales and Administration Costs	137.60	137.60	0.00	USD
Inventory (Commercial)	372.12	148.54	223.59	USD
Inventory Valuation	234.52	10.94	223.59	USD

Figure 7.3: Standard cost estimate using costing variant ZPC1

Figure 7.4 shows the dates used when the cost estimate was created. The highlighted area shows the period during which the cost estimate becomes active.

Figure 7.4: Dates tab for cost estimate

Figure 7.5 shows the COSTING DATA tab of the cost estimate. At this stage in the process, the cost estimate status is KA COSTED WITHOUT ERRORS.

215

Figure 7.5: Initial costing status KA

7.1.1 Marking the standard cost estimate

The two-step process for updating the standard cost from a cost estimate begins with marking. This process changes the status of the cost estimate to VO (marked) and updates the COSTING 2 tab of the material master with the future price, the fiscal period and year corresponding to the costing date of the cost estimate. The marking step is performed by the Release Material Cost Estimates Fiori tile. SAPGUI transaction CK24 performs the same function. The initial display shows the data entry window for marking a cost estimate (see Figure 7.6).

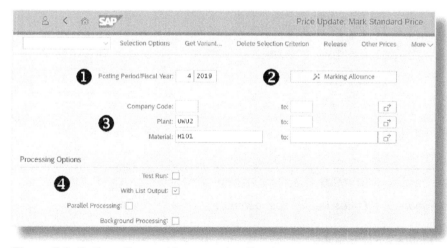

Figure 7.6: Options for marking a cost estimate

Area ❶ is used to specify the period and year for marking the cost estimate. To enable marking, the costing date of the cost estimate must match the posting period and year selected. This can be the current period or some future period. Marking in a past period is not allowed.

Area ❷ contains the MARKING ALLOWANCE button. A cost estimate with a specific costing variant and costing version cannot be marked unless it is explicitly allowed for the period and year selected. Only one costing variant and version can be enabled for the period within each company code. Click on the MARKING ALLOWANCE button to determine if marking has been enabled for the company code for the selected fiscal period. Figure 7.7 shows the two company codes for Universal Writing Utensils. Both have a red "stoplight" next to them, indicating that marking is not enabled for period 4.

Figure 7.7: Marking allowance by company code for period 4

Plant UWU2 is in company code K102. Click on the company code to enter the parameters required to enable marking. The window in Figure 7.8 is then displayed.

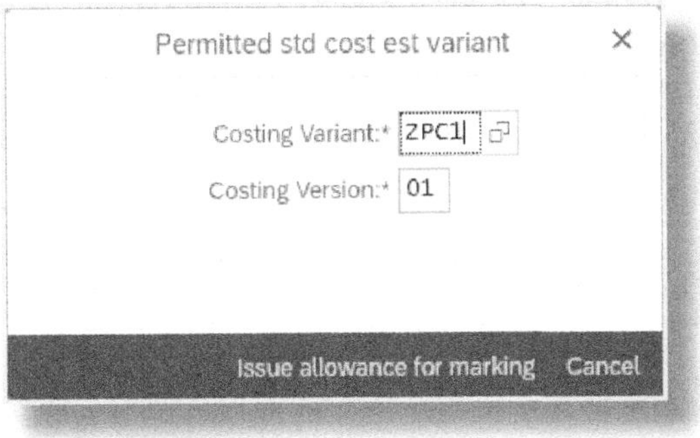

Figure 7.8: Costing variant and version for marking

Once a costing variant and version are entered for the company code, they cannot be changed. Only cost estimates with that costing variant and version are allowed to be marked and released for that company code and period. Click on ISSUE ALLOWANCE FOR MARKING (▣) to enable marking for the period in the selected company code. The stoplight then turns green for that company code. If the stoplight for the company code is already green, marking for that period has already been enabled. Exit to the previous menu.

Area ❸ of Figure 7.6 is used for entering the materials to be marked. All three selections are optional. For example, if PLANT is specified, there is no need to enter a company code because the plant can only belong to one company code. If the COMPANY CODE field is populated and PLANT is left blank, then the selected materials for all plants in that company code will be processed, assuming they have valid cost estimates ready for marking. If MATERIAL is left blank, then all materials for a selected company code or plant will be processed.

Area ❹ determines how marking is processed. If TEST RUN is selected, then the system processes the marking operation but does not update any date in the cost estimate or the material master. Erroneous costs can be reviewed and corrected before making the update run. The WITH LIST OUTPUT checkbox determines whether a listing file with the marked prices is to be displayed. This can be reviewed to see if there are any gross errors in the cost estimates. If this is not selected, then only log messages are displayed. When PARALLEL PROCESSING is selected, another field is displayed requesting a server group (e.g. parallel_generators) and a number of concurrent processes to be entered. If a large number of cost estimates is being processed, this can speed up processing. Selecting BACKGROUND PROCESSING allows the actual execution of the marking step to be run as a background job. Using background processing frees up the current session for other work. Because background jobs do not have to be run immediately, they can also be used to schedule the marking of cost estimates at a future time.

Using parallel processing

Check with the Basis team before using parallel processing as it can slow down the system if too many processes are chosen. A typical number of processes to use is 5, but this may vary based on the system load.

When all the options for marking have been entered, click on the `Execute` button (SAPGUI ⊕) or press [F8]. A log list is displayed to indicate success or failure (see Figure 7.9).

⚠	M	Material	Plnt	AppAr	MsgNo	Message Text
■	I		CK	790	************** Summary : *****************
■	I		CK	705	Of 1 materials, 1 cost estimates were updated successfully

Figure 7.9: Log for marking

If WITH LIST OUTPUT was selected, a report showing all of the marked costs is displayed after exiting the log. Figure 7.10 shows the report, which displays the new status (VO) along with the marked price in company code and controlling area currencies.

Exe...	Material	Plant	V...	Cos...	Fut. pln...	Standard pr...	Price unit	Currency	Valuation View	With Qty ...	Description
■	H101	UWU2		VO	234.52	227.02	100	USD	Legal Valuation	✓	Red Ink
■	H101	UWU2		VO	187.62	181.62	100	EUR	Legal Valuation	✓	Red Ink

Figure 7.10: Report showing result of marking

If TEST RUN is not selected, then both the cost estimate and the material master are updated. Figure 7.11 shows that the status on the COSTING DATA tab of the cost estimate has changed from KA to VO MARKED WITHOUT ERRORS.

Figure 7.11: Cost estimate status VO after marking

Figure 7.12 shows that the value of the marked cost estimate has been written to the COSTING 2 tab of the material master as the future planned price. The period corresponds to the marking period.

Figure 7.12: Marked cost in Costing 2 tab of material master

7.1.2 Releasing the standard cost estimate

The second step for updating a standard cost estimate in the material master is called releasing. A standard cost estimate can only be released during the period for which it was marked for release. If the period for releasing the cost estimate has passed, it is necessary to create a new cost estimate to be both marked and released using the current date or a future date.

Releasing standard costs

 A standard cost estimate should be released at the beginning of a fiscal period to ensure consistent goods movement valuation throughout the period. When PRICE DETERMINATION is set to 3 (SINGLE-/MULTILEVEL for actual costing) in the ACCOUNTING 1 tab of the material master, the release fails if it occurs after the first goods movement of the period. If, in that case, it is absolutely necessary to release a cost estimate in the middle of the period, this can be done using transaction MR21 with OK code set to LTPC (late price change). See SAP Note 2483836—"MR21 with LTPC with 'Default Planned Prices'." for more details.

To switch to the release process in the Release Material Cost Estimates transaction, click on the RELEASE button shown in Figure 7.13.

Figure 7.13: Selecting the release processing

The parameters in the release window are basically the same as the parameters required for marking. The standard cost is used for valuing inventory. Therefore, if there is a price change, then any inventory associated with that material must have its value updated. Because releasing a cost estimate can cause these changes, documents are created which display the valuation changes for each material processed. A field has been included to specify the number of materials to be processed in each price change document that is created (see Figure 7.14). Valuation changes are tracked in the price change document that is created as part of the release. Every material that is processed by the release has an entry in the document. If there is no inventory for the material, or if there is no price change, then no accounting posting is made. If there is inventory, then a posting is made to the inventory account associated with the material, with the offset posted to the account assigned to transaction/event key UMB.

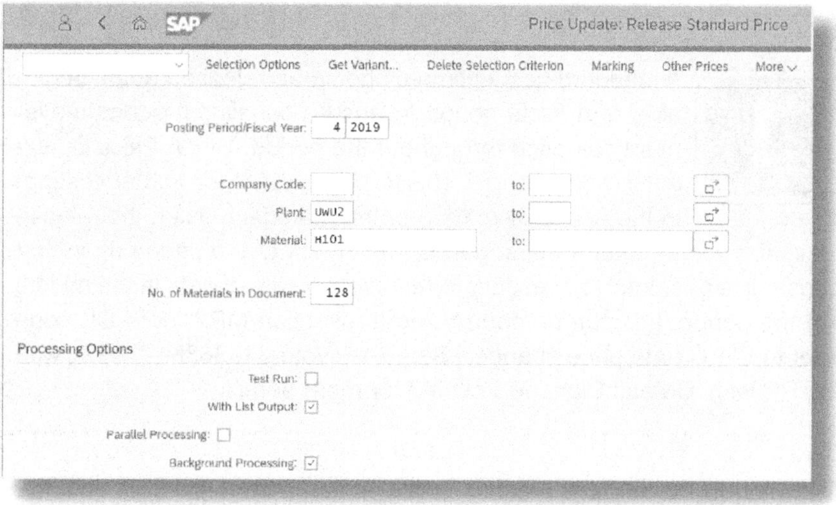

Figure 7.14: Window for entering release options

Enter the material information and the processing options. Unless the standard cost is being released in the current period, BACKGROUND PROCESSING should always be selected. This allows the batch job to be scheduled just after midnight on the first day of the marked period. For releases in the current period, either option can be used. A log similar to the marking log is generated when the release job runs, and if WITH LIST OUTPUT is selected, a listing of all released costs is also produced. When a standard price is successfully released, updates are made to the previous cost estimate, the current cost estimate, and the COSTING 2 tab of the material master. Figure 7.15 shows that the costing status for the latest cost estimate is changed to FR RELEASED WITHOUT ERRORS.

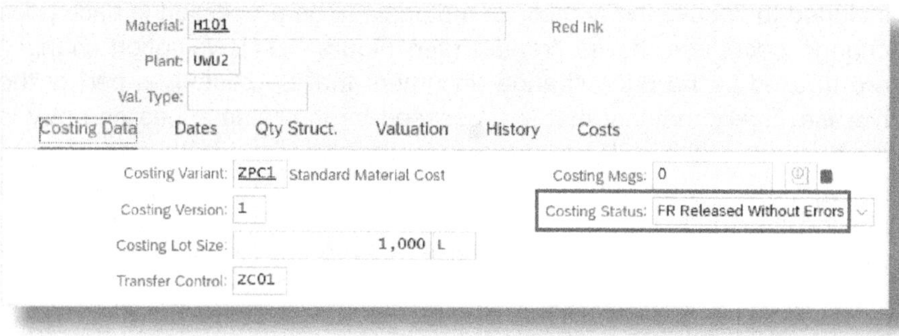

Figure 7.15: Current cost estimate status FR after releasing

There is also a change made to the cost estimate that was previously used as the standard. Figure 7.16 shows the DATES tab of the cost estimate that was previously used as the standard. The date changes to the date just before the current standard became effective.

Figure 7.16: Date change for previous standard cost estimate

There are also changes made to the COSTING 2 tab of the material master. These changes are shown in Figure 7.17.

Figure 7.17: Costing 2 tab after standard cost estimate release

Area ❶ shows that the future cost estimate period and price information has been removed. The marked cost estimate has now become the current standard. Area ❷ shows the value of the now current cost estimate that has been moved over from the future fields. Compare this with Figure 7.12. In addition, the STANDARD PRICE field takes on the value of the cost estimate. Area ❸ is now updated with what was previously the current cost estimate. The cost estimate information that was previously in this location

223

is no longer available in the material master, but it has not been deleted from the system and can still be viewed with the Display Material Cost Estimate Fiori tile or via SAPGUI transaction CK13N.

7.2 Updating other prices

Nine different fields, other than the standard cost, can be updated in the material master. The six tax-based and commercial inventory fields are found on the ACCOUNTING 2 tab of the material master. The three planned price fields are found on the COSTING 2 tab of the material master. Costing type also defines which fields can be updated for cost estimates using specific costing variants. Unlike the standard cost update, there is no requirement to mark the cost estimate, and the costs are updated at the time the transaction is executed. The same Release Material Cost Estimates Fiori tile (SAPGUI transaction CK24) is used to update these costs.

7.2.1 Inventory cost estimates

SAP allows for the update of special inventory cost estimates using the lowest-value method of price determination. This method looks at various methods associated with goods movements and pricing history for raw materials to help determine a value that more accurately reflects the true worth of those purchased items. Using the values calculated for the purchased materials, inventory cost estimates can be made for manufactured materials to include these raw material values in order to get a truer picture of the costs of these intermediate materials and finished products. Special costing variants are created to generate these cost estimates, and the results can be updated in special fields on the ACCOUNTING 2 tab of the material master. Two sets of three values can be updated. There are three tax-based and three commercial inventory prices that use the lowest-value method when updating the costs. Some countries distinguish between the tax-based and commercial valuations, but for others, there is no distinction between the two.

To update the tax-based prices, the costing variant must use a costing type that explicitly specifies the update of the tax-based prices, as shown in Figure 7.18.

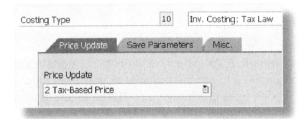

Figure 7.18: Costing type for updating tax-based inventory price

Commercial inventory-based cost estimates must use a different costing variant with a costing type that enables the specific update of the commercial inventory prices (see Figure 7.19).

Figure 7.19: Costing type for updating commercial inventory price

In the ACCOUNTING 2 tab, special balance sheet valuation procedures are used to update the raw material inventory prices for those materials, based on the lowest-value method. The valuation variants associated with the inventory cost estimates should use raw material valuation strategies referring to the prices loaded on the ACCOUNTING 2 tab. These are strategies A through F. See Section 5.2.1 for a description of these strategies. The resulting intermediate and finished goods cost estimates then pull the special inventory prices from the raw materials as the material components. Other adjustments can be made with special costing relevancy factors for both BOM items and routing operations. The costs associated with the

INVENTORY (TAX-BASED) cost component view are used for updating the tax-based inventory prices, and the INVENTORY (COMMERCIAL) cost component view costs update the commercial inventory prices.

The following examples illustrate how the inventory cost estimates are updated in the material master using the DETERMINATION OF LOWEST VALUE method. Two cost estimates for material H101 at plant UWU2 are created. The first one uses costing variant ZTAX, which is intended to update the tax-based fields in the ACCOUNTING 2 tab of the material master (see Figure 7.20, area ❶). The second one uses costing variant ZCOM to update the commercial inventory fields (see Figure 7.20, area ❷). Prior to updating these cost estimates, the ACCOUNTING 2 tab of the material master has no values in either sets of the inventory price fields.

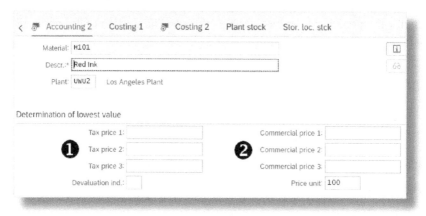

Figure 7.20: Determination of lowest value on Accounting 2

The resulting cost estimate using the ZTAX costing variant is shown in Figure 7.21. The tax-based inventory cost component view is highlighted, and the cost estimate display is set to costs based on price unit of the material (PRICE UNIT), which in this case is 100 L.

The Release Material Cost Estimates Fiori tile (SAPGUI transaction CK24) is used to update the inventory-based costs. When entering the application, the marking window is first displayed. Inventory cost estimates are directly updated in the material master and do not require marking. Click on the OTHER PRICES button, shown in Figure 7.22, to enable the update of the auxiliary price fields in the material master.

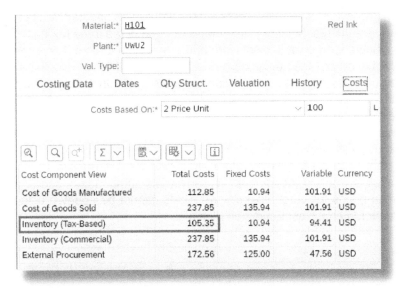

Figure 7.21: Tax-based cost estimate using costing variant ZTAX

Figure 7.22: Other prices selection button

Transaction CKU1

 CKU1 is a transaction that only updates the auxiliary price fields in the material master. Run this transaction instead of the Release Material Cost Estimates tile or transaction CK24 to go directly to the OTHER PRICES window.

The system displays an alternative window, providing the ability to select fields to update in the material master. Figure 7.23 shows the expanded window for updating other prices. In addition to entering the material information, the costing data in area ❶ must also be entered in order to specify which cost estimate is being updated. The COSTING VARIANT determines which fields can be updated. ZTAX uses costing type 10, which is set up for tax-based inventory field updates (see Figure 7.18). Therefore, only one of the three tax-based price fields in area ❷ can be updated. Multiple fields can be selected, but if any field that is not one of the three tax-based fields is selected, an error is displayed, and the system does not proceed until only the proper field or fields are selected. The MAT. COMP. PRICES checkbox can also be selected in order to update prices in the purchased materials that are included in the exploded BOM of the cost estimate. For tax-based and commercial inventory prices, this selection is ignored, because the prices for these materials are updated separately using special transactions available in the BALANCE SHEET VALUATION menu area. These special transactions use the standard strategies for determining lowest value based on goods movements and inventory turns. Tax-based and commercial prices for purchased raw materials cannot be updated using the Release Material Cost Estimates Fiori tile.

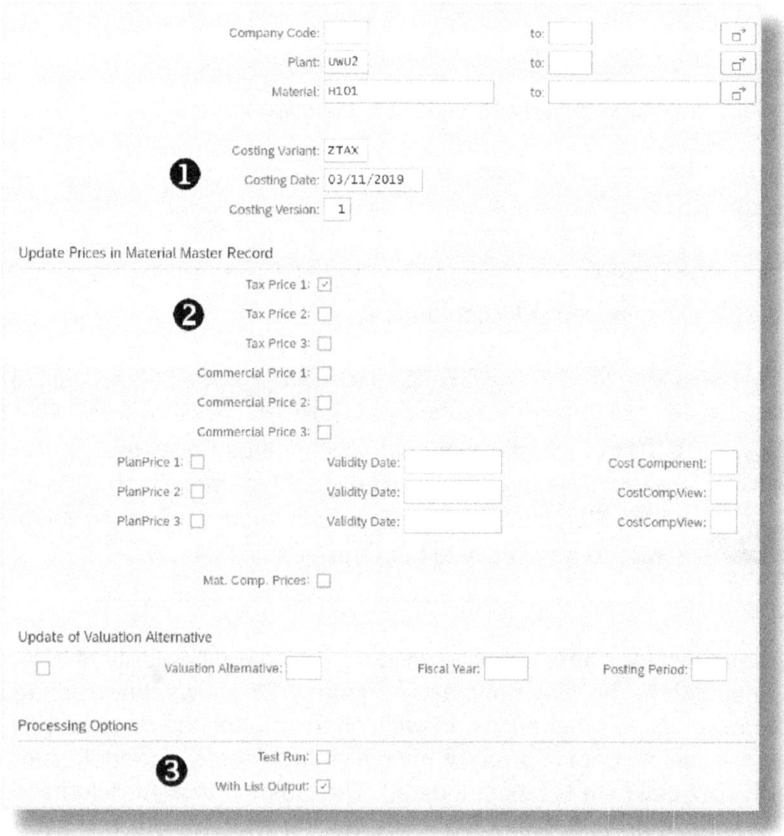

Figure 7.23: Updating tax-based inventory cost estimate price

Click on the Execute button or press F8 to update the prices for the selected materials. If With List Output is selected, a report is generated with
all the selected prices. Figure 7.24 shows that a value of 105.35 USD per
100 L was used as the value updated in the Tax price 1 field of the material master. This matches the Inventory (Tax-Based) cost component view
value shown in Figure 7.21.

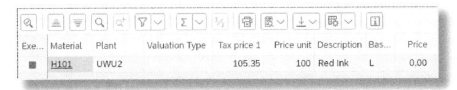

Exe...	Material	Plant	Valuation Type	Tax price 1	Price unit	Description	Bas...	Price
■	H101	UWU2		105.35	100	Red Ink	L	0.00

Figure 7.24: List display for tax price update

Figure 7.25 shows the updated material master.

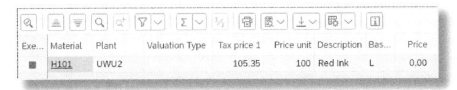

Figure 7.25: Material H101 with tax price update

Although this update seemed straightforward, there is some hidden logic
behind the scenes. The value from the cost estimate was only updated
because it was lower than the value calculated using the lowest value
method. Another cost estimate for material H101 was created to update
the Commercial price 1 field using the ZCOM costing variant. Figure 7.26
shows that the cost estimate for material H101 using the Inventory (Commercial) cost component view is 269.35 USD per 100 L.

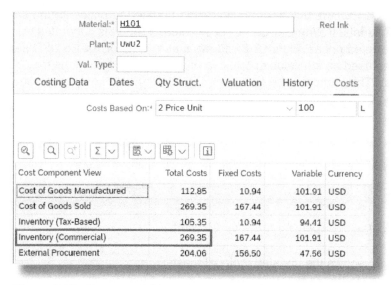

Material:*	H101					Red Ink	

Plant:*	UwU2

Val. Type:	

Costing Data	Dates	Qty Struct.	Valuation	History	Costs

Costs Based On:*	2 Price Unit		100	L

Cost Component View	Total Costs	Fixed Costs	Variable	Currency
Cost of Goods Manufactured	112.85	10.94	101.91	USD
Cost of Goods Sold	269.35	167.44	101.91	USD
Inventory (Tax-Based)	105.35	10.94	94.41	USD
Inventory (Commercial)	269.35	167.44	101.91	USD
External Procurement	204.06	156.50	47.56	USD

Figure 7.26: Commercial inventory cost estimate using ZCOM

Once the cost estimate is saved, it can be used to update the material master. Figure 7.27 shows the selections.

Company Code:		to:	
Plant:	UwU2	to:	
Material:	H101	to:	

Costing Variant:	ZCOM
Costing Date:	03/11/2019
Costing Version:	1

Update Prices in Material Master Record

Tax Price 1:	☐
Tax Price 2:	☐
Tax Price 3:	☐
Commercial Price 1:	☑
Commercial Price 2:	☐
Commercial Price 3:	☐

Figure 7.27: Price update selections for commercial inventory

Note that in Figure 7.28, the value assigned to COMMERCIAL PRICE 1 is only 200.00 USD per 100 L instead of the expected 269.35 USD per 100 L. This is because the lowest price determination strategies have found a price lower than the cost estimate price, and this price is used to update the material master.

Figure 7.28: List display for commercial price update

Figure 7.29 shows the updated material master with the 200.00 USD price in the COMMERCIAL PRICE 1 FIELD. Because the determination of lowest value method is used, the price updated may differ from the price in the cost estimate.

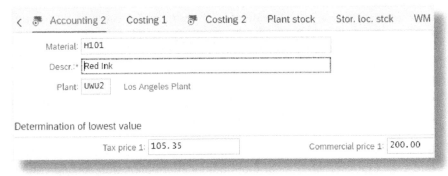

Figure 7.29: Material H101 with commercial price update

7.2.2   Other prices

There are nine price fields in the material master that can be updated from the calculation of cost estimates. These include the six inventory prices on the ACCOUNTING 2 tab and the three planned price fields in the COSTING 2 tab. Costing type Z0, shown in Figure 7.30, is defined with a PRICE UPDATE setting PRICES OTHER THAN STANDARD PRICE. Cost estimates created with a costing variant and defined with a costing type with this setting can update any of the nine fields. When prices are updated in the tax-based or commercial inventory fields in ACCOUNTING 2, the logic used to determine the lowest value is not used. Therefore, whatever price is calculated in the cost estimate is always used to update the material master.

Figure 7.30: Costing type for updating other price fields

The ZOTH costing variant has been created using costing type Z0. A cost estimate for material H101 at plant UWU2 is created and saved. Figure 7.31 shows the cost component views of the cost estimate created with costing variant ZOTH. The intention is to update four separate fields in the material master from this cost estimate. First, TAX PRICE 3 on the ACCOUNTING 2 tab should receive the value of the INVENTORY (TAX-BASED) cost component view (i.e. 105.35 USD). The COMMERCIAL PRICE 3 field, on the same tab, should be updated with the value from the INVENTORY (COMMERCIAL) view (i.e. 237.85 USD). Finally, the PLANNED PRICE 2 and PLANNED PRICE 3 fields on the COSTING 2 tab should be updated with the COST OF GOODS MANUFACTURED value and the EXTERNAL PROCUREMENT value respectively (i.e. 112.85 USD and 172.56 USD). This is shown below.

Execute Release Material Cost Estimates or SAPGUI transaction CK24 and select OTHER PRICES. After the material information and costing variant information have been entered, select the fields to update in the UPDATE PRICES IN MATERIAL MASTER section of the window. Note the selections in Figure 7.32. When selecting one of the planned price checkboxes (PLAN-PRICE), a date and a cost component view are required. This allows the planned price fields to contain the values of different cost component views of the cost estimate. A date is required when updating a price in one of the planned price fields and becomes important if one of these fields is used in another cost estimate to determine the value of the material. The tax price fields are always updated with the INVENTORY (TAX-BASED) cost component view and the commercial price fields always use the INVENTORY (COMMERCIAL) cost component view.

Material:* H101
Red Ink
Plant:* UWU2
Val. Type:
Costing Data
Dates
Qty Struct.
Valuation
History
Costs
Costs Based On:* 2 Price Unit
100
L
Cost Component View
Total Costs
Fixed Costs
Variable
Currency
Cost of Goods Manufactured 112.85 10.94 101.91 USD
Cost of Goods Sold 237.85 135.94 101.91 USD
Inventory (Tax-Based) 105.35 10.94 94.41 USD
Inventory (Commercial) 237.85 135.94 101.91 USD
External Procurement 172.56 125.00 47.56 USD

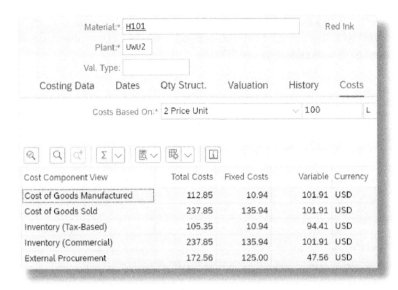

Figure 7.31: Cost estimate using costing variant ZOTH

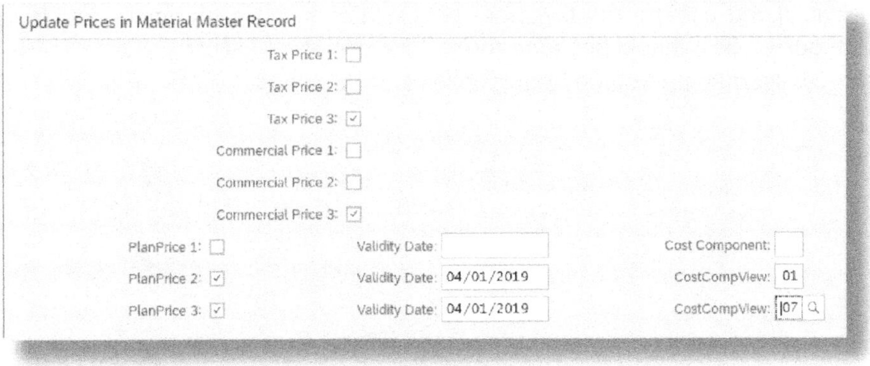

Update Prices in Material Master Record
Tax Price 1:
Tax Price 2:
Tax Price 3:
Commercial Price 1:
Commercial Price 2:
Commercial Price 3:
PlanPrice 1:
PlanPrice 2:
PlanPrice 3:
Validity Date:
Validity Date: 04/01/2019
Validity Date: 04/01/2019
Cost Component:
CostCompView: 01
CostCompView: 07

Figure 7.32: General price update selections

Figure 7.33 shows all the fields that were updated after executing the cost release.

Exe...
Material
Plant
V...
Planned price 2
Planned price date 2
Planned price 3
Planned price date 3
Price Unit/Planned Price
Tax price 3
Commercial price 3
Price unit
Description
Bas
H101
UWU2
112.85
04/01/2019
172.56
04/01/2019
100
105.35
237.85
100
Red Ink
L

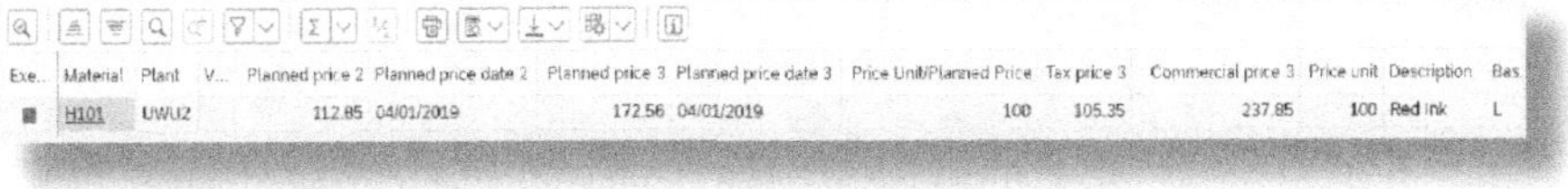

Figure 7.33: Detail list when updating multiple fields

The ACCOUNTING 2 tab now shows the TAX PRICE 3 and COMMERCIAL PRICE 3 fields updated with the values from their respective cost component views from the cost estimate (see Figure 7.34).

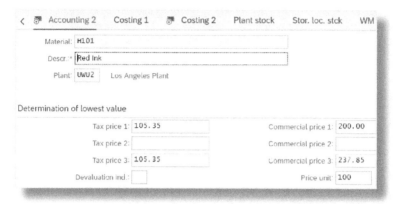

Figure 7.34: Accounting 2 tab after updating of ZOTH prices

Note that the value in COMMERCIAL PRICE 3 shows the full amount of the calculated cost for the INVENTORY (COMMERCIAL) cost component view from Figure 7.31. This is because the determination of lowest value logic was bypassed as part of the update for this costing type.

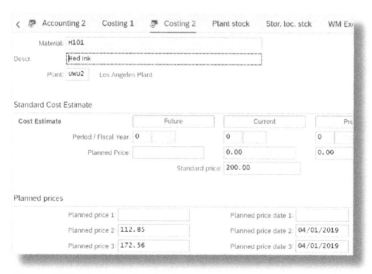

Figure 7.35: Costing 2 tab after updating ZOTH prices

Figure 7.35 shows the Costing 2 tab of the material master after the price updates. A wide variety of prices that are useful for making cost comparisons can be updated in the material master when using a costing type with Price Update set to Prices Other Than Standard Price.

You have finished the book.

A The Author

Tom King is a graduate of Northwestern University and recently retired from being a senior business analyst with a focus on controlling and product costing. He has over 10 years of experience with the SAP FI-CO modules, mostly as an internal consultant. Prior to that, he was involved in the modeling and design of an Activity Based Costing system using a different ERP system for his company's European operations. He has spoken at conferences on several topics relating to the CO module and is also the author of "Practical Guide to SAP® CO Templates", published by Espresso Tutorials.

B Index

C Disclaimer

This publication contains references to the products of SAP SE.

SAP, R/3, SAP NetWeaver, Duet, PartnerEdge, ByDesign, SAP Business-Objects Explorer, StreamWork, and other SAP products and services mentioned herein as well as their respective logos are trademarks or registered trademarks of SAP SE in Germany and other countries.

Business Objects and the Business Objects logo, BusinessObjects, Crystal Reports, Crystal Decisions, Web Intelligence, Xcelsius, and other Business Objects products and services mentioned herein as well as their respective logos are trademarks or registered trademarks of Business Objects Software Ltd. Business Objects is an SAP company.

Sybase and Adaptive Server, iAnywhere, Sybase 365, SQL Anywhere, and other Sybase products and services mentioned herein as well as their respective logos are trademarks or registered trademarks of Sybase, Inc. Sybase is an SAP company.

SAP SE is neither the author nor the publisher of this publication and is not responsible for its content. SAP Group shall not be liable for errors or omissions with respect to the materials. The only warranties for SAP Group products and services are those that are set forth in the express warranty statements accompanying such products and services, if any. Nothing herein should be construed as constituting an additional warranty.

More Espresso Tutorials Books

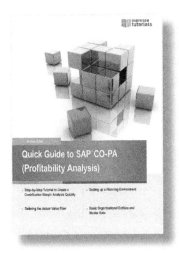

Stefan Eifler:

Quick Guide to CO-PA (Profitability Analysis)

- ▶ Familiarize yourself with basic organizational entities and master data in CO-PA
- ▶ Define the actual value flow
- ▶ Set up a planning environment
- ▶ Create your own reports

http://5018.espresso-tutorials.com

Paul Ovigele:

Reconciling SAP CO-PA to the General Ledger

- ▶ Learn the Difference between Costing-based and Accounting-based CO-PA
- ▶ Walk through Various Value Flows into CO-PA
- ▶ Match the Cost-of-Sales Account with Corresponding Value Fields in CO-PA

http://5040.espresso-tutorials.com

Ashish Sampat:

First Steps in SAP Controlling (CO)

▶ Cost center and product cost planning, actual cost flow

▶ Best practices for cost absorption using Product Cost Controlling

▶ Month-end closing activities in SAP Controlling

▶ Examples and screenshots based on a case study approach

http://5069.espresso-tutorials.com

Marjorie Wright:

Practical Guide to SAP Internal Orders (CO-OM)

▶ Concepts and daily postings to internal orders

▶ Master data configuration

▶ Streamlining period-end close activities

▶ Reporting options and summarization hierarchies in SAP CO

http://5139.espresso-tutorials.com

Ashish Sampat:

Expert tips to Unleash the Full Potential of SAP Controlling

▶ Optimize SAP ERP Controlling configuration, reconciliation, and reporting

▶ Transaction processing tips to ensure accurate data capture

▶ Instructions for avoiding common month-end close pain points

▶ Reporting and reconciliation best practices

http://5140.espresso-tutorials.com

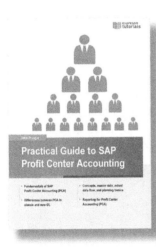

John Pringle:

Practical Guide to SAP Profit Center Accounting

▶ Fundamentals of SAP Profit Center Accounting (PCA)

▶ Concepts, master data, actual data flow, and planning basics

▶ Differences between PCA in classic and new GL

▶ Reporting for Profit Center Accounting (PCA)

http://5144.espresso-tutorials.com

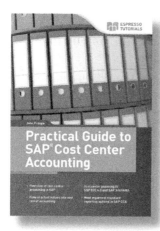

John Pringle:

Practical Guide to SAP Cost Center Accounting

► Overview of cost center accounting in SAP
► Flow of actual values into cost center accounting
► Cost center planning in SAP ECC 6.0 and SAP S/4HANA
► Most important standard reporting options in SAP CCA

http://5192.espresso-tutorials.com

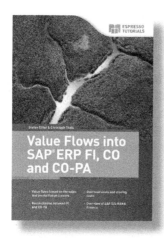

Stefan Eifler, Christoph Theis:

Value Flows into SAP ERP FI, CO, and CO-PA

► Value flows based on the sales and production processes
► Reconciliation between FI and CO-PA
► Overhead costs and closing tasks
► Overview of SAP S/4 HANA Finance

http://5199.espresso-tutorials.com

Tom King:

Practical Guide to SAP CO Templates

▶ Implement and properly use templates

▶ Scenarios for using templates in SAP Product Costing and Cost Object Controlling

▶ Template configuration tasks

▶ Easy cost planning applications

http://5262.espresso-tutorials.com

Made in United States
Orlando, FL
09 August 2023